ABOUT THIS PUBLICATION

FOR SERVICE ASSISTANCE

Customer Service
1.704.898.0770

North Carolina General Statues is published by The Muliti-Media Group of Greater Charlotte in Charlotte, North Carolina. Copyright 2015 by the Multi-Media Group of Greater Charlotte. This book or parts thereof may not be reproduced in any form, stored in a retrieval system, or transmitted in any form by any means—electronic, mechanical, photocopy, recording or otherwise—without prior written permission of the publisher, except as provided by United States of America copyright law.

The records required by U.S. Code 2257(a) through (c) and the pertinent regulations 28 C.F.R. Cli. 1, Part 75 with respect to this publication and all materials associated with such records are maintained by The Multi-Media Group of Greater Charlotte, Publisher and available for review by Attorney General.

www.visionbooks.org

Copyright © 2015 by MMGGC
All rights reserved!

TID: 5061522
ISBN (10) digit: 1502913720
ISBN (13) digit: 978-1502913722

123-4-56789-01239-Paperback
123-4-56789-01239-Hardback

First Edition

090520140547

Printed in the United States of America

2015 EDITION

North Carolina Criminal Law And Procedure-Pamphlet # 41

Printed In conjunction with the Administration of the Courts

North Carolina Criminal Law and Procedure
Pamphlet Reference Guide

Chapters	Pamphlet
Chapter 1 Civil Procedure	1
Chapter 1 Civil Procedure (Continue)	2
Chapter 1A Rules of Civil Procedure	2
Chapter 1B Contribution.	2
Chapter 1C Enforcement of Judgments.	2
Chapter 1D Punitive Damages.	2
Chapter 1E Eastern Band of Cherokee Indians.	2
Chapter 1F North Carolina Uniform Interstate Depositions and Discovery Act.	2
Chapter 2 - Clerk of Superior Court [Repealed and Transferred.]	3
Chapter 3 - Commissioners of Affidavits and Deeds [Repealed.]	3
Chapter 4 - Common Law	3
Chapter 5 - Contempt [Repealed.]	3
Chapter 5A - Contempt	3
Chapter 6 - Liability for Court Costs	3
Chapter 7 - Courts [Repealed and Transferred.]	3
Chapter 7A - Judicial Department	3
Chapter 7A – Continuation (Judicial Department)	4
Chapter 7A – Continuation (Judicial Department)	5
Chapter 7B - Juvenile Code	5
Chapter 8 - Evidence	6
Chapter 8A - Interpreters for Deaf Persons [Recodified.]	6
Chapter 8B - Interpreters for Deaf Persons	6
Chapter 8C - Evidence Code	6
Chapter 9 - Jurors	6
Chapter 10 - Notaries [Repealed.]	6
Chapter 10A - Notaries [Recodified.]	6
Chapter 10B - Notaries	6
Chapter 11 - Oaths	6
Chapter 12 - Statutory Construction	6
Chapter 13 - Citizenship Restored	6
Chapter 14 - Criminal Law	7
Chapter 14 –Criminal Law (Continuation)	8
Chapter 15 - Criminal Procedure	9
Chapter 15A - Criminal Procedure Act (Continuation)	10
Chapter 15A - Criminal Procedure Act (Continuation)	11
Chapter 15B - Victims Compensation	11
Chapter 15C - Address Confidentiality Program	11
Chapter 16 - Gaming Contracts and Futures	11
Chapter 17 - Habeas Corpus	11

Chapter 17A - Law-Enforcement Officers [Recodified.]	11
Chapter 17B - North Carolina Criminal Justice Education and Training System [Recodified.] Chapter 17C - North Carolina Criminal Justice Education and Training Standards Commission	11 11
Chapter 17D - North Carolina Justice Academy	11
Chapter 17E - North Carolina Sheriffs' Education and Training Standards Commission	11
Chapter 18 - Regulation of Intoxicating Liquors [Repealed.]	12
Chapter 18A - Regulation of Intoxicating Liquors [Repealed.]	12
Chapter 18B - Regulation of Alcoholic Beverages	12
Chapter 18C - North Carolina State Lottery	12
Chapter 19 - Offenses against Public Morals	12
Chapter 19A - Protection of Animals	12
Chapter 20 - Motor Vehicles	13
Chapter 20 - Motor Vehicles (Continuation)	14
Chapter 20 - Motor Vehicles (Continuation)	15
Chapter 20 - Motor Vehicles (Continuation)	16
Chapter 21 - Bills of Lading	17
Chapter 22 - Contracts Requiring Writing	17
Chapter 22A - Signatures	17
Chapter 22B - Contracts Against Public Policy	17
Chapter 22C - Payments to Subcontractors	17
Chapter 23 - Debtor and Creditor.	17
Chapter 24 – Interest	17
Chapter 25 – Uniform Commercial Code	18
Chapter 25 – Uniform Commercial Code (Continuation)	19
Chapter 25A – Retail Installment Sales Act	20
Chapter 25B - Credit	20
Chapter 25C - Sales of Artwork	20
Chapter 26 - Suretyship	20
Chapter 27 - Warehouse Receipts [Repealed.]	20
Chapter 28 - Administration [Repealed.]	20
Chapter 28A - Administration of Decedents' Estates	20
Chapter 28B - Estates of Absentees in Military Service	20
Chapter 28C - Estates of Missing Persons	20
Chapter 29 - Intestate Succession	21
Chapter 30 - Surviving Spouses	21
Chapter 31 - Wills	21
Chapter 31A - Acts Barring Property Rights	21
Chapter 31B - Renunciation of Property and Renunciation of Fiduciary Powers Act	21
Chapter 31C - Uniform Disposition of Community Property Rights at Death Act	21
Chapter 32 - Fiduciaries	21
Chapter 32A - Powers of Attorney	21
Chapter 33 - Guardian and Ward [Repealed and Recodified.]	21

Chapter 33A - North Carolina Uniform Transfers to Minors Act	21
Chapter 33B - North Carolina Uniform Custodial Trust Act	21
Chapter 34 - Veterans' Guardianship Act	22
Chapter 35 - Sterilization Procedures	22
Chapter 35A - Incompetency and Guardianship	22
Chapter 36 - Trusts and Trustees [Repealed.]	22
Chapter 36A - Trusts and Trustees	22
Chapter 36B - Uniform Management of Institutional Funds Act [Repealed.]	22
Chapter 36C - North Carolina Uniform Trust Code	22
Chapter 36D - North Carolina Community Third Party Trusts, Pooled Trusts	23
Chapter 36E - Uniform Prudent Management of Institutional Funds Act	23
Chapter 37 - Allocation of Principal and Income [Repealed.]	23
Chapter 37A - Uniform Principal and Income Act	23
Chapter 38 - Boundaries	23
Chapter 38A - Landowner Liability	23
Chapter 39 - Conveyances	23
Chapter 39A - Transfer Fee Covenants Prohibited	23
Chapter 40 - Eminent Domain [Repealed.]	23
Chapter 40A - Eminent Domain	23
Chapter 41 - Estates	23
Chapter 41A - State Fair Housing Act	23
Chapter 42 - Landlord and Tenant	23
Chapter 42A - Vacation Rental Act	23
Chapter 43 - Land Registration	23
Chapter 44 - Liens	24
Chapter 44A - Statutory Liens and Charges	24
Chapter 45 - Mortgages and Deeds of Trust	24
Chapter 45A - Good Funds Settlement Act	24
Chapter 46 - Partition	24
Chapter 47 - Probate and Registration	25
Chapter 47A - Unit Ownership	25
Chapter 47B - Real Property Marketable Title Act	25
Chapter 47C - North Carolina Condominium Act	25
Chapter 47D - Notice of Settlement Act [Expired.]	25
Chapter 47E - Residential Property Disclosure Act	25
Chapter 47F - North Carolina Planned Community Act	25
Chapter 47G - Option to Purchase Contracts	25
Chapter 47H - Contracts for Deed	25
Chapter 48 - Adoptions +	26
Chapter 48A - Minors	26
Chapter 49 - Bastardy	26
Chapter 49A - Rights of Children	26
Chapter 50 - Divorce and Alimony	26
Chapter 50A - Uniform Child-Custody Jurisdiction and	

Enforcement Act	26
Chapter 50B - Domestic Violence	26
Chapter 50C - Civil No-Contact Orders	26
Chapter 51 - Marriage	26
Chapter 52 - Powers and Liabilities of Married Persons	27
Chapter 52A - Uniform Reciprocal Enforcement of Support Act [Repealed.]	27
Chapter 52B - Uniform Premarital Agreement Act	27
Chapter 52C - Uniform Interstate Family Support Act	27
Chapter 53 - Banks	27
Chapter 53A - Business Development Corporations and North Carolina Capital Resource Corporations	28
Chapter 53B - Financial Privacy Act	28
Chapter 54 - Cooperative Organizations	28
Chapter 54A - Capital Stock Savings and Loan Associations [Repealed.]	28
Chapter 54B - Savings and Loan Associations	29
Chapter 54C - Savings Banks	29
Chapter 55 - North Carolina Business Corporation Act	30
Chapter 55A - North Carolina Nonprofit Corporation Act	31
Chapter 55B - Professional Corporation Act	31
Chapter 55C - Foreign Trade Zones	31
Chapter 55D - Filings, Names, and Registered Agents for Corporations, Nonprofit Corporations, and Partnerships	31
Chapter 56 - Electric, Telegraph and Power Companies [Repealed.]	31
Chapter 57 - Hospital, Medical and Dental Service Corporations [Recodified.]	31
Chapter 57A - Health Maintenance Organization Act [Recodified.]	31
Chapter 57B - Health Maintenance Organization Act [Recodified.]	31
Chapter 57C - North Carolina Limited Liability Company Act.	31
Chapter 58 - Insurance.	32
Chapter 58 - Insurance (Continuation)	33
Chapter 58 - Insurance (Continuation)	34
Chapter 58 - Insurance (Continuation)	35
Chapter 58 - Insurance (Continuation)	36
Chapter 58 - Insurance (Continuation)	37
Chapter 58 - Insurance (Continuation)	38
Chapter 58A - North Carolina Health Insurance Trust Commission [Recodified.]	38
Chapter 59 - Partnership.	39
Chapter 59B - Uniform Unincorporated Nonprofit Association Act.	39
Chapter 60 - Railroads and Other Carriers [Repealed and Transferred.]	39
Chapter 61 - Religious Societies	39
Chapter 62 - Public Utilities	39

Chapter 62 - Public Utilities (Continuation)	40
Chapter 62A - Public Safety Telephone Service And Wireless Telephone Service	40
Chapter 63 - Aeronautics	40
Chapter 63A - North Carolina Global TransPark Authority	40
Chapter 64 - Aliens	40
Chapter 65 – Cemeteries	40
Chapter 66 - Commerce and Business	41
Chapter 67 - Dogs	41
Chapter 68 - Fences and Stock Law	41
Chapter 69 - Fire Protection	41
Chapter 70 - Indian Antiquities, Archaeological Resources and Unmarked Human Skeletal Remains Protection	42
Chapter 71 - Indians [Repealed.]	42
Chapter 71A - Indians	42
Chapter 72 - Inns, Hotels and Restaurants	42
Chapter 73 - Mills	42
Chapter 74 - Mines and Quarries	42
Chapter 74A - Company Police [Repealed.]	42
Chapter 74B - Private Protective Services Act [Repealed.]	42
Chapter 74C - Private Protective Services	42
Chapter 74D - Alarm Systems	42
Chapter 74E - Company Police Act	42
Chapter 74F - Locksmith Licensing Act	42
Chapter 74G - Campus Police Act	42
Chapter 75 - Monopolies, Trusts and Consumer Protection	42
Chapter 75A - Boating and Water Safety	43
Chapter 75B - Discrimination in Business	43
Chapter 75C - Motion Picture Fair Competition Act	43
Chapter 75D - Racketeer Influenced and Corrupt Organizations	43
Chapter 75E - Unlawful Activities in Connection With Certain Corporate Transactions	43
Chapter 76 - Navigation	43
Chapter 76A - Navigation and Pilotage Commissions	43
Chapter 77 - Rivers, Creeks, and Coastal Waters	43
Chapter 78 - Securities Law [Repealed.]	43
Chapter 78A - North Carolina Securities Act	43
Chapter 78B - Tender Offer Disclosure Act [Repealed.]	43
Chapter 78C - Investment Advisers	43
Chapter 78D - Commodities Act	43
Chapter 79 - Strays [Repealed.]	43
Chapter 80 - Trademarks, Brands, etc.	44
Chapter 81 - Weights and Measures [Recodified.]	44
Chapter 81A - Weights and Measures Act of 1975.	44
Chapter 82 - Wrecks [Repealed.]	44
Chapter 83 - Architects [Recodified.]	44

Chapter 83A - Architects	44
Chapter 84 - Attorneys-at-Law	44
Chapter 84A - Foreign Legal Consultants	44
Chapter 85 - Auctions and Auctioneers [Repealed.]	44
Chapter 85A - Bail Bondsmen and Runners [Recodified.]	44
Chapter 85B - Auctions and Auctioneers	44
Chapter 85C - Bail Bondsmen and Runners [Recodified.]	44
Chapter 86 - Barbers [Recodified.]	44
Chapter 86A - Barbers	44
Chapter 87 - Contractors	44
Chapter 88 - Cosmetic Art [Repealed.]	44
Chapter 88A - Electrolysis Practice Act	44
Chapter 88B - Cosmetic Art	45
Chapter 89 - Engineering and Land Surveying [Recodified.]	45
Chapter 89A - Landscape Architects	45
Chapter 89B - Foresters	45
Chapter 89C - Engineering and Land Surveying	45
Chapter 89D - Landscape Contractors	45
Chapter 89E - Geologists Licensing Act	45
Chapter 89F - North Carolina Soil Scientist Licensing Act	45
Chapter 89G - Irrigation Contractors	45
Chapter 90 - Medicine and Allied Occupations	45
Chapter 90 - Medicine and Allied Occupations (Continuation)	46
Chapter 90 - Medicine and Allied Occupations (Continuation)	47
Chapter 90 - Medicine and Allied Occupations (Continuation)	48
Chapter 90A - Sanitarians and Water and Wastewater Treatment Facility Operators	48
Chapter 90B - Social Worker Certification and Licensure Act	48
Chapter 90C - North Carolina Recreational Therapy Licensure Act	48
Chapter 90D - Interpreters and Transliterators	48
Chapter 91 - Pawnbrokers [Repealed.]	48
Chapter 91A - Pawnbrokers Modernization Act of 1989	48
Chapter 92 - Photographers [Deleted.]	48
Chapter 93 - Certified Public Accountants	48
Chapter 93A - Real Estate License Law	49
Chapter 93B - Occupational Licensing Boards	49
Chapter 93C - Watchmakers [Repealed.]	49
Chapter 93D - North Carolina State Hearing Aid Dealers and Fitters Board.	49
Chapter 93E - North Carolina Appraisers Act	49
Chapter 94 - Apprenticeship	49
Chapter 95 - Department of Labor and Labor Regulations	49
Chapter 95 - Department of Labor and Labor Regulations (Continuation)	50
Chapter 96 - Employment Security	50
Chapter 97 - Workers' Compensation Act	50
Chapter 97 - Workers' Compensation Act (Continuation)	51

Chapter 98 - Burnt and Lost Records	51
Chapter 99 - Libel and Slander	51
Chapter 99A - Civil Remedies for Criminal Actions	51
Chapter 99B - Products Liability	51
Chapter 99C - Actions Relating to Winter Sports Safety and Accidents	51
Chapter 99D - Civil Rights	51
Chapter 99E - Special Liability Provisions	51
Chapter 100 - Monuments, Memorials and Parks	51
Chapter 101 - Names of Persons	51
Chapter 102 - Official Survey Base	51
Chapter 103 - Sundays, Holidays and Special Days	51
Chapter 104 - United States Lands	51
Chapter 104A - Degrees of Kinship	51
Chapter 104B - Hurricanes or Other Acts of Nature	51
Chapter 104C - Atomic Energy, Radioactivity and Ionizing Radiation [Repealed and Recodified.]	51
Chapter 104D - Southern States Energy Compact	51
Chapter 104E - North Carolina Radiation Protection Act	51
Chapter 104F - Southeast Interstate Low-Level Radioactive Waste Management Compact [Repealed]	51
Chapter 104G - North Carolina Low-Level Radioactive Waste Management Authority Act of 1987 [Repealed]	51
Chapter 105 - Taxation	51
Chapter 105 - Taxation (Continuation)	52
Chapter 105 - Taxation (Continuation)	53
Chapter 105 - Taxation (Continuation)	54
Chapter 105A - Setoff Debt Collection Act	55
Chapter 105B - Defaulted Student Loan Recovery Act	55
Chapter 106 - Agriculture	55
Chapter 106 - Agriculture (Continue)	56
Chapter 106 - Agriculture (Continue)	57
Chapter 107 - Agricultural Development Districts [Repealed.]	57
Chapter 108 - Social Services [Repealed and Recodified.]	57
Chapter 108A - Social Services	57
Chapter 108B - Community Action Programs	58
Chapter 108C Medicaid and Health Choice Provider Requirements.	58
Chapter 108D Medicaid Managed Care for Behavioral Health Services.	58
Chapter 109 - Bonds [Recodified.]	58
Chapter 110 - Child Welfare	58
Chapter 111 - Aid to the Blind	58
Chapter 112 - Confederate Homes and Pensions [Repealed.]	58
Chapter 113 - Conservation and Development	58
Chapter 113 - Conservation and Development (Continuation)	59

Chapter 113A - Pollution Control and Environment	59
Chapter 113A - Pollution Control and Environment (Continuation)	60
Chapter 113B - North Carolina Energy Policy Act of 1975	60
Chapter 114 - Department of Justice	60
Chapter 115 - Elementary and Secondary Education [Repealed.]	60
Chapter 115A - Community Colleges, Technical Institutes, and Industrial Education Centers [Repealed.]	60
Chapter 115B - Tuition and Fee Waivers	60
Chapter 115C - Elementary and Secondary Education	60
Chapter 115C - Elementary and Secondary Education (Continuation)	61
Chapter 115C - Elementary and Secondary Education (Continuation)	62
Chapter 115C - Elementary and Secondary Education (Continuation)	63
Chapter 115D - Community Colleges	63
Chapter 115E - Private Educational Facilities Finance Act [Recodified]	63
Chapter 116 - Higher Education	63
Chapter 116 - Higher Education (Continuation)	63
Chapter 116A - Escheats and Abandoned Property [Repealed.]	64
Chapter 116B - Escheats and Abandoned Property	64
Chapter 116C - Continuum of Education Programs	64
Chapter 116D - Higher Education Bonds	64
Chapter 117 - Electrification	64
Chapter 118 - Firemen's and Rescue Squad Workers' Relief and Pension Funds [Recodified.]	64
Chapter 118A - Firemen's Death Benefit Act [Repealed.]	64
Chapter 118B - Members of a Rescue Squad Death Benefit Act [Repealed.]	64
Chapter 119 - Gasoline and Oil Inspection and Regulation	64
Chapter 120 - General Assembly	65
Chapter 120 - General Assembly (Continuation)	66
Chapter 120 - General Assembly (Continuation)	67
Chapter 120C - Lobbying	67
Chapter 121 - Archives and History	67
Chapter 122 - Hospitals for the Mentally Disordered [Repealed.]	67
Chapter 122A - North Carolina Housing Finance Agency	67
Chapter 122B - North Carolina Agricultural Facilities Finance Act [Repealed.]	67
Chapter 122C - Mental Health, Developmental Disabilities, and Substance Abuse Act of 1985	67
Chapter 122C - Mental Health, Developmental Disabilities, and Substance Abuse Act of 1985 (Continuation)	68
Chapter 122D - North Carolina Agricultural Finance Act	68

Chapter 122E - North Carolina Housing Trust and Oil Overcharge Act	68
Chapter 123 - Impeachment	69
Chapter 123A - Industrial Development [Repealed.]	69
Chapter 124 - Internal Improvements	69
Chapter 125 - Libraries	69
Chapter 126 - State Personnel System	69
Chapter 127 - Militia [Repealed.]	69
Chapter 127A - Militia	69
Chapter 127B - Military Affairs	69
Chapter 127C - Advisory Commission on Military Affairs	69
Chapter 128 - Offices and Public Officers	69
Chapter 128 - Offices and Public Officers (Continuation)	70
Chapter 129 - Public Buildings and Grounds	70
Chapter 130 - Public Health [Repealed.]	70
Chapter 130A - Public Health	70
Chapter 130A - Public Health (Continuation)	71
Chapter 130A - Public Health (Continuation)	72
Chapter 130B - Hazardous Waste Management Commission [Repealed.]	72
Chapter 131 - Public Hospitals [Repealed.]	72
Chapter 131A - Health Care Facilities Finance Act	72
Chapter 131B - Licensing of Ambulatory Surgical Facilities [Repealed.]	72
Chapter 131C - Charitable Solicitation Licensure Act [Repealed.]	72
Chapter 131D - Inspection and Licensing of Facilities	72
Chapter 131E - Health Care Facilities and Services	72
Chapter 131E - Health Care Facilities and Services (Continuation)	73
Chapter 131F - Solicitation of Contributions	73
Chapter 132 - Public Records	73
Chapter 133 - Public Works	74
Chapter 134 - Youth Development [Recodified.]	74
Chapter 134A - Youth Services [Repealed.]	74
Chapter 135 - Retirement System for Teachers and State Employees; Social Security; Health Insurance Program for Children	74
Chapter 135 - Retirement System for Teachers and State Employees; Social Security; Health Insurance Program for Children	75
Chapter 136 - Transportation	75
Chapter 136 - Transportation (Continuation)	76
Chapter 137 - Rural Rehabilitation [Repealed.]	76
Chapter 138 - Salaries, Fees and Allowances	76
Chapter 138A - State Government Ethics Act	76
Chapter 139 - Soil and Water Conservation Districts	76

Chapter 140 - State Art Museum; Symphony and Art Societies	76
Chapter 140A - State Awards System	76
Chapter 141 - State Boundaries	76
Chapter 142 - State Debt	76
Chapter 143 - State Departments, Institutions, and Commissions	77
Chapter 143 - State Departments, Institutions, and Commissions (Continuation)	78
Chapter 143 - State Departments, Institutions, and Commissions (Continuation)	79
Chapter 143 - State Departments, Institutions, and Commissions (Continuation)	80
Chapter 143A - State Government Reorganization	80
Chapter 143B - Executive Organization Act of 1973	80
Chapter 143B - Executive Organization Act of 1973 (Continuation)	81
Chapter 143B - Executive Organization Act of 1973 (Continuation)	82
Chapter 143C - State Budget Act	83
Chapter 143D - The State Governmental Accountability and Internal Control Act	83
Chapter 144 - State Flag, Official Governmental Flags, Motto, and Colors	83
Chapter 145 - State Symbols and Other Official Adoptions.	83
Chapter 146 - State Lands	83
Chapter 147 - State Officers	83
Chapter 148 - State Prison System	84
Chapter 149 - State Song and Toast	84
Chapter 150 - Uniform Revocation of Licenses [Repealed.]	84
Chapter 150A - Administrative Procedure Act [Recodified.]	84
Chapter 150B - Administrative Procedure Act	84
Chapter 151 - Constables [Repealed.]	84
Chapter 152 - Coroners	84
Chapter 152A - County Medical Examiner [Repealed.]	84
Chapter 152A - County Medical Examiner [Repealed.] (Continuation)	85
Chapter 153 - Counties and County Commissioners [Repealed.]	85
Chapter 153A - Counties	85
Chapter 153B - Mountain Resources Planning Act	85
Chapter 153C - Uwharrie Regional Resources Act	85
Chapter 154 - County Surveyor [Repealed.]	85
Chapter 155 - County Treasurer [Repealed.]	85
Chapter 156 - Drainage	85
Chapter 156 – Drainage (Continuation)	86

Chapter	Page
Chapter 157 - Housing Authorities and Projects	86
Chapter 157A - Historic Properties Commissions [Transferred.]	86
Chapter 158 - Local Development	86
Chapter 159 - Local Government Finance	86
Chapter 159 - Local Government Finance (Continuation)	87
Chapter 159A - Pollution Abatement and Industrial Facilities Financing Act [Unconstitutional.]	87
Chapter 159B - Joint Municipal Electric Power and Energy Act	87
Chapter 159C - Industrial and Pollution Control Facilities Financing Act	87
Chapter 159D - The North Carolina Capital Facilities Financing Act	87
Chapter 159E - Registered Public Obligations Act	87
Chapter 159F - North Carolina Energy Development Authority [Repealed.]	87
Chapter 159G - Water Infrastructure	87
Chapter 159H - [Reserved.]	87
Chapter 159I - Solid Waste Management Loan Program and Local Government Special Obligation Bonds	87
Chapter 160 - Municipal Corporations [Repealed And Transferred.]	87
Chapter 160A - Cities and Towns	88
Chapter 160A - Cities and Towns (Continuation)	89
Chapter 160B - Consolidated City-County Act	89
Chapter 160C - Baseball Park Districts [Repealed.]	90
Chapter 161 - Register of Deeds	90
Chapter 162 - Sheriff	90
Chapter 162A - Water and Sewer Systems	90
Chapter 162B Continuity of Local Government in Emergency.	90
Chapter 163 Elections and Election Laws.	90
Chapter 163 Elections and Election Laws. (Continuation)	91
Chapter 164 Concerning the General Statutes of North Carolina.	92
Chapter 165 Veterans.	92
Chapter 166 Civil Preparedness Agencies [Repealed.]	92
Chapter 166A North Carolina Emergency Management Act.	92
Chapter 167 State Civil Air Patrol [Repealed.]	92
Chapter 168 Persons with Disabilities.	92
Chapter 168A Persons With Disabilities Protection Act.	92

Chapter 66.

Commerce and Business.

Article 1.

Regulation and Inspection.

§ 66-1. County commissioners to appoint inspectors.

The board of county commissioners may appoint for their county or any township thereof inspectors for any article of commerce the inspection of which is not otherwise provided for by law, who shall hold office for the term of five years after their employment. (Rev., ss. 4637, 4669; C.S., s. 5068.)

§ 66-2. Repealed by Session Laws 1973, c. 108, s. 22.

§ 66-3. Bond of inspector; fees.

The said inspector shall enter into bond in the sum of five hundred dollars ($500.00), payable to the State of North Carolina, conditioned for the faithful performance of the duties of his office, which bond the board shall take; and he shall be entitled to such fees as may be prescribed by the board. (1848, c. 43, s. 3; R.C., c. 60, s. 76; Code, s. 3053; Rev., s. 4671; C.S., s. 5071.)

§ 66-4. Falsely acting as inspector.

If any person, who is not a legal or sworn inspector of lumber or other articles, presume to act as such, he shall forfeit and pay one hundred dollars ($100.00), and be guilty of a Class 1 misdemeanor. (1824, c. 1254, s. 3; R.C., c. 60, s. 69; Code, s. 3046; Rev., s. 3580; C.S., s. 5072; 1993, c. 539, s. 503; 1994, Ex. Sess., c. 24, s. 14(c).)

§ 66-5. Penalty for sale without inspection.

If any person shall sell any article of forage or provision, of which inspection is required in accordance with this Article, without the same having been inspected as required, he shall, for every offense, forfeit and pay one hundred dollars ($100.00).

The clear proceeds of penalties provided for in this section shall be remitted to the Civil Penalty and Forfeiture Fund in accordance with G.S. 115C-457.2. (1850, c. 74, s. 2; R.C., c. 60, s. 77; Code, s. 3054; Rev., s. 4672; C.S., s. 5073; 1998-215, s. 40.)

§ 66-6. Penalty on master receiving without inspection.

No master or commander of any vessel shall take on board any cask or barrel or other commodity, liable to inspection as aforesaid, without its being inspected and branded as required, under the penalty of two hundred dollars ($200.00) for each offense.

The clear proceeds of penalties provided for in this section shall be remitted to the Civil Penalty and Forfeiture Fund in accordance with G.S. 115C-457.2. (1784, c. 206, s. 6; R.C., c. 60, s. 59; Code, ss. 3036, 3037; Rev., ss. 4657, 4658; C.S., s. 5074; 1998-215, s. 41.)

§ 66-7. Who to pay inspectors' fees; penalty for extortion.

The fees of inspectors shall be paid by the purchaser or exporter of the articles inspected, and if any inspector shall receive any greater fees than are by law allowed, he shall forfeit and pay ten dollars ($10.00) for every offense to any person suing for the same. (1824, c. 1254, ss. 1, 2; R.C., c. 60, s. 79; Code, s. 3055; Rev., s. 4673; C.S., s. 5075.)

§ 66-8: Repealed by Session Laws 1995, c. 379, s. 18.3.

§ 66-9. Gas and electric light bills to show reading of meter.

It shall be the duty of all gas companies and electric light companies selling gas and electricity to the public to show, among other things, on all statements or bills rendered to consumers, the reading of the meter at the end of the preceding month, and the reading of the meter at the end of the current month, and the amount of electricity, in kilowatt hours, and of gas, in feet, consumed for the current month; provided, however, that nothing herein contained shall be construed to prohibit any gas or electric company from adopting any method of and times of reading meters and rendering bills that may be approved by the North Carolina Utilities Commission.

Any gas or electric light company failing to render bills or statements, as provided for in this section, shall be subject to a penalty of ten dollars ($10.00) for each violation of this section or failure to render such statements, recoverable in the district court by any person suing for the same; but this section shall not apply to bills and accounts rendered customers on flat rate contracts. (1915, c. 259; C.S., s. 5082; 1959, c. 987; 1973, c. 108, s. 23.)

§ 66-10. Failure of dealers of scrap, salvage, or surplus to keep record of purchases of certain items misdemeanor.

(a) Every person, firm, or corporation buying rubber or leather, rubber belts, and belting, as scrap, salvage, or surplus shall keep a register containing a true and accurate record of each purchase, including the description of the article purchased, the name from whom purchased, the amount paid for the article purchased, the date of the purchase, and any and all marks or brands upon the rubber or leather, rubber belts, and belting. This register and the rubber, leather, rubber belts, and belting purchased shall be at all times open to the inspection of the public. A failure to comply with these requirements or the making of a false entry concerning the rubber or leather, rubber belts, or belting shall constitute a Class 1 misdemeanor.

(b) Every person, firm, or corporation engaged in the business of buying or dealing in scrap, salvage, or surplus, including glass, waste paper, burlap, cloth, cordage, rubber, leather, or belting of every kind, in addition to the above requirements under subsection (a) of this section, shall make and keep a record of the name and address of the person from whom this scrap, salvage, or surplus is purchased and the license number, if any, and if there is no license, a description of the vehicle in which this scrap, salvage, or surplus is delivered. Any person, firm, or corporation which fails to comply with the requirements of this subsection shall be guilty of a Class 3 misdemeanor and upon conviction shall only be fined not in excess of fifty dollars ($50.00) in the discretion of the court. (1917, c. 46; C.S., s. 5090; 1957, c. 791; 1993, c. 295, s. 1, c. 539, s. 504; 1994, Ex. Sess., c. 24, s. 14(c).)

§ 66-11: Repealed by Session Laws 2012-46, s. 26, effective October 1, 2012, and applicable to offenses committed on or after that date.

§ 66-11.1: Repealed by Session Laws 2012-46, s. 26, effective October 1, 2012, and applicable to offenses committed on or after that date.

§ 66-11.2: Recodified as G.S. 66-426 by Session Laws 2012-46, s. 27, effective October 1, 2012, and applicable to offenses committed on or after that date.

Article 2.

Manufacture and Sale of Matches and Lighters.

§ 66-12. Requirements for matches permitted to be sold.

No person, association, or corporation shall manufacture, store, offer for sale, sell or otherwise dispose of or distribute white phosphorous, single-dipped, strike-anywhere matches of the type popularly known as "parlor matches"; nor manufacture, store, sell, offer for sale, or otherwise dispose of, or distribute, white phosphorous, double-dipped, strike-anywhere matches or any other type of double-dipped matches, unless the bulb or first dip of such match is composed of a so-called safety or inert composition, nonignitible as an abrasive surface; nor manufacture, store, sell, or offer for sale, or otherwise dispose of or distribute matches which when packed in a carton of 500 approximate capacity and placed in an oven maintained at a constant temperature of 200 degrees F., will ignite in eight hours; nor manufacture, store, offer for sale, sell or otherwise dispose of, or distribute, blazer, or so-called wind matches, whether of the so-called safety or strike-anywhere type. (1915, c. 109, s. 12, I; C.S., s. 5113.)

§ 66-13. Packages to be marked.

No person, association, or corporation shall offer for sale, sell or otherwise dispose of, or distribute, any matches, unless the package or container in which such matches are packed bears, plainly marked on the outside thereof, the name of the manufacturer and the brand or trademark under which the matches are sold, disposed of, or distributed. (1915, c. 109, s. 12, II; C.S., s. 5114.)

§ 66-14. Storage and packing regulated.

No more than one case of each brand of matches of any type or manufacture shall be opened at any one time in the retail store where matches are sold or otherwise disposed of; nor shall loose boxes or paper-wrapped packages of matches be kept on shelves or stored in such retail stores at a height exceeding five feet from the floor; all matches when stored in warehouses must be kept only in properly secured cases, and not piled to a height exceeding 10 feet from the floor; nor be stored within a horizontal distance of 10 feet from any boiler, furnace, stove, or other like heating apparatus; nor within a horizontal distance of 25 feet from any explosive material kept or stored on the same floor. All matches shall be packed in boxes or suitable packages, containing not more than 700 matches in any one box or package: Provided, however, that when more than 300 matches are packed in any one box or package the said matches shall be arranged in two nearly equal portions, the heads of the matches in the two portions shall be placed in opposite directions, and all boxes containing 350 or more matches shall have placed over the matches a center-holding or protecting strip, made of chip board, not less than one and one-quarter inches wide; said strip shall be flanged down to hold the matches in position when the box is nested into the shuck or withdrawn from it. (1915, c. 109, s. 12, II; C.S., s. 5115.)

§ 66-15. Shipping containers regulated.

All match boxes or packages shall be packed in strong shipping containers or cases; maximum number of match boxes or packages contained in any one shipping container or case shall not exceed the following number:

Number of Matches per Box	Nominal Number of Boxes
1/2 gross	700
1 gross	500
2 gross	400
3 gross	300
5 gross	200
12 gross	100
20 gross over 50 and under	100
25 gross under	50

No shipping container or case constructed of fiber board, corrugated fiber board, or wood, nailed or wirebound, shall exceed a weight, including its contents, of 75 pounds; and no lock-cornered wooden case containing matches shall have a weight, including its contents, exceeding 85 pounds; nor shall any other article or commodity be packed with matches in any such container or case; and all such containers and cases in which matches are packed shall have plainly marked on the outside of the container or case the words "Strike-Anywhere Matches" or "Strike-on-the-Box Matches." (1915, c. 109, s. 12, III; C.S., s. 5116.)

§ 66-16. Violation of Article a misdemeanor.

Any person, association, or corporation violating any of the provisions of this Article, other than G.S. 66-16.1, shall be guilty of a Class 3 misdemeanor and shall only be fined for the first offense not less than five dollars ($5.00) nor more than twenty-five dollars ($25.00), and for each subsequent violation not less than twenty-five dollars ($25.00). (1915, c. 109, s. 12, IV; C.S., s. 5117; 1993, c. 539, s. 507; 1994, Ex. Sess., c. 24, s. 14(c); 2009-230, s. 2.)

§ 66-16.1. Retail sale of novelty lighters prohibited.

(a)   Definition. - As used in this section, the term "novelty lighter" means a mechanical or electrical device typically used for lighting cigarettes, cigars, or pipes, that is designed to resemble a cartoon character, toy, gun, watch, musical instrument, vehicle, animal, food or beverage, or similar articles, or that plays musical notes. A novelty lighter may operate on any fuel, including butane, isobutene, or liquid fuel.

(b)   Prohibition. - It shall be unlawful to sell at retail, offer to sell at retail, or give, or distribute for retail sale or promotion, a novelty lighter in this State. This prohibition does not apply to the transportation of novelty lighters through this State or to the storage of novelty lighters in a warehouse or distribution center in this State that is closed to the public for purposes of retail sales.

(c)   Exceptions. - The prohibition in this section does not apply to any of the following:

(1)   A lighter manufactured prior to January 1, 1980.

(2)   Any mechanical or electrical device primarily used to ignite fuel for fireplaces or charcoal or gas grills.

(3)   Standard disposable or refillable lighters that are printed or decorated with logos, labels, decals or artwork, or heat shrinkable sleeves, but which do not otherwise resemble a novelty lighter.

(d) Penalty. - A violation of this section is an infraction and shall subject a violator to a penalty of five hundred dollars ($500.00) for each violation. The clear proceeds of any penalties imposed under this section shall be remitted in accordance with G.S. 115C-452. (2009-230, s. 3.)

Article 3.

Candy and Similar Products.

§§ 66-17 through 66-22: Repealed by Session Laws 1998-98, s. 37.

Article 4.

Electrical Materials, Devices, Appliances and Equipment.

§ 66-23. Sale of electrical goods regulated.

Every person, firm or corporation before selling, offering for sale, assigning, or disposing of by gift as premiums or in any similar manner any electrical material, devices, appliances or equipment shall first determine if such electrical materials, devices, appliances and equipment comply with the provision of this Article. (1933, c. 555, s. 1; 1989, c. 681, s. 1.)

§ 66-24. Identification marks required.

All electrical materials, devices, appliances and equipment shall have the maker's name, trademark, or other identification symbol placed thereon, together with such other markings giving voltage, current, wattage, or other appropriate ratings as may be necessary to determine the character of the material, device, appliance or equipment and the use for which it is intended; and it shall be unlawful for any person, firm or corporation to remove, alter, change or deface the maker's name, trademark or other identification symbol. (1933, c. 555, s. 2; 1989, c. 681, s. 1.)

§ 66-25. Acceptable listings as to safety of goods.

(a) All electrical materials, devices, appliances, and equipment shall be evaluated for safety and suitability for intended use. Except as provided in subsection (b) of this section, this evaluation shall be conducted in accordance with nationally recognized standards and shall be conducted by a qualified testing laboratory. The Commissioner of Insurance, through the Engineering Division of the Department of Insurance, shall implement the procedures necessary to approve suitable national standards and to approve suitable qualified testing laboratories. The Commissioner may assign his authority to implement the procedures for specific materials, devices, appliances, or equipment to other agencies or bodies when they would be uniquely qualified to implement those procedures.

In the event that the Commissioner determines that electrical materials, devices, appliances, or equipment in question cannot be adequately evaluated through the use of approved national standards or by approved qualified testing laboratories, the Engineering Division of the Department of Insurance shall specify any alternative evaluations which safety requires.

The Engineering Division of the Department of Insurance shall keep in file, where practical, copies of all approved national standards and resumes of approved qualified testing laboratories.

(b) Electrical devices, appliances, or equipment used by the Division of Adult Correction of the Department of Public Safety shall be evaluated for safety and suitability by the Central Engineering Section of the Department of Public Safety. The evaluation shall be conducted in accordance with nationally recognized standards. (1933, c. 555, s. 3; 1989, c. 681, s. 1; 2013-289, s. 11.)

§ 66-26. Legal responsibility of proper installations unaffected.

This Article shall not be construed to relieve from or to lessen the responsibility or liability of any party owning, operating, controlling or installing any electrical materials, devices, appliances or equipment for damages to persons or property caused by any defect therein, nor shall the electrical inspector, the Commissioner, or agents of the Commissioner be held as assuming any such liability by reason of the approval of any material, device, appliance or equipment authorized herein. (1933, c. 555, s. 4; 1989, c. 681, s. 1.)

§ 66-27. Violation made misdemeanor.

Any person, firm or corporation who shall violate any of the provisions of this Article shall be guilty of a Class 2 misdemeanor. (1933, c. 555, s. 5; 1989, c. 681, s. 1; 1993, c. 539, s. 509; 1994, Ex. Sess., c. 24, s. 14(c).)

§ 66-27.01. Enforcement.

The Commissioner or his designee or the electrical inspector of any State or local governing agency may initiate any appropriate action or proceedings to prevent, restrain, or correct any violation of this Article. The Commissioner or his designee, upon showing proper credentials and in discharge of his duties pursuant to this Article may, at reasonable times and without advance notice, enter and inspect any facility within the State in which there is reasonable cause to suspect that electrical materials, devices, appliances, or equipment not in conformance with the requirements of this Article are being sold, offered for sale, assigned, or disposed of by gift, as premiums, or in any other similar manner. (1989, c. 681, s. 1; 1997-456, s. 27.)

Article 4A.

Safety Features of Hot Water Heaters.

§ 66-27.1. Certain automatic hot water tanks or heaters to have approved relief valves; installation or sale of unapproved relief valves forbidden.

(a) No individual, firm, corporation or business shall install, sell or offer for sale any automatic hot water tank or heater of 120-gallon capacity or less, except for a tankless water heater, which does not have installed thereon by the manufacturer of the tank or heater an American Society of Mechanical

Engineers and National Board of Boiler and Pressure Vessel Inspectors approved type pressure-temperature relief valve set at or below the safe working pressure of the tank as indicated, and so labeled by the manufacturer's identification stamped or cast upon the tank or heater or upon a plate secured to it.

(b)   No individual, firm, corporation or business shall install, sell, or offer for sale any relief valve, whether it be pressure type, temperature type or pressure-temperature type, which does not carry the stamp of approval of the American Society of Mechanical Engineers and the National Board of Boiler and Pressure Vessel Inspectors. (1965, c. 860, s. 1; 1967, c. 453; 2004-199, s. 24.)

§ 66-27.1A. Water heater thermostat settings.

(a)   The thermostat of any new residential water heater offered for sale or lease for use in a single-family or multifamily dwelling in the State shall be preset by the manufacturer or installer no higher than approximately 120 degrees Fahrenheit (or 49 degrees Celsius). A water heater reservoir temperature may be set higher if it is supplying space heaters that require higher temperatures. For purposes of this section, a water heater shall mean the primary source of hot water for any single-family or multifamily residential dwelling including, but not limited to any solar or other hot water heating systems.

(b)   Nothing in this section shall prohibit the occupant of a single-family or multiunit residential dwelling with an individual water heater from resetting or having reset the thermostat on the water heater. Any such resetting shall relieve the manufacturer or installer of the water heater and, in the case of a residential dwelling that is leased or rented, also the unit's owner, from liability for damages attributed to the resetting.

(c)   A warning tag or sticker shall be placed on or near the operating thermostat control of any residential water heater. This tag or sticker shall state that the thermostat settings above the preset temperature may cause severe burns. This tag or sticker may carry such other appropriate warnings as may be agreed upon by manufacturers, installers, and other interested parties. (1991, c. 190, s. 1.)

§ 66-27.2. Certain hot water supply storage tank or heater baffles, heat traps, etc., to be tested before installation or sale.

(a) No individual, firm, corporation or business shall install, sell or offer for sale any hot water supply storage tanks or heaters of 120-gallon capacity or less which utilize dip tubes, supply and hot water nipples, supply water baffles or heat traps that have not been tested to withstand a temperature of 400 degrees Fahrenheit without deteriorating in any manner, and such tank or heater so labeled by the manufacturer.

(b) No individual, firm, corporation or business shall install, sell, or offer for sale any water baffles or heat traps, which are not constructed and tested to withstand a temperature of 400 degrees Fahrenheit without deterioration in any manner and such baffles or heat traps to be so labeled by the manufacturer. (1965, c. 860, s. 2.)

§ 66-27.3. Violation of Article made misdemeanor.

Violation of any provision of this Article is hereby made a Class 1 misdemeanor. (1965, c. 860, s. 3; 1993, c. 539, s. 510; 1994, Ex. Sess., c. 24, s. 14(c).)

§ 66-27.4. Local regulation of hot water heater safety features.

Nothing in this Article shall be interpreted as relieving any individual, firm, corporation or business from complying with additional protective regulations relating to the safety features of hot water heaters as may be prescribed by local law, county or municipal charter or ordinance; provided, however, that no local law, county or municipal charter or ordinance shall fix or govern the temperature or pressure settings of a pressure-temperature relief valve on an automatic hot water tank or heater covered by this Article if there is installed on such tank or heater a pressure-temperature relief valve having settings in compliance with the North Carolina Building Code. (1965, c. 860, s. 4.)

Article 4B.

Safety Features of Trailers.

§ 66-27.5. House trailers to have two doors.

(a)   In order to provide greater protection from the dangers of fire, every new house trailer having a body length exceeding 32 feet and manufactured or assembled after January 1, 1970, and sold in this State shall, if such house trailer is to be used as a residence or dwelling within this State, be equipped with at least two doors. These doors shall be located in the vicinity of the front and rear rooms of the house trailer. Provided, however, this section shall not apply: to any (i) travel trailer which is factory equipped for the road and designed to be used as a dwelling for travel, recreational or vacation use, if such travel trailer does not exceed 32 feet in length; (ii) to any house trailer of any length sold in North Carolina for use in a state other than North Carolina.

(b)   It shall be unlawful for any dealer to sell in this State any house trailer manufactured or assembled after January 1, 1970, having a body length exceeding 32 feet which does not conform to the specifications set forth in subsection (a). Any dealer who violates this section shall be guilty of a Class 3 misdemeanor. (1969, c. 463; 1993, c. 539, s. 511; 1994, Ex. Sess., c. 24, s. 14(c).)

§ 66-27A: Recodified as 66-27.01 by Session Laws 1997-456, s. 27.

Article 5.

Sale of Phonograph Records or Electrical Transcriptions.

§ 66-28. Prohibition of rights to further restrict or to collect royalties on commercial use.

When any phonograph record or electrical transcription, upon which musical performances are embodied, is sold in commerce for use within this State, all asserted common-law rights to further restrict or to collect royalties on the commercial use made of such recorded performances by any person is hereby abrogated and expressly repealed. When such article or chattel has been sold in commerce, any asserted intangible rights shall be deemed to have passed to the purchaser upon the purchase of the chattel itself, and the right to further restrict the use made of phonograph records or electrical transcriptions, whose sole value is in their use, is hereby forbidden and abrogated.

Nothing in this section shall be deemed to deny the rights granted any person by the United States copyright laws. The sole intendment of this enactment is to abolish any common-law rights attaching to phonograph records and electrical transcriptions, whose sole value is in their use, and to forbid further restrictions of the collection of subsequent fees and royalties on phonograph records and electrical transcriptions by performers who were paid for the initial performance at the recording thereof. (1939, c. 113.)

Article 6.

Sale of Nursery Stock.

§ 66-29: Repealed by Session Laws 1973, c. 918.

Article 7.

Tagging Secondhand Watches.

§§ 66-30 through 66-34: Repealed by Session Laws 1995, c. 379, s. 18.4.

Article 8.

Public Warehouses.

§ 66-35. Who may become public warehousemen.

Any person or any corporation organized under the laws of this State whose charter authorizes it to engage in the business of a warehouseman may become a public warehouseman and authorized to keep and maintain public warehouses for the storage of cotton, goods, wares, and other merchandise as hereinafter prescribed upon giving the bond hereinafter required. (1901, c. 678; Rev., s. 3029; 1919, c. 212; C.S., s. 5118.)

§ 66-36. Bond required.

Every person or every corporation organized under G.S. 66-35, to become a public warehouseman, except such as shall have a capital stock of not less than five thousand dollars ($5,000), shall give bond in a reliable bonding or surety company, or an individual bond with sufficient sureties, payable to the State of North Carolina, in an amount not less than ten thousand dollars ($10,000), to be approved, filed with and recorded by the clerk of the superior court of the county in which the warehouse is located, for the faithful performance of the duties of a public warehouseman; but if such person or corporation has a capital stock of not less than five thousand dollars ($5,000), then it shall not be required to give the bond mentioned in this section. (1901, c. 678, s. 2; 1905, c. 540; Rev., s. 3030; 1908, c. 56; 1919, c. 212; C.S., s. 5119.)

§ 66-37. Person injured may sue on bond.

Whenever such warehouseman fails to perform any duty or violates any of the provisions of this Article, any person injured by such failure or violation may bring an action in his name and to his own use in any court of competent jurisdiction on the bond of said warehouseman. (1901, c. 678, s. 3; Rev., s. 3031; C.S., s. 5120.)

§ 66-38. When insurance required; storage receipts.

Every such warehouseman shall, when requested thereto in writing by a party placing property with it on storage, cause such property to be insured; every such warehouseman shall give to each person depositing property with it for storage a receipt therefor. (1901, c. 678, s. 4; 1905, c. 540, s. 2; Rev., s. 3032; C.S., s. 5121.)

§ 66-39. Books of account kept; open to inspection.

Every such warehouseman shall keep a book in which shall be entered an account of all its transactions relating to warehousing, storing, and insuring cotton, goods, wares and merchandise, and to the issuing of receipts therefor, which books shall be open to the inspection of any person actually interested in the property to which such entry relates. (1901, c. 678, s. 7; Rev., s. 3035; C.S., s. 5122.)

§ 66-40. Unlawful disposition of property stored.

If any person unlawfully sells, pledges, lends, or in any other way disposes of or permits or is a party to the unlawful selling, pledging, lending, or other disposition of any goods, wares, merchandise, or anything deposited in a public warehouse, without the authority of the party who deposited the same, he shall be punished by a fine not to exceed two thousand dollars ($2,000) and by imprisonment in the State's prison for not more than three years; but no officer, manager, or agent of such public warehouse shall be liable to the penalties provided in this section unless, with the intent to injure or defraud any person, he so sells, pledges, lends, or in any other way disposes of the same, or is a party to the selling, pledging, lending, or other disposition of any goods, wares, merchandise, article, or thing so deposited. (1901, c. 678, s. 11; Rev., s. 3831; C.S., s. 5123.)

Article 9.

Collection of Accounts.

§§ 66-41 through 66-49: Recodified as §§ 66-49.24 through 66-49.50.

Article 9A

Private Detectives.

§§ 66-49.1 through 66-49.8: Repealed by Session Laws 1977, c. 712, s. 2.

Article 9B

Motor Clubs and Associations.

§§ 66-49.9 through 66-49.23: Recodified as Article 69 of Chapter 58.

Article 9C.

Collection Agencies.

§§ 66-49.24 through 66-49.50: Recodified as Article 70 of Chapter 58.

Article 10.

Fair Trade.

§§ 66-50 through 66-57. Repealed by Session Laws 1975, c. 172.

Article 10A.

Inventions Developed by Employee.

§ 66-57.1. Employee's right to certain inventions.

Any provision in an employment agreement which provides that the employee shall assign or offer to assign any of his rights in an invention to his employer shall not apply to an invention that the employee developed entirely on his own time without using the employer's equipment, supplies, facility or trade secret information except for those inventions that (i) relate to the employer's business or actual or demonstrably anticipated research or development, or (ii) result from any work performed by the employee for the employer. To the extent a provision in an employment agreement purports to apply to the type of invention described, it is against the public policy of this State and is unenforceable. The employee shall bear the burden of proof in establishing that his invention qualifies under this section. (1981, c. 488, s. 1.)

§ 66-57.2. Employer's rights.

An employer may not require a provision of an employment agreement made unenforceable under G.S. 66-57.1 as a condition of employment or continued employment. An employer, in an employment agreement, may require that the employee report all inventions developed by the employee, solely or jointly, during the term of his employment to the employer, including those asserted by the employee as nonassignable, for the purpose of determining employee or employer rights. If required by a contract between the employer and the United States or its agencies, the employer may require that full title to certain patents and inventions be in the United States. (1981, c. 488, s. 1.)

Article 11.

Government in Business.

§ 66-58. Sale of merchandise or services by governmental units.

(a) Except as may be provided in this section, it shall be unlawful for any unit, department or agency of the State government, or any division or subdivision of the unit, department or agency, or any individual employee or employees of the unit, department or agency in his, or her, or their capacity as employee or employees thereof, to engage directly or indirectly in the sale of goods, wares or merchandise in competition with citizens of the State, or to engage in the operation of restaurants, cafeterias or other eating places in any building owned by or leased in the name of the State, or to maintain service establishments for the rendering of services to the public ordinarily and customarily rendered by private enterprises, or to provide transportation services, or to contract with any person, firm or corporation for the operation or rendering of the businesses or services on behalf of the unit, department or agency, or to purchase for or sell to any person, firm or corporation any article of merchandise in competition with private enterprise. The leasing or subleasing of space in any building owned, leased or operated by any unit, department or agency or division or subdivision thereof of the State for the purpose of operating or rendering of any of the businesses or services herein referred to is hereby prohibited.

(b) The provisions of subsection (a) of this section shall not apply to:

(1) Counties and municipalities.

(2) The Department of Health and Human Services or the Department of Agriculture and Consumer Services for the sale of serums, vaccines, and other like products.

(3) The Department of Administration, except that the agency shall not exceed the authority granted in the act creating the agency.

(4) The State hospitals for the mentally ill.

(5) The Department of Health and Human Services.

(6) The North Carolina School for the Blind at Raleigh.

(6a) The Division of Juvenile Justice of the Department of Public Safety.

(7) The North Carolina Schools for the Deaf.

(8) The University of North Carolina with regard to:

a. The University's utilities and other services operated by it prior to January 1, 2005.

b. The sale of articles produced incident to the operation of instructional departments, articles incident to educational research, articles of merchandise incident to classroom work, meals, books, or to articles of merchandise when sold to members of the educational staff or staff auxiliary to education or to duly enrolled students or occasionally to immediate members of the families of members of the educational staff or of duly enrolled students.

c. The sale of meals or merchandise to persons attending meetings or conventions as invited guests.

d. The operation by the University of North Carolina of an inn or hotel and dining and other facilities usually connected with a hotel or inn.

e. The hospital and Medical School of the University of North Carolina.

f. The Coliseum of North Carolina State University at Raleigh, and the other schools and colleges for higher education maintained or supported by the State.

g. The Centennial Campus of North Carolina State University at Raleigh.

h. The Horace Williams Campus of the University of North Carolina at Chapel Hill.

i. A Millennial Campus of a constituent institution of The University of North Carolina.

j. The comprehensive student health services or the comprehensive student infirmaries maintained by the constituent institutions of the University of North Carolina.

k. Agreements by the University of North Carolina School of the Arts to the use of that school's facilities, equipment, and services of students, faculty, and staff for the creation of commercial materials and productions that may be unrelated to educational purposes, so long as the proceeds from those agreements are used for the benefit of the educational mission of the University of North Carolina School of the Arts.

l. Activities that further the mission of the University as stated in G.S. 116-1.

m. Activities that serve students or employees of the University or members of the immediate families or guests of students or employees.

n. Activities that provide University-related services or market University-related merchandise to alumni of the University and members of their immediate families.

o. Activities that enable the community in which the constituent institution or other University entity is located, or the people of the State to utilize the University's facilities, equipment, or expertise. If the University proposes to engage in a new type of activity under this subdivision, then the University shall provide electronic notice of the proposal to the persons who have requested to be included in the registry created pursuant to subdivision (j)(2) of this section prior to engaging in the new type of activity.

(8a) The University of North Carolina with regard to the operation of gift shops, snack bars, and food service facilities physically connected to any of The University of North Carolina's public exhibition spaces, including the North Carolina Arboretum, provided that the resulting profits are used to support the operation of the public exhibition space.

(9) The Department of Environment and Natural Resources, except that the Department shall not construct, maintain, operate or lease a hotel or tourist inn in any park over which it has jurisdiction. The North Carolina Wildlife Resources Commission may sell wildlife memorabilia as a service to members of the public interested in wildlife conservation.

(9a) The North Carolina Forest Service.

(9b) The Department of Cultural Resources for the sale of food pursuant to G.S. 111-47.2 and the sale of books, crafts, gifts, and other tourism-related items at historic sites and museums administered by the Department.

(10) Child-caring institutions or orphanages receiving State aid.

(11) Highlands School in Macon County.

(12) The North Carolina State Fair.

(13) Rural electric memberships corporations.

(13a) Repealed by Session Laws 2006-264, s. 8, effective August 27, 2006.

(13b) The Department of Agriculture and Consumer Services with regard to its lessees at farmers' markets operated by the Department.

(13c) The Western North Carolina Agricultural Center.

(13d) Agricultural centers or livestock facilities operated by the Department of Agriculture and Consumer Services.

(14) Nothing herein contained shall be construed to prohibit the engagement in any of the activities described in subsection (a) hereof by a firm, corporation or person who or which is a lessee of space only of the State of North Carolina or any of its departments or agencies; provided the leases shall be awarded by the Department of Administration to the highest bidder, as provided by law in the case of State contracts and which lease shall be for a term of not less than one year and not more than five years.

(15) The Division of Adult Correction of the Department of Public Safety is authorized to purchase and install automobile license tag plant equipment for the purpose of manufacturing license tags for the State and local governments and for such other purposes as the Division may direct.

The Commissioner of Motor Vehicles, or such other authority as may exercise the authority to purchase automobile license tags is hereby directed to purchase from, and to contract with, the Division of Adult Correction of the Department of Public Safety for the State automobile license tag requirements from year to year.

The price to be paid to the Division of Adult Correction of the Department of Public Safety for the tags shall be fixed and agreed upon by the Governor, the State Division of Adult Correction of the Department of Public Safety, and the Motor Vehicle Commissioner, or such authority as may be authorized to purchase the supplies.

(16) Laundry services performed by the Division of Adult Correction of the Department of Public Safety may be provided only for agencies and instrumentalities of the State which are supported by State funds and for county or municipally controlled and supported hospitals presently being served by the Division of Adult Correction of the Department of Public Safety, or for which services have been contracted or applied for in writing, as of May 22, 1973. In addition to the prior sentence, laundry services performed by the Division of Adult Correction of the Department of Public Safety may be provided for VA Medical Centers of the United States Department of Veterans Affairs, the Governor Morehead School, and the North Carolina School for the Deaf.

The services shall be limited to wet-washing, drying and ironing of flatwear or flat goods such as towels, sheets and bedding, linens and those uniforms prescribed for wear by the institutions and further limited to only flat goods or apparel owned, distributed or controlled entirely by the institutions and shall not include processing by any dry-cleaning methods; provided, however, those garments and items presently being serviced by wet-washing, drying and ironing may in the future, at the election of the Division of Adult Correction of the Department of Public Safety, be processed by a dry-cleaning method.

(17)   The North Carolina Global TransPark Authority or a lessee of the Authority.

(18)   The activities and products of private enterprise carried on or manufactured within a State prison facility pursuant to G.S. 148-70.

(19)   The North Carolina Justice Academy.

(20)   The Department of Transportation, or any nonprofit lessee of the Department, for the sale of books, crafts, gifts, and other tourism-related items at visitor centers owned by the Department.

(21)   Repealed by Session Laws 2008-134, s. 73(b), effective July 28, 2008.

(22)   The North Carolina State Highway Patrol.

(23)   The North Carolina State Lottery Commission.

(24)   The North Carolina National Guard, for the operation of post exchanges.

(25)   The gift or sale of any craft items made by inmates in the custody of the Division of Adult Correction of the Department of Public Safety as part of a program or initiative established by the Section of Prisons of the Division of Adult Correction.

(26)   The North Carolina Zoological Park.

(27)   The North Carolina Office of Economic Recovery and Investment and State agencies in the implementation of the American Recovery and Reinvestment Act of 2009 (Public Law 111-5) funded projects.

(c)   The provisions of subsection (a) shall not prohibit:

(1)   The sale of products of experiment stations or test farms.

(1a) The sale of products raised or produced incident to the operation of a community college viticulture/enology program as authorized by G.S. 18B-1114.4.

(1b) The sale by North Carolina State University at University-owned facilities of dairy products, including ice cream, cheeses, milk-based beverages, and the by-products of heavy cream, produced by the Dairy and Process Applications Laboratory, so long as any profits are used to support the Department of Food Science and College of Agriculture and Life Sciences at North Carolina State University.

(2) The sale of learned journals, works of art, books or publications of the Department of Cultural Resources or other agencies, or the Supreme Court Reports or Session Laws of the General Assembly.

(3) The business operation of endowment funds established for the purpose of producing income for educational purposes; for purposes of this section, the phrase "operation of endowment funds" shall include the operation by constituent institutions of The University of North Carolina of campus stores, the profits from which are used exclusively for awarding scholarships to defray the expenses of students attending the institution; provided, that the operation of the stores must be approved by the board of trustees of the institution, and the merchandise sold shall be limited to educational materials and supplies, gift items and miscellaneous personal-use articles. Provided further that, notwithstanding this subsection, profits from a campus store operated by the endowment of the North Carolina School of Science and Mathematics are used exclusively for student activities, athletics, and other programs to enhance student life. Provided further that sales at campus stores are limited to employees of the institution and members of their immediate families, to duly enrolled students of the campus at which a campus store is located and their immediate families, to duly enrolled students of other campuses of the University of North Carolina other than the campus at which the campus store is located, to other campus stores and to other persons who are on campus other than for the purpose of purchasing merchandise from campus stores. It is the intent of this subdivision that campus stores be established and operated for the purpose of assuring the availability of merchandise described in this Article for sale to persons enumerated herein and not for the purpose of competing with stores operated in the communities surrounding the campuses of the University of North Carolina.

(3a) The use of community college personnel or facilities, with the consent of the trustees of that college, in support of or by a private business enterprise located on a community college campus or in the service area of a community college for one or more of the following specific services in support of economic development:

a. Small business incubators. - As used in this sub-subdivision, the term "small business incubators" means sites for new business ventures in the service area of the community college that are in need of the support and assistance provided by the college; and, without which, the likelihood of success of the business would be greatly diminished. The services of the small business incubator shall not extend to any such new business venture for a period of more than 48 months.

b. Product testing services.

c. Videoconferencing services provided to the public for occasional use.

(3b) The operation of a military business center by a community college. For the purposes of this subdivision, the term "military business center" means a facility that serves to coordinate and facilitate interactions between the Armed Forces of the United States; military personnel, veterans, and their families; and private businesses.

(3c) The use of the personnel and facilities of Western Piedmont Community College, with the consent of the trustees of the college, in support of economic development through the operation of the East Campus and its companion facilities as an event venue.

(3d) The use of community college facilities by a private business enterprise that has loaned or donated instructional equipment to the college to demonstrate that equipment to customers. This use of college facilities shall be in accordance with policies adopted by the board of trustees of the college.

(3e) The use of personnel, equipment, and facilities relating to Interactive Three Dimensional (Advanced Visualization) technology and Tele-presence technology at Fayetteville Technical Community College. Proceeds generated must be used either to continue the function of this program or to support the educational mission of the school.

(4)   The operation of lunch counters by the Department of Health and Human Services as blind enterprises of the type operated on January 1, 1951, in State buildings in the City of Raleigh.

(5)   The operation of a snack bar and cafeteria in the State Legislative Building, and a snack bar in the Legislative Office Building.

(6)   The maintenance by the prison system authorities of eating and sleeping facilities at units of the State prison system for prisoners and for members of the prison staff while on duty, or the maintenance by the highway system authorities of eating and sleeping facilities for working crews on highway construction or maintenance when actually engaged in such work on parts of the highway system.

(7)   The operation by penal, correctional or facilities operated by the Department of Health and Human Services, the Division of Juvenile Justice of the Department of Public Safety, or by the Department of Agriculture and Consumer Services, of dining rooms for the inmates or clients or members of the staff while on duty and for the accommodation of persons visiting the inmates or clients, and other bona fide visitors.

(8)   The sale by the Department of Agriculture and Consumer Services of livestock, poultry and publications in keeping with its present livestock and farm program.

(9)   The operation by the public schools of school cafeterias.

(9a)   The use of a public school bus or public school activity bus for a purpose allowed under G.S. 115C-242 or the use of a public school activity bus for a purpose authorized by G.S. 115C-247.

(9b)   The use of a public school activity bus by a nonprofit corporation or a unit of local government to provide transportation services for school-aged and preschool-aged children, their caretakers, and their instructors to or from activities being held on the property of a nonprofit corporation or a unit of local government. The local board of education that owns the bus shall ensure that the person driving the bus is licensed to operate the bus and that the lessee has adequate liability insurance to cover the use and operation of the leased bus.

(10) Sale by any State correctional or other institution of farm, dairy, livestock or poultry products raised or produced by it in its normal operations as authorized by the act creating it.

(11) The sale of textbooks, library books, forms, bulletins, and instructional supplies by the State Board of Education, State Department of Public Instruction, and local school authorities.

(12) The sale of North Carolina flags by or through the auspices of the Department of Administration, to the citizens of North Carolina.

(13) The operation by the Division of Adult Correction of the Department of Public Safety of forestry management programs on State-owned lands, including the sale on the open market of timber cut as a part of the management program.

(14) The operation by the Division of Adult Correction of the Department of Public Safety of facilities to manufacture and produce traffic and street name signs for use on the public streets and highways of the State.

(15) The operation by the Division of Adult Correction of the Department of Public Safety of facilities to manufacture and produce paint for use on the public streets and highways of the State.

(16) The performance by the Department of Transportation of dredging services for a unit of local government.

(17) The sale by the State Board of Elections to political committees and candidate committees of computer software designed by or for the State Board of Elections to provide a uniform system of electronic filing of the campaign finance reports required by Article 22A of Chapter 163 of the General Statutes and to facilitate the State Board's monitoring of compliance with that Article. This computer software for electronic filing of campaign finance reports shall not exceed a cost of one hundred dollars ($100.00) to any political committee or candidate committee without the State Board of Elections first notifying in writing the Joint Legislative Commission on Governmental Operations.

(18) Repealed by Session Laws 2009-329, s. 2.2, effective July 24, 2009.

(19) The use of the North Carolina Museum of Art's conservation lab by the Regional Conservation Services Program of the North Carolina Museum of Art

Foundation for the provision of conservation treatment services on privately owned works of art. However, when providing this service, the Regional Conservation Services Program shall give priority to publicly owned works of art.

(20) The sale by the State Board of Education of NCVPS courses to home schools, private schools, and out-of-state educational entities.

(d) A department, agency or educational unit named in subsection (b) shall not perform any of the prohibited acts for or on behalf of any other department, agency or educational unit.

(e) Any person, whether employee of the State of North Carolina or not, who shall violate, or participate in the violation of this section, shall be guilty of a Class 1 misdemeanor.

(f) Notwithstanding the provisions of G.S. 66-58(a), the operation by the Division of Adult Correction of the Department of Public Safety of facilities for the manufacture of any product or the providing of any service pursuant to Article 14 of Chapter 148 of the General Statutes not regulated by the provisions of subsection (c) of this section shall be subject to the prior approval of the Governor, with biennial review by the General Assembly, at the beginning of each fiscal year commencing after October 1, 1975. The Division of Adult Correction of the Department of Public Safety shall file with the Director of the Budget quarterly reports detailing prison enterprise operations in such a format as shall be required by the Director of the Budget.

(g) Repealed by Session Laws 2006-66, s. 9.11(x), effective July 1, 2007.

(h) Notwithstanding the provisions of G.S. 66-58(b)(8), The University of North Carolina, its constituent institutions, the Centennial Campus of North Carolina State University, the Horace Williams Campus of the University of North Carolina at Chapel Hill, a Millennial Campus of a constituent institution of The University of North Carolina, or any corporation or other legal entity created or directly controlled by and using land owned by The University of North Carolina shall consult with and provide the following information to the Joint Legislative Commission on Governmental Operations before issuing debt or executing a contract for a golf course or for any transient accommodations facility, including a hotel or motel:

(1) Architectural concepts.

(2) Financial and debt service projections.

(3) Business plans.

(4) Operating plans.

(5) Feasibililty studies and consultant reports.

(i) The Board of Governors of The University of North Carolina shall establish a panel to determine whether The University of North Carolina is authorized pursuant to sub-subdivisions m., n., and o. of subdivision (8) of subsection (b) of this section to undertake an activity in competition with an existing or proposed nongovernmental entity. Pursuant to G.S. 138-5, panel members shall receive the same per diem and reimbursement for travel expenses as members of State boards and commissions. The University of North Carolina shall be responsible for staffing and paying the expenses of the panel. The panel shall consist of nine members as follows:

(1) Two members who are familiar with the interests of the business community of the State appointed by the Governor.

(2) Two members who are familiar with the interests of the business community of the State appointed by the General Assembly upon the recommendation of the Speaker of the House of Representatives under G.S. 120-121.

(3) Two members who are familiar with the interests of the business community of the State appointed by the General Assembly upon the recommendation of the President Pro Tempore of the Senate under G.S. 120-121.

(4) Three members who are not employees of The University of North Carolina appointed by the Board of Governors.

The panel may make the determination whether a proposed or ongoing activity undertaken under sub-subdivisions m. or n. of subdivision (8) of subsection (b) of this section is unauthorized competition. The panel may also make a determination whether a proposed or ongoing activity undertaken under sub-subdivision o. of subdivision (8) of subsection (b) of this section is either unauthorized or unfair competition. The University will be bound by a decision of the panel that a proposed or ongoing activity is not justified by the exceptions set out in sub-subdivisions m., n., or o. of subdivision (8) of subsection (b) of this section.

The panel established by this subsection shall report to the Joint Legislative Economic Development Oversight Committee. The panel shall report to the Committee by May 1 of each year on the number and types of determinations made during the preceding year.

(j) The Board of Governors shall establish and publish procedures to be used by the panel created under subsection (i) of this section in making determinations. The procedures shall:

(1) Include that a determination may be initiated based on a request from any nongovernmental entity in the State that is in or proposes to be in the same or a similar or competing business or based on a request from the constituent institution or other university system entity engaging in or proposing to engage in the activity.

(2) Require the panel to maintain a registry of all parties that request to receive notification of the panel's proceedings. The notification may be electronic and shall be given to all parties that have requested to be notified at least seven days prior to the panel's meeting. The notice shall include the name of the constituent institution or other university system entity engaging in or proposing to engage in the activity and the nature of the activity. The panel shall provide the documents relating to any agenda item to anyone requesting them in advance of the panel's proceedings.

(3) Provide that the agendas for the panel's meetings, the minutes of the meetings, and the determinations of the panel shall be posted on The University of North Carolina Web site.

(k) The University of North Carolina and its employees may rely on a determination made by the panel created under subsection (i) of this section as to whether an activity violates this section, and a determination that an activity is authorized shall be an absolute defense in any prosecution for any activity undertaken before a contrary determination is made by a court or by an opinion of the Attorney General. The panel shall not have the power to overrule a prior determination of the Attorney General.

(l) The proceeds of any activity undertaken under sub-subdivisions m., n., or o. of subdivision (8) of subsection (b) of this section shall be placed in an institutional trust fund pursuant to G.S. 116-36.1 and shall be used to continue to conduct the activity that generated the proceeds or to further the mission of the constituent institution or other University entity engaging in the activity.

(m) Any person, firm, or corporation who or which is injured or suffers damages as a result of a violation of this section may maintain an action in the Wake County Superior Court for injunctive relief against any unit, department or agency of the State government, or any division or subdivision of the unit, department or agency, or any individual employee or employees of the unit, department or agency, in his or her, or their capacity as employee or employees, who or which has committed a violation. In a proceeding under this subsection, the court shall determine whether a violation has been committed and enter any judgment or decree necessary to remove the effects of any violation it finds and to prevent continuation or renewal of the violation in the future. Upon a judicial finding that any contract or contractual obligation is in violation of this section, such contract or contractual obligation shall be null and void. Any person, firm, or corporation who or which believes that a proposed activity will be in violation of this section may request a declaratory judgment under G.S. 1-253 or injunctive relief or both, notwithstanding the fact that such activity has not been commenced. (1929, c. 221, s. 1; 1933, c. 172, s. 18; 1939, c. 122; 1941, c. 36; 1951, c. 1090, s. 1; 1957, c. 349, ss. 6, 10; 1967, c. 996, s. 13; 1973, c. 476, ss. 48, 128, 143; c. 671, s. 1; c. 965; c. 1262, s. 86; c. 1294; c. 1457, s. 7; 1975, c. 730, ss. 2-5; c. 840; c. 879, s. 46; 1977, cc. 355, 715; c. 771, s. 4; 1979, c. 830, s. 4; 1981, c. 635, s. 3; 1983, c. 8; c. 476; c. 717, s. 13; c. 761, s. 168; 1985, c. 589, s. 28; c. 757, s. 206(d); 1989, c. 727, s. 218(9); 1989 (Reg. Sess., 1990), c. 1004, s. 1; 1991, c. 749, s. 7; 1991 (Reg. Sess., 1992), c. 902, s. 3; 1993, c. 539, s. 513; 1994, Ex. Sess., c. 24, s. 14(c); 1993 (Reg. Sess., 1994), c. 769, s. 17.15; c. 777, s. 4(e); 1995, c. 247, s. 2; c. 507, s. 13.1(a); 1997-258, s. 1; 1997-261, ss. 4-6; 1997-315, s. 1; 1997-443, s. 11A.21; 1997-456, s. 55.2A; 1997-527, s. 1; 1998-202, s. 4(d), (e); 1998-212, ss. 9.9, 13.3; 1999-234, s. 9; 1999-237, ss. 19.7, 27.23A; 2000-137, ss. 4(f), 4(g); 2000-148, s. 6; 2000-177, s. 10; 2001-41, s. 2; 2001-127, s. 1; 2001-368, s. 1; 2002-102, s. 3; 2002-109, s. 1; 2002-126, ss. 9.15(a), 18.5; 2004-124, ss. 8.17(b), 9.13; 2005-20, s. 1; 2005-63, s. 1; 2005-247, s. 1; 2005-344, s. 5; 2005-397, ss. 1, 2, 4; 2006-66, ss. 9.11(w), (x); 2006-264, s. 8; 2007-60, s. 1; 2007-280, ss. 4.1, 5; 2007-398, s. 5; 2008-134, s. 73(b); 2008-192, s. 12; 2009-207, s. 1; 2009-281, s. 1; 2009-329, ss. 2.1, 2.2; 2009-475, s. 9; 2011-145, ss. 7.22(l), 19.1(h), (j), (l); 2011-183, s. 50; 2011-331, s. 1; 2011-398, s. 61.3; 2012-83, s. 33; 2012-194, s. 60; 2013-360, s. 19.3(c).)

Article 11A.

Electronic Commerce in Government.

§ 66-58.1. Title; purpose.

This Article shall be known and may be cited as the Electronic Commerce Act. The purpose of this Article is to facilitate electronic commerce with public agencies and regulate the application of electronic signatures when used in commerce with public agencies. (1998-127, s. 1.)

§ 66-58.2. Definitions.

The following definitions apply in this Article:

(1)   "Certification authority" means a person authorized by the Secretary to facilitate electronic commerce by vouching for the relationship between a person or public agency and that person's or public agency's electronic signature.

(2)   "Electronic signature" means any identifier or authentication technique attached to or logically associated with an electronic record which is intended by the party using it to have the same force and effect as the party's manual signature.

(3)   "Person" means any individual, firm, partnership, corporation, or combination thereof of whatsoever form or character.

(4)   "Public agencies" means and includes every public office, public officer or official (State or local, elected or appointed), institution, board, commission, bureau, council, department, authority, or other unit of government of the State or of any county, unit, special district, or other political subdivision of government.

(5)   "Secretary" means Secretary of State.

(6) "Transaction" means an electronic transmission of data between a person and a public agency, or between public agencies, including, but not limited to, contracts, filings, and legally operative documents. (1998-127, s. 1.)

§ 66-58.3. Certification authority licensing.

All persons acting as a certification authority with respect to transactions under this Article shall be licensed by the Secretary prior to representing themselves or acting as a certification authority under this Article. Certification authority licensing standards set by the Secretary may include, but are not limited to, technical, physical, procedural, and personnel security controls, repository obligations, and financial responsibility standards. Upon payment of the required fees, a certification authority meeting the standards adopted by the Secretary by rule shall be licensed for a period of one year. Licenses of certification authorities complying with the standards adopted by the Secretary may be renewed for additional one-year terms upon payment of the required renewal fee. (1998-127, s. 1.)

§ 66-58.4. Use of electronic signatures.

All public agencies may use and accept electronic signatures pursuant to this Article, pursuant to Article 40 of this Chapter (the Uniform Electronic Transactions Act), or pursuant to other law. (1998-127, s. 1; 2003-233, s. 1; 2007-119, s. 1.)

§ 66-58.5. Validity of electronic signatures.

(a) An electronic signature contained in a transaction undertaken pursuant to this Article between a person and a public agency, or between public agencies, shall have the same force and effect as a manual signature provided all of the following requirements are met:

(1) The public agency involved in the transaction requests or requires the use of electronic signatures.

(2) The electronic signature contained in the transaction embodies all of the following attributes:

a. It is unique to the person using it;

b. It is capable of certification;

c. It is under sole control of the person using it;

d. It is linked to data in such a manner that if the data are changed, the electronic signature is invalidated; and

e. It conforms to rules adopted by the Secretary pursuant to this Article.

(b) A transaction undertaken pursuant to this Article between a person and a public agency, or between public agencies, is not unenforceable, nor is it inadmissible into evidence, on the sole ground that the transaction is evidenced by an electronic record or that it has been signed with an electronic signature.

(c) This Article does not affect the validity of, presumptions relating to, or burdens of proof regarding an electronic signature that is accepted pursuant to Article 40 of this Chapter or other law. (1998-127, s. 1; 2003-233, s. 2.)

§ 66-58.6. Enforcement.

(a) The Secretary may investigate complaints or other information indicating fraudulent or unlawful conduct that violates this Article or the rules promulgated thereunder.

(b) The Superior Court Division of the General Court of Justice has jurisdiction and authority upon application of the Secretary to enjoin or restrain violations of this Article.

(c) It shall be the duty of the Attorney General, when requested, to represent the Secretary in actions or proceedings in connection with this Article.

(d) Nothing in this Article shall adversely affect any rights or the enforcement of any rights acquired by any person or public agency under any other statute or at common law with respect to matters also covered by this Article. (1998-127, s. 1.)

§ 66-58.7. Civil penalty.

The Secretary may assess a civil penalty of not more than five thousand dollars ($5,000) per violation against any certification authority that violates a provision of this Article or any rule promulgated thereunder. In determining the amount of a penalty under this section, the Secretary shall give due consideration to each of the following factors:

(1) The organizational size of the certification authority cited;

(2) The good faith of the certification authority cited;

(3) The gravity of the violation;

(4) The prior record of the violator in complying or failing to comply with this Article or a rule adopted pursuant to this Article; and

(5) The risk of harm caused by the violation.

Chapter 150B of the General Statutes governs the imposition of a civil penalty under this section. A civil penalty owed under this section may be recovered in a civil action brought by the Secretary or the Attorney General. (1998-127, s. 1.)

§ 66-58.8. Criminal penalty.

(a) Any person who willfully violates any provision of this Article, or who willfully violates any rule or order under this Article, with intent to defraud, is guilty of a Class I felony.

(b) The Secretary shall provide such evidence as is available concerning criminal violations of this Article or of any rule or order promulgated hereunder to the proper district attorney, who may, with or without such a reference, institute appropriate criminal proceedings under this Article.

(c)   Nothing in this Article limits the power of the State to punish any person for any conduct which constitutes a crime by statute or common law. (1998-127, s. 1.)

§ 66-58.9. Exemptions.

This Article shall not apply to any of the following:

(1)   Electronic signatures and facsimile signatures that are otherwise allowed by law.

(2)   The execution of documents filed with, issued, or entered by a court of the General Court of Justice. However, a document or transaction validly executed under this Article is not rendered invalid because it is filed with, or attached to, a document issued or entered by a court of the General Court of Justice.

(3)   Transactions where a public agency is not a party. (1998-127, s. 1.)

§ 66-58.10. Rule making.

(a)   The Secretary may promulgate rules under this Article. Such rules may include, but are not limited to:

(1)   Definitions, including, but not limited to, more technical definitions of "certification authority" and "electronic signature";

(2)   The creation, accreditation, bonding, licensing, operation, regulation, and sanctioning of certification authorities;

(3)   The imposition of licensing and renewal fees in amounts not to exceed five thousand dollars ($5,000) per year; and

(4)   The imposition of civil monetary penalties for noncompliance with this Article or the rules promulgated thereunder.

(b) Notwithstanding G.S. 150B-21.1(a), the Secretary may adopt temporary rules to implement the certification authority technology provisions of this Article using the procedure for adoption of temporary rules under G.S. 150B-21.1(a2).

(c) The Secretary shall deposit licensing and renewal fees in the General Fund. (1998-127, s. 1.)

§ 66-58.11. Reciprocal agreements.

The Secretary is hereby authorized to enter into reciprocal arrangements with appropriate and duly authorized public agencies of other jurisdictions having a law substantially similar to this Article so as to further the purpose of this Article. (1998-127, s. 1.)

§ 66-58.12. Agencies may provide access to services through electronic and digital transactions; fees authorized.

(a) Public agencies are encouraged to maximize citizen and business access to their services through the use of electronic and digital transactions. A public agency may determine, through program and transaction analysis, which of its services may be made available to the public through electronic means, including the Internet. The agency shall identify any inhibitors to electronic transactions between the agency and the public, including legal, policy, financial, or privacy concerns and specific inhibitors unique to the agency or type of transaction. An agency shall not provide a transaction through the Internet that is impractical, unreasonable, or not permitted by laws pertaining to privacy or security.

(b) An agency may charge a fee to cover its costs of permitting a person to complete a transaction through the World Wide Web or other means of electronic access. The fee may be applied on a per transaction basis and may be calculated either as a flat fee or a percentage fee, as determined under an agreement between a person and a public agency. The fee may be collected by the agency or by its third party agent.

(c) The fee imposed under subsection (b) of this section must be approved by the Office of State Budget and Management, in consultation with the State

Chief Information Officer and the Joint Legislative Commission on Governmental Operations. The revenue derived from the fee must be credited to a nonreverting agency reserve account. The funds in the account may be expended only for e-commerce initiatives and projects approved by the State Chief Information Officer, in consultation with the Joint Legislative Oversight Committee on Information Technology. For purposes of this subsection, the term "public agencies" does not include a county, unit, special district, or other political subdivision of government.

(d) This section does not apply to the Judicial Department. (2000-109, s. 8; 2004-129, s. 27; 2005-92, s. 1.)

§§ 66-58.13 through 66-58.19. Reserved for future codification purposes.

Article 11B.

Electronic Access to State Services.

§ 66-58.20. Development and implementation of Web portals; public agency links.

(a) The Office of Information Technology Services (ITS) shall develop the architecture, requirements, and standards for the development, implementation and operation of one or more centralized Web portals that will allow persons to access State government services on a 24-hour basis. ITS shall submit its plan for the implementation of the Web portals to the State Chief Information Officer for review and approval. When the plan is approved by the State Chief Information Officer, ITS shall move forward with development and implementation of the statewide Web Portal system.

(b) Each State department, agency, and institution under the review of the State Chief Information Officer shall functionally link its Internet or electronic services to a centralized Web portal system established pursuant to subsection (a) of this section. (2000-67, s. 7.9; 2004-129, s. 28.)

Article 12.

Coupons for Products of Photography.

§§ 66-59 through 66-64: Repealed by Session Laws 1995, c. 379, s. 18.5.

Article 13

Miscellaneous Provisions.

§ 66-65. Indemnity bonds required of agents, etc., to state maximum liability and period of liability.

Wherever any person, firm, or corporation, engaged in the business of merchandising any articles whatsoever, shall require of its agents, solicitors, salesmen, representatives, consignees, or peddlers, or other persons selling or handling its merchandise, as a condition precedent to selling or handling any of the merchandise of said person, firm, or corporation, that such agents, solicitors, salesmen, representatives, consignees, or peddlers should furnish and provide a bond or guaranty or indemnity contract guaranteeing the full and faithful accounting of moneys collected from such merchandise, such bond or indemnity contract shall state specifically therein the maximum amount of money or other liability which the principal and the sureties or guarantors thereof undertake thereby to pay in event of default of said bond or indemnity or guaranty contract; and said bond or indemnity or guaranty contract shall also state specifically the period of time during which liability may be incurred on account of any default in said bond or indemnity or guaranty contract.

Any bond or indemnity or guaranty contract which does not comply with the provisions of this section shall be null and void and no action may be maintained against the surety or guarantor to recover any sum due thereon in any court of this State. (1943, c. 604, ss. 1, 2.)

§ 66-66. Manufacture or sale of antifreeze solutions compounded with inorganic salts or petroleum distillates prohibited.

The manufacture or sale of antifreeze solutions which are designated, intended, advertised, or recommended by the manufacturer or seller for use in the cooling systems of motor vehicles or gasoline combustion engines, and which are compounded with calcium chloride, magnesium chloride, sodium chloride, or other inorganic salts or with petroleum distillates is hereby prohibited.

Any person, firm, or corporation violating the provisions of this section shall be guilty of a Class 1 misdemeanor. (1943, c. 625, ss. 1, 2; 1993, c. 539, s. 515; 1994, Ex. Sess., c. 24, s. 14(c).)

§ 66-67. Disposition by laundries and dry cleaning establishments of certain unclaimed clothing.

(a)   If any person fails to claim any garment, clothing, household article or other article delivered for laundering, cleaning or pressing to any laundry or dry cleaning establishment as defined in G.S. 105-85, or any dry cleaning establishment as defined in G.S. 105-74, for a period of 90 days after the surrender of such articles for processing, the laundry or dry cleaning establishment may dispose of such garments, clothing, household articles or other articles by whatever means it may choose, without liability or responsibility to the owner, 30 days after a notice has been mailed by certified mail, return receipt requested, to the last known address of the owner of the garment, clothing, or other article, stating that the article will be disposed of unless it is redeemed within 30 days of the mailing of the notice. Provided, however, that before such laundry or dry cleaning establishment may claim the benefit of this section it shall at the time of receiving such garments, clothing, household articles or other articles, have a notice of dimensions of not less than eight and one-half by 11 inches, prominently displayed in a conspicuous place in the office, branch office or retail outlet where said clothes, garments or articles are received, if the same be received at an office, on which notice shall appear the words "NOT RESPONSIBLE FOR GOODS LEFT ON HAND FOR MORE THAN 90 DAYS".

(b)   If any person fails to claim any garment, clothing, household article or other article delivered to any laundry or dry cleaning establishment described in subsection (a) of this section and displaying the notice described in that subsection, for a period of 180 days, the laundry or dry cleaning establishment may, without giving notice to the owner, dispose of such garment, clothing, household article, or other article by whatever means it may choose, without liability or responsibility to the owner.

(c) The provisions of this section shall also be applicable with respect to the storage of garments, furs, rugs, clothing or other articles after the completion of the period for which storage was agreed to be provided. (1947, c. 975; 1953, c. 1054; 1967, c. 931; 1987, c. 158; 1991, c. 531, s. 1.)

§ 66-67.1. Disposal by repair businesses of certain unclaimed property.

(a) Disposal Authorized. - Notwithstanding the provisions of Article 1 of Chapter 44A of the General Statutes, a person who repairs, alters, treats, or improves personal property in the ordinary course of his business pursuant to an express or implied contract with an owner or legal possessor of the personal property may, upon compliance with the notice requirement of subsection (b), dispose of any personal property of a value of five hundred dollars ($500.00) or less, other than a motor vehicle, that has not been claimed by the owner or legal possessor for a period of sixty days or more after his receipt of written notice that the property is ready to be claimed.

(b) Notice Requirement. - The repair business shall, at the time the property is surrendered, have a written notice of dimensions of not less than eight and one-half by eleven inches prominently displayed in a conspicuous place in the office or shop where the property was surrendered containing the following message: "NOT RESPONSIBLE FOR GOODS LEFT ON HAND FOR MORE THAN 60 DAYS". When the property has been repaired or otherwise processed, the repair business shall notify the owner or legal possessor of the property, by certified mail with return receipt requested, that the property is ready to be claimed.

(c) Liability. - A person who disposes of property in accordance with this section is not liable for damages to the owner of the property disposed of.

(d) Definitions. - As used in this section, the terms "legal possessor" and "owner" have the meanings provided in G.S. 44A-1. (1987, c. 386.)

§ 66-67.2. Persons who sell used goods on consignment must keep certain records.

(a)   A person who is engaged in the business of selling used tangible personal property on consignment must keep a record of each piece of property consigned to that person for sale. The record must contain all of the following information:

(1)   A description of the property, including any model or serial number of the property.

(2)   The name, residence address, telephone number, and drivers license number or other identifying number of the owner of the property.

(3)   The date the property was consigned.

(4)   The owner's stated value of the property.

(b)   The consignee shall provide the owner with a copy of the record required by subsection (a) of this section.

(c)   A person who fails to keep the records required by this section is guilty of a Class 2 misdemeanor. A law enforcement agency may examine the records required to be kept under this section during business hours.

(d)   This section does not apply to a motor vehicle.

(e)   This section does not apply to any nonprofit organization exempt from taxation under section 501(c)(3) of the Internal Revenue Code (26 U.S.C. § 501(c)(3)). (1991, c. 536; 1993, c. 539, s. 516; 1994, Ex. Sess., c. 24, s. 14(c).)

§ 66-67.3. Disposal of dies, molds, forms, and patterns.

(a)   Definitions. - The following definitions apply in this section:

(1)   Customer. - Either of the following:

a.   A person who causes or caused a molder to fabricate, cast, or otherwise make a die, mold, form, or pattern.

b. A person who causes or caused a molder to use a die, mold, form, or pattern to manufacture, assemble, or otherwise make a product.

(2) Molder. - A tool or die maker or any other person who does either of the following:

a. Fabricates, casts, or otherwise makes a die, mold, form, or pattern.

b. Uses a die, mold, form, or pattern to manufacture, assemble, or otherwise make a product.

(b) Ownership and Transfer. - A customer has all rights, title, and interest to a die, mold, form, or pattern made or used by a molder on behalf of the customer unless an agreement provides otherwise. If the customer does not claim possession of the die, mold, form, or pattern from the molder within three years after the last time it is used, the molder may choose to obtain all rights, title, and interest to the die, mold, form, or pattern by operation of law unless a written agreement provides otherwise.

(c) Procedure. - If a molder chooses to have all rights, title, and interest to a die, mold, form, or pattern transferred to the molder by operation of law, the molder must send a written notice, by registered mail, return receipt requested, to the customer and to any known secured creditor. The notice must state that the molder intends to terminate the customer's rights, title, and interest in a mold, die, form, or pattern by having those rights, title, and interest transferred to the molder by operation of law pursuant to this section. The notice to the customer must be sent to the customer's last known address or, if the customer has designated in writing a different address for receipt of the notice, to the designated address. If a return receipt cannot be obtained for a notice that is mailed, the molder may give notice by publication in accordance with G.S. 1A-1, Rule 4(j1). The rights, title, and interest in a die, mold, form, or pattern are transferred by operation of law to a molder who gives notice as required by this section unless, within 30 days after the date the molder receives acknowledgement of the return receipt of a notice that is mailed or 45 days after the date of first publication of a notice made by publication, the customer takes possession of the die, mold, form, or pattern, or makes other contractual arrangements with the molder for taking possession of or for storing the die, mold, form, or pattern.

(d) Use Upon Transfer. - A molder to whom the rights, title, and interest in a die, mold, form, or pattern is transferred by operation of law under this section may destroy or otherwise dispose of the die, mold, form, or pattern as the molder's own property without any risk of liability to the customer. The molder may not use the die, mold, form, or pattern for any other purpose.

(e) Scope. - This section does not affect a right of a customer under federal patent or copyright law or any state or federal law pertaining to unfair competition. (1993, c. 541, s. 9.)

§ 66-67.4. Film and photographic print processor or computer technician to report film or computer images containing pictures of a minor engaging in sexual activity.

(a) As used in this section:

(1) "Computer technician" means any person who repairs, installs, or otherwise services any computer or computer network or system for compensation.

(2) "Minor" has the same meaning as in G.S. 14-190.13.

(3) "Processor of photographic images" means any person who, for compensation: (i) develops exposed photographic film into negatives, slides, or prints; (ii) makes prints from negatives, slides, digital images, or video; or (iii) develops, processes, transfers, edits, or enhances video or digital images.

(4) "Sexual activity" has the same meaning as in G.S. 14-190.13.

(b) Any processor of photographic images or any computer technician who, within the person's scope of employment, observes an image of a minor or a person who reasonably appears to be a minor engaging in sexual activity shall report the name and address of the person requesting the processing of the film or photographs or the owner or person in possession of the computer or computer network or system to the Cyber Tip Line at the National Center for Missing and Exploited Children or to the appropriate law enforcement official in the county or municipality in which the image or film was submitted.

(c) An employee of a processor of photographic images or computer technician may satisfy the requirements of this section by reporting the required information to a person designated by the employer. The person designated by the employer shall then report as required by subsection (b) of this section.

(d) Any person, their employer, or a third party complying with this section in good faith shall be immune from any civil or criminal liability that might otherwise be incurred as a result of the report. In any proceeding involving liability, good faith is presumed. (2007-263, s. 1.)

§ 66-67.5. Requirements for maintenance fees for gift cards.

(a) Disclosure. - The seller or issuer of a gift card must conspicuously disclose any maintenance fee charges at the time of purchase. The disclosure must be visible on the gift card itself. No person, firm, or corporation engaged in commerce shall charge any maintenance fee on a gift card for one calendar year following the date of the purchase of the gift card.

(b) Penalty. - A seller or issuer of a gift card who violates this section commits an unfair trade practice under G.S. 75-1.1 and is subject to a civil penalty in accordance with G.S. 75-15.2.

(c) Definitions. - As used in this section, the following terms mean:

(1) Gift card. - A record evidencing a promise, made for monetary consideration, by a seller or issuer that goods or services will be provided to the owner of the record to the value shown in the record. A gift card includes a record that contains a microprocessor chip, magnetic strip, or other storage medium that is prefunded and for which the value is adjusted upon each use, a gift certificate, a stored-value card or certificate, a store card, or a prepaid long-distance telephone service that is activated by a prepaid card that required dialing an access number or an access code in addition to dialing the phone number to which the user of the prepaid card seeks to connect.

(2) Maintenance fee. - Any fee that the owner of the gift card is subject to when the gift card is redeemed, including a service or inactivity fee.

(d) Limitation. - The provisions of this section shall not apply to gift cards that are issued by a financial institution or its operating subsidiary and that are usable at multiple unaffiliated sellers of goods or services. (2007-363, s. 1.)

Article 14.

Business under Assumed Name Regulated.

§ 66-68. Certificate to be filed; contents; exemption of certain partnerships and limited liability companies engaged in rendering professional services; withdrawal or transfer of assumed name.

(a) Unless exempt under subsection (e) hereof, before any person or partnership engages in business in any county in this State under an assumed name or under any designation, name or style other than the real name of the owner or owners thereof, before any limited partnership engaged in business in any county in this State other than under the name set out in the Certificate filed with the Office of the Secretary of State, before any limited liability company engages in business in any county other than under the name set out in the articles of organization filed with the Office of the Secretary of State, or before a corporation engages in business in any county other than under its corporate name, such person, partnership, limited partnership, limited liability company, or corporation must file in the office of the register of deeds of such county a certificate giving the following information:

(1) The name under which the business is to be conducted; and

(2) The name and address of the owner, or if there is more than one owner, the name and address of each.

(b) If the owner is an individual or a partnership, the certificate must be signed and duly acknowledged by the individual owner, or by each general partner. If the owner is a corporation or limited liability company, it must be signed in the name of the corporation or limited liability company and duly acknowledged as provided by G.S. 47-41.01 or G.S. 47-41.02.

(c) Whenever a general partner withdraws from or a new general partner joins a partnership, a new certificate shall be filed. For limited partnerships, the requirement of this subsection (c) shall be deemed satisfied if the partnership is identified as the owner as provided in subsection (a) and the partnership's certificate of limited partnership is amended as provided in G.S. 59-202.

(d) It is not necessary that any person, partnership, limited liability company, or corporation file such certificate in any county where no place of business is maintained and where the only business done in such county is the sale of goods by sample or by traveling agents or by mail.

(e) Any partnership or limited liability company engaged in rendering professional services, as defined in G.S. 55B-2(6), in this State, shall be exempt from the requirements of this section if it shall file annually with the licensing board responsible for regulating the rendering of such professional services, or at such intervals as shall be designated from time to time by such licensing board, a listing of the names and addresses of its partners or members. The listing shall be open to public inspection during normal working hours.

(f) Any person, partnership, limited liability company, or corporation executing and filing a certificate of assumed name as required by this section may, upon ceasing to engage in business in this State under the assumed name, withdraw the assumed name or transfer the assumed name to any other person, partnership, or corporation by filing in the office of the register of deeds of the county in which the certificate of assumed name is filed a certificate of withdrawal or a certificate of transfer executed as provided in subsection (b) of this section and setting forth:

(1) The assumed name being withdrawn or transferred;

(2) The date of filing of the certificate of assumed name;

(3) The name and address of the owner or owners of the business;

(4) A statement that such owner or owners have ceased engaging in business under the assumed name;

(5) If the assumed name is to be withdrawn, the effective date (which shall be a date certain but not more than 20 days from the date of filing) of the withdrawal if it is not to be effective upon the filing of the certificate of withdrawal; and

(6) If the assumed name is to be transferred, the name and address of the transferee or transferees, and the effective date (which shall be a date certain

but not more than 20 days from the date of filing) of the transfer if it is not to be effective upon the filing of the certificate of transfer. This subsection does not relieve a transferee of the obligation to file a certificate of assumed name as required by this Article. (1913, c. 77, s. 1; C.S., s. 3288; 1951, c. 381, ss. 3, 7; 1967, c. 823, s. 28; 1977, c. 384; 1985, c. 264; 1987, c. 723, ss. 1, 2; 1987 (Reg. Sess., 1988), c. 1031, s. 4; 1991 (Reg. Sess., 1992), c. 1030, s. 18; 1999-189, s. 6; 2000-140, s. 101(t).)

§ 66-69. Index of certificates kept by register of deeds.

Each register of deeds of this State shall keep an index which will show alphabetically every assumed name with respect to which a certificate is hereafter so filed in his county. The index shall also contain notations of any certificates of withdrawal or certificates of transfer filed in the county. (1913, c. 77, s. 2; C.S., s. 3299; 1951, c. 381, ss. 4, 7; 1967, c. 823, s. 29; 1987, c. 723, s. 3.)

§ 66-69.1. Copy of certificate prima facie evidence.

A copy of such certificate duly certified by the register of deeds in whose office it has been filed shall be prima facie evidence of the facts required to be stated herein. (1913, c. 77, s. 2; C.S., s. 3299; 1951, c. 381, ss. 5, 7; 1967, c. 823, s. 30.)

§ 66-70. Repealed by Session Laws 1969, c. 751, s. 45.

§ 66-71. Violation of Article a misdemeanor; civil penalty.

(a) Any person, partner or corporation failing to file the certificate as required by G.S. 66-68(a) or G.S. 66-68(c) -

(1) Shall be guilty of a Class 3 misdemeanor, and

(2) Shall be liable in the amount of fifty dollars ($50.00) to any person demanding that such certificate be filed if he fails to file the certificate within seven days after such demand. Such penalty may be collected in a civil action therefor.

(b) The failure of any person to comply with the provisions of this Article does not prevent a recovery by such person in any civil action brought in any of the courts of this State. (1913, c. 77, s. 4; 1919, c. 2; C.S., s. 3291; 1951, c. 381, ss. 6, 7; 1987, c. 723, s. 4; 1993, c. 539, s. 517; 1994, Ex. Sess., c. 24, s. 14(c).)

Article 15.

Person Trading as "Company" or "Agent."

§ 66-72. Person trading as "company" or "agent" to disclose real parties.

If any person shall transact business as trader or merchant, with the addition of the words "factor," "agent," "& Company" or "& Co.," or shall conduct such business under any name or style other than his own, except in case of a corporation, and fail to disclose the name of his principal or partner by a sign placed conspicuously at the place wherein such business is conducted, then all the property, stock of goods and merchandise, and choses in action purchased, used and contracted in the course of such business shall, as to creditors, be liable for the debts contracted in the course of such business by the person in charge of same. Provided, this section shall not apply to any person transacting business under license as an auctioneer, broker, or commission merchant; in all actions under this section it is incumbent on such trader or merchant to prove compliance with the same. (1905, c. 443; Rev., s. 2118; C.S., s. 3292; 1951, c. 381, s. 8.)

Article 16.

Unfair Trade Practices in Diamond Industry.

§ 66-73. Definitions.

For the purpose of this Article:

(1)   A "diamond" is a natural mineral consisting essentially of pure carbon crystallized in the isometric system and is found in many colors. Its hardness is 10; its specific gravity approximately 3.52; and it has a refractive index 2.42.

(2)   "A member of the diamond industry" shall be construed to mean any person, firm, corporation or organization engaged in the business of selling, offering for sale, or distributing in commerce, diamonds (other than industrial diamonds), whether cut, polished, or in the rough, synthetic diamonds and imitation diamonds, and of any jewelry items or other products containing diamonds, synthetic diamonds, or imitation diamonds.

(3)   "The diamond industry" or "the industry" as used in this Article is a trade, industry or business which shall be construed to embrace all persons, firms, corporations and organizations engaged in selling, offering for sale, or the distribution in commerce of diamonds (other than industrial diamonds), whether cut, polished or in the rough, synthetic diamonds and imitation diamonds, and of any jewelry item or other products containing diamonds, synthetic diamonds or imitation diamonds.

(4)   "Unfair trade practices" as referred to herein are unfair methods of competition, unfair or deceptive acts or practices and other illegal practices which are prohibited by law. (1957, c. 585, s. 1.)

§ 66-74. What constitutes unfair trade practice.

It is an unfair trade practice for any member of the diamond industry:

(1)   To use, or cause or promote the use of, any trade promotional literature, advertising matter, guarantee, warranty, mark, brand, label, trade name, picture, design or device, designation, or other type of oral or written representation, however disseminated or published, which has the capacity and tendency or effect of misleading or deceiving purchasers or prospective purchasers with respect to the type, kind, grade, quality, color, cut, quantity, size, weight, nature, substance, durability, serviceability, origin, preparation, production, manufacture, distribution, or customary or regular price, of any diamond or other product of the industry, or which has the capacity and tendency or effect of

misleading or deceiving the purchasing or consuming public in any other material respect.

(2)   In the sale, offering for sale, or distribution of products of the industry to use the unqualified word "diamond" as descriptive of or as an identification for any object or product not meeting the requirement specified in the definition of diamond hereinabove set forth, or which, though meeting such requirements, has not been symmetrically fashioned with at least 17 polished facets.

The foregoing provisions of subdivision (2) have application to the unqualified use of the word "diamond." They are not to be construed as inhibiting:

a.   The use of the words "rough diamond" as descriptive of or as a designation for, uncut or unfaceted objects or products meeting the requirements specified in the mentioned definition of diamond; or

b.   The use of the word "diamond" as descriptive of or as a designation for objects or products meeting the requirements of said definition of diamond, but which have not been symmetrically fashioned with at least 17 polished facets when in immediate conjunction with the word "diamond," there is either a disclosure of the number of facets and shape of the diamond or the name of a type of diamond which denotes shape and which usually has less than 17 facets (e.g., "rose diamond"); or

c.   The use of the words "imitation diamond" as descriptive of or as a designation for objects or products which do not meet the requirements of said definition of diamond but have an appearance similar to that of a cut and polished diamond.

When the word "diamond" is so used, the qualifying word or words shall be of at least equal conspicuousness as the word "diamond."

(3)   To use the words "reproduction," "replica," "diamond-like," or similar terms as descriptive of imitation diamonds.

(4)   To use the term "synthetic diamond" as descriptive of any object or product unless such object or product has in fact been artificially created and is of similar appearance and of essentially the same optical and physical properties and chemical structure as a diamond, or to apply the term "diamond" to any man-made objects or products unless it is immediately preceded in each instance with equal conspicuity by the word "synthetic."

(5) To use the word "perfect" or any other word, expression or representation of similar import, as descriptive of any diamond which discloses flaws, cracks, carbon spots, clouds, or other blemishes or imperfection of any sort when examined in normal daylight, or its equivalent, by a trained eye under a 10-power corrected diamond eye loupe or other equal magnifier.

The use with respect to a stone which is not perfect of any phase (such as "commercially perfect") containing the word "perfect" or "perfectly" is regarded as misleading and in violation of this subdivision, and this subdivision shall not be construed as approving of the use of the word "perfect," or any word or representation of like import, as descriptive of any diamond that is of inferior color or make. Nothing is to be construed as inhibiting the use of the word "flawless" as descriptive of a diamond which meets the requirements for "perfect" set forth in this subdivision.

(6) In connection with the offering of any ring or rings or other articles of jewelry having a perfect center stone or stones, and side or supplementary stones which are not of such quality, to use the word "perfect" without clearly disclosing that such description applies only to the center stone or center stones.

(7) To use the term "blue white" or any other term, expression or representation of similar import as descriptive of any diamond which under normal, north daylight or its equivalent, shows any color or any trace of any color, other than blue or bluish.

(8) To advertise, offer for sale, or sell any diamond which has been artificially colored or tinted by coating, irradiating, or heating, or by use of nuclear bombardment, or by any other means, without disclosure of such fact to purchasers or prospective purchasers, or without disclosure that such artificial coloring or tinting is not permanent, if such is the fact.

(9) To use the terms "properly cut," "proper cut," "modern cut," "well made," or expressions of similar import, to describe any diamond that is lopsided or so thick or so thin in depth as materially to detract from the brilliance of the stone.

(10) To use the unqualified expressions "brilliant," or "brilliant cut," or "full cut" to describe, identify or refer to any diamond except a round diamond which has at least 32 facets, plus the table above the girdle and at least 24 facets below.

Such terms should not be applied to single or rose-cut diamonds, either with or without qualification. They may be applied to emerald (rectangular) cut and marquise (pointed oval) cut diamonds meeting the above stated facet requirements when, in immediate conjunction with the term used, disclosure is made of the fact that the diamond is of emerald or marquise form.

(11)   To use the terms "clean," "eye clean," "commercially clean," "commercially white," or any other terms, expressions, or representations of similar import in advertising, labeling, representing, or describing any diamond when such terms are used for the purpose, or with the capacity and tendency or effect, of misleading or deceiving purchasers, prospective purchasers, or the consuming public.

(12)   To misrepresent the weight of any diamond or to deceive purchasers or prospective purchasers as to the weight of any diamond.

The standard unit for designation of the weight of a diamond is the carat, which is equivalent to 200 milligrams (one-fifth gram). While advertisements may state the approximate weight or range of weights of a group of products, all weight representations regarding individual products shall state the exact weight of the stone or stones and be accurate to within 1/200th of a carat (one-half "point").

(13)   To state or otherwise represent the weight of all diamonds contained in a ring or other article of jewelry unless such weight figure is accompanied with equal conspicuity by the words "total weight" or words of similar import, so as to indicate clearly that the weight shown is that of all stones in the article and not that of the center or largest stone.

(14)   To use the word "gem" to describe, identify or refer to any diamond which does not possess the requisite beauty, brilliance, value and other qualities necessary for classification as a gem.

Not all diamonds are gems. For example: Small pieces of diamond rough or melee weighing only one or two points are not to be described as "gems." Neither should stones which are grossly imperfect or of decidedly poor color be so classified unless they are of such a size as to be rare and desirable and valuable for that reason.

No imitation diamond can be described as a gem under any circumstances.

(15) In connection with the offering for sale, sale, or distribution of diamonds or articles set with diamonds, to use as part of any advertisement, label, packaging material, or other sales promotion literature, any illustration, picture, diagram or other depiction which either alone or in conjunction with accompanying words or phrases has the capacity and tendency or effect of misleading or deceiving purchasers or prospective purchasers concerning the type, kind, grade, color, cut, quality, size, weight, or character of any diamond, or which has the capacity and tendency or effect of misleading the purchasing or consuming public in any other material respect.

(16) To use as part of any advertisement, label, packaging material, or other sales promotion literature, any illustration which exaggerates the size of a diamond inset or enlarges it out of proper proportion to the mounting, without clearly and conspicuously stating either the amount that the diamond has been enlarged in the illustration, or that the diamond in the illustration has been "enlarged to show detail."

(17) To represent, directly or indirectly, through the use of any statement or representation in advertising or through the use of any word or term in a corporate or trade name, or otherwise, that said member is a producer, cutter, or importer of diamonds, or owns or controls a cutting plant, or has connections abroad, through which importations of rough or cut stones are secured, or maintains offices abroad, when such is not the fact, or in any other manner to misrepresent the character, extent, volume, or type of business being conducted.

(18) To publish or circulate false or misleading price quotations, price lists, terms or conditions of sale or reports as to production or sales which have the capacity and tendency or effect of misleading purchasers, prospective purchasers, or the consuming public, or to advertise, sell or offer to sell diamonds or articles set with diamonds at prices purporting to be reduced from what are, in fact, fictitious or exaggerated manufacturer's or distributor's suggested retail selling price, or that contains what purport to be bona fide price quotations which are in fact higher than the prices at which such products are regularly and customarily sold in bona fide retail transactions. It is likewise an unfair trade practice to distribute, sell or offer for sale to the consuming public in such manner diamonds or articles set with diamonds bearing such false, fictitious, or exaggerated price tags or labels.

(19) To offer for sale, sell, advertise, describe, or otherwise represent diamonds or diamond-set merchandise as "close-outs," "discontinued lines," or

"special bargains," by use of such terms or by words or representations of similar import, when such is not true in fact; or to offer for sale, sell, advertise, describe or otherwise represent such articles where the capacity and tendency or effect thereof is to lead the purchasing or consuming public to believe the same are being offered for sale or sold at greatly reduced prices, or at so-called "bargain" prices when such is not the fact.

(20)   To advertise a particular style or type of product for sale when purchasers or prospective purchasers responding to such advertisement cannot readily purchase the advertised style or type of product from the industry member and the purpose of the advertisement is to obtain prospects for the sale of a different style or type of product than that advertised.

(21)   To use sale practices or methods which:

a.   Deprive prospective customers of a fair opportunity to purchase any advertised style or type of product; or

b.   To falsely disparage any advertised style or type of product or, without the knowledge of the customer, to substitute other styles or types of products which the advertiser intends to sell instead of the advertised style or type of product.

(22)   To advertise or offer for sale a grossly inadequate supply of products at reduced or bargain prices without disclosure of the inadequacy of the supply available at such prices when such advertisement or offer has the capacity and tendency or effect of misleading or deceiving purchasers or prospective purchasers.

(23)   To describe, identify or refer to a diamond as "certified," or to use respecting it any other word or words of similar meaning or import unless:

a.   The identity of the certifier and the specific matters or qualities certified are clearly disclosed in conjunction therewith; and

b.   The certifier has examined such diamond, has made such certification and is qualified to certify as to such matters and qualities; and

c.   There is furnished the purchaser a certificate setting forth clearly and nondeceptively the name of the certifier and the matters and qualities certified.

(24) To aid, abet, coerce or induce another, directly or indirectly, to use or promote the use of any unfair trade practice specified in this Article. (1957, c. 585, s. 2.)

§ 66-75. Penalty for violation; each practice a separate offense.

Any person, firm, corporation or organization engaging in any unfair trade practice, as defined in this Article, shall be guilty of a Class 1 misdemeanor; and each and every unfair trade practice engaged in shall be deemed a separate offense. (1957, c. 585, s. 3; 1993, c. 539, s. 518; 1994, Ex. Sess., c. 24, s. 14(c).)

Article 17.

Closing-Out Sales.

§ 66-76. Definitions.

For the purposes of this Article, "closing-out sale" shall mean and include all sales advertised, represented or held forth under the designation of "going out of business," "discontinuance of business," "selling out," "liquidation," "lost our lease," "must vacate," "forced out," "removal," or any other designation of like meaning; "distress sale" shall mean and include all sales in which it is represented or implied that going out of business is possible or anticipated, in which closing out is referred to in any way, or in which it is implied that business conditions are so difficult that the seller is forced to conduct the sale; and "person" shall mean and include individuals, partnerships, voluntary associations and corporations. (1957, c. 1058, s. 1; 1981, c. 633, s. 1.)

§ 66-77. License required; contents of applications; inventory required; fees; bond; extension of licenses; records; false statements.

(a) No person shall advertise or offer for sale a stock of goods, wares or merchandise under the description of closing-out sale, or a sale of goods, wares or merchandise damaged by fire, smoke, water or otherwise, or a distress sale unless he shall have obtained a license to conduct such sale from the clerk of the city or town in which he proposes to conduct such a sale or from the officer designated by the Board of County Commissioners if the sale is conducted in an unincorporated area. The applicant for such a license shall make to such clerk an application therefor, in writing and under oath at least seven days prior to the opening date of sale, showing all the facts relating to the reasons and character of such sale, including the opening and terminating dates of the proposed sale, the opening and terminating dates of any previous distress sale or closing-out sale held by the applicant within that county during the preceding 12 months, a complete inventory of the goods, wares or merchandise actually on hand in the place whereat such sale is to be conducted, and all details necessary to locate exactly and identify fully the goods, wares or merchandise to be sold. Provided, the seller in a distress sale need not file an inventory.

(b) If such clerk shall be satisfied from said application that the proposed sale is of the character which the applicant desires to advertise and conduct, the clerk shall issue a license, upon the payment of a fee of fifty dollars ($50.00) therefor, together with a bond, payable to the city or town or county in the penal sum of five hundred dollars ($500.00), conditioned upon compliance with this Article, to the applicant authorizing him to advertise and conduct a sale of the particular kind mentioned in the application. The license fee provided for herein shall be good for a period of 30 days from its date, and if the applicant shall not complete said sale within said 30-day period then the applicant shall make application to such clerk for a license for a new permit, which shall be good for an additional period of 30 days, and shall pay therefor the sum of fifty dollars ($50.00), and a second extension period of 30 days may be similarly applied for and granted by the clerk upon payment of an additional fee of fifty dollars ($50.00) and upon the clerk being satisfied that the applicant is holding a bona fide sale of the kind contemplated by this Article and is acting in a bona fide manner; provided, however, that the clerk may not grant an extension period as provided in this subsection if (i) the applicant conducted a distress sale immediately preceding the current sale for which the extension is applied for and (ii) the period of the extension applied for, when added to the period of the preceding sale and the period of the current sale, will exceed 120 days. No additional bond shall be required in the event of one or more extensions as herein provided for. Any merchant who shall have been conducting a business in the same location where the sale is to be held for a period of not less than one year, prior to the date of holding such sale, or any merchant who shall have been conducting a business in one location for such period but who shall, by reason of the building being untenantable or by reason of the fact that said merchant shall have no existing lease or ownership of the building and shall be forced to hold such sale at another location, shall be exempted from the payment of the fees and the filing of the bond herein provided for.

(c) Every city or town or county to whom application is made shall endorse upon such application the date of its filing, and shall preserve the same as a record of his office, and shall make an abstract of the facts set forth in such application, and shall indicate whether the license was granted or refused.

(d) Any person making a false statement in the application provided for in this section shall, upon conviction, be deemed guilty of perjury. (1957, c. 1058, s. 2; 1981, c. 633, ss. 2-4; 1987, c. 387, s. 1.)

§ 66-78. Additions to stock in contemplation of sale prohibited.

No person in contemplation of a closing-out sale shall order any goods, wares or merchandise for the purpose of selling and disposing of the same at such sale, and any unusual purchase and additions to the stock of such goods, wares or merchandise within 60 days prior to the filing of application for a license to conduct such sale shall be presumptive evidence that such purchases and additions to stock were made in contemplation of such sale. (1957, c. 1058, s. 3; 1981, c. 633, s. 5.)

§ 66-79. Replenishment of stock prohibited.

No person carrying on or conducting a closing-out sale or a sale of goods, wares or merchandise damaged by fire, smoke, water or otherwise, shall, during the continuance of such sale, add any goods, wares or merchandise to the damaged stock inventoried in his original application for such license, and no goods, wares or merchandise shall be sold as damaged merchandise at or during such sale, excepting the goods, wares or merchandise described and inventoried in such original application. (1957, c. 1058, s. 4; 1981, c. 633, s. 5.)

§ 66-80. Continuation of sale or business beyond termination date.

No person shall conduct a closing-out sale or a sale of goods, wares or merchandise damaged by fire, smoke, water or otherwise or a distress sale beyond the termination date specified for such sale, except as otherwise provided for in subsection (b) of G.S. 66-77; nor shall any person, upon conclusion of such sale, continue that business which had been represented as closing out or going out of business under the same name, or under a different name, at the same location, or elsewhere in the same city or town where the inventory for such sale was filed for a period of 12 months; nor shall any person, upon conclusion of such sale, continue business contrary to the designation of such sale. As used in this section, the term "person" includes individuals, partnerships, corporations, and other business entities. If a business entity that is prohibited from continuing a business under this section reformulates itself as a new entity or as an individual, whether by sale, merger, acquisition, bankruptcy, dissolution, or any other transaction, for the purpose of continuing the business, the successor entity or individual shall be considered the same person as the original entity for the purpose of this section. If an individual who is prohibited from continuing a business under this section forms a new business entity to continue the business, that entity shall be considered the same person as the individual for the purpose of this section. (1957, c. 1058, s. 5; 1981, c. 633, s. 6; 1987, c. 387, s. 2.)

§ 66-81. Advertising or conducting sale contrary to Article; penalty.

Any person who shall advertise, hold, conduct or carry on any sale of goods, wares or merchandise under the description of closing-out sale or a sale of goods, wares or merchandise damaged by fire, smoke, water or otherwise or a distress sale, contrary to the provisions of this Article, or who shall violate any of the provisions of this Article shall be deemed guilty of a Class 1 misdemeanor. (1957, c. 1058, s. 6; 1981, c. 633, s. 7; 1993, c. 539, s. 519; 1994, Ex. Sess., c. 24, s. 14(c).)

§ 66-82. Sales excepted; liability for dissemination of false advertisement.

The provisions of this Article shall not apply to sheriffs, constables or other public or court officers, or to any other person or persons acting under the license, direction or authority of any court, State or federal, selling goods, wares or merchandise in the course of their official duties; provided, however, that no newspaper publisher, radio-broadcast licensee, television-broadcast licensee, or other agency or medium for the dissemination of advertising shall be liable under this Article by reason of the dissemination of any false advertisement prohibited by this Article, unless he has refused, on the written request of any law-enforcement officer or agency of this State, to furnish to such officer or agency the name and address of the person who caused the dissemination of such advertisement. (1957, c. 1058, s. 7.)

§ 66-83. Restraining or enjoining illegal act.

Upon complaint of any person the superior court shall have jurisdiction to restrain and enjoin any act forbidden or declared illegal by any provisions of this Article. (1957, c. 1058, s. 8.)

§ 66-84: Repealed by Session Laws 1981, c. 633, s. 8.

Article 18.

Labeling of Household Cleaners.

§ 66-85. Labeling cleaners containing volatile substances capable of producing toxic effects; definition.

It shall be unlawful for any person, firm, or corporation manufacturing household cleaners which contain volatile substances capable of producing toxic effects in or on their users when used for their intended domestic purposes to sell or offer for sale any such cleaner unless such cleaner shall be labeled with the word "caution" or other word of similar import and unless directions shall plainly appear thereon as to the safe and proper use of the contents. Such label shall identify the particular substance contained therein. The phrase "volatile substances capable of producing toxic effect" as used herein shall include, but shall not be limited to, the following: benzene (benzol), toluene (toluol), coal tar naphtha, carbon tetrachloride, trichlorethylene, tetrachlorethylene (perchlorethylene), tetrachlorethane, methyl alcohol, and aromatic and chlorinated hydrocarbons of comparable volatility and toxicity. (1957, c. 1241, s. 1.)

§ 66-86. Penalty for selling product in violation of Article.

Any person, firm or corporation selling or offering to sell any product in violation of the terms of this Article shall be guilty of a Class 1 misdemeanor. (1957, c. 1241, s. 2; 1993, c. 539, s. 520; 1994, Ex. Sess., c. 24, s. 14(c).)

§ 66-87. Injunctions.

Upon complaint by the Department of Health and Human Services, the superior court shall have jurisdiction to enjoin any sale or offer of sale which is in violation of the provisions of this Article. (1957, c. 1241, s. 3; 1973, c. 476, s. 128; 1997-443, s. 11A.118(a).)

§ 66-88. Application of Article after enactment of federal legislation.

If the Congress of the United States shall, at any time hereafter, enact in any form legislation designed to regulate the interstate distribution, labeling and sale of hazardous articles in packages suitable for or intended for household use, the Department of Health and Human Services shall, upon so determining, issue a proclamation to such effect and, from and after the date of such proclamation, this Article shall be applicable only with respect to intrastate manufacture, distribution, sale and labeling by persons, firms or corporations who do not comply with the federal legislation as to interstate distribution, labeling and sale of the materials or articles described in G.S. 66-85. (1957, c. 1241, s. 31/2; 1973, c. 476, s. 128; 1997-443, s. 11A.118(a).)

§§ 66-89 through 66-93. Reserved for future codification purposes.

Article 19.

Business Opportunity Sales.

§ 66-94. Definition.

For purposes of this Article, "business opportunity" means the sale or lease of any products, equipment, supplies or services for the purpose of enabling the purchaser to start a business, and in which the seller represents:

(1) That the seller will provide locations or assist the purchaser in finding locations for the use or operation of vending machines, racks, display cases or other similar devices, or currency-operated amusement machines or devices, on premises neither owned nor leased by the purchaser or seller; or

(2) That it may, in the ordinary course of business, purchase any or all products made, produced, fabricated, grown, bred or modified by the purchaser using in whole or in part the supplies, services or chattels sold to the purchaser; or

(3) The seller guarantees that the purchaser will derive income from the business opportunity which exceeds the price paid for the business opportunity; or that the seller will refund all or part of the price paid for the business opportunity, or repurchase any of the products, equipment, supplies or chattels supplied by the seller, if the purchaser is unsatisfied with the business opportunity and pays to the seller an initial, required consideration which exceeds two hundred dollars ($200.00); or

(4) That it will provide a sales program or marketing program which will enable the purchaser to derive income from the business opportunity which exceeds the price paid for the business opportunity, provided that this subsection shall not apply to the sale of a marketing program made in conjunction with the licensing of a federally registered trademark or a federally registered service mark, or when the purchaser pays less than two hundred dollars ($200.00).

Provided, that "business opportunity" does not include the sale of an on-going business when the owner of that business sells and intends to sell only that one business opportunity; nor does it include the not-for-profit sale of sales demonstration equipment, materials, or samples, for a total price of two hundred dollars ($200.00) or less. (1977, c. 884, s. 1; 1981, c. 817, s. 1; 1983, c. 421, s. 2; 1991, c. 74, s. 1.)

§ 66-94.1. Responsible sellers exemption.

(a) The provisions of Article 19 shall not apply to the sale or lease of any products, equipment, supplies or services where:

(1) The seller has not derived net income from such sales within the State during either of its two previous fiscal years, and does not intend to derive net income from such sales during its current fiscal year; and

(2) The primary commercial activity of the seller or its affiliate is substantially different from the sale of the goods or services to the purchaser, and the gross revenues received by the seller from all such sales during the current and each of the two previous fiscal years do not exceed ten percent (10%) of the total gross revenues from all operations for the same period of the seller and any other affiliated entity contractually obligated to compensate the purchaser for the purchaser's business activities arising from the sale; and

(3) The sale results in an improvement to realty owned or leased by the purchaser which enables the purchaser to receive goods on consignment from the seller or its affiliate. An "improvement to realty" occurs when a building or other structure is constructed or when significant improvements to an existing building or structure are made; and

(4) The seller has either a net worth on a consolidated basis, according to its most recent audited financial statement, of not less than five million dollars ($5,000,000) or has obtained a surety bond from a surety company authorized to do business in this State in an amount equal to or greater than the gross revenues received from the sale or lease of products, equipment, supplies or services in this State during the preceding 12-month period which enabled the purchaser to start a business.

(b) The provisions of Article 19 shall not apply to the sale or lease of any products, equipment, supplies, or services where:

(1) The seller has a net worth on a consolidated basis, according to its most recent audited financial statement, of not less than five million dollars ($5,000,000); and

(2) The primary commercial activity of the seller is motor carrier transportation and the seller is subject to the jurisdiction of the Interstate Commerce Commission or any other federal agency that regulates motor carrier transportation.

(c) Any seller satisfying the requirements of subsections (a) or (b) of this section shall file with the Secretary of State two copies of a document signed under oath by the seller or one authorized to sign on behalf of the seller containing the following information:

(1) The name of the seller and whether the seller is doing business as an individual, partnership, or corporation;

(2) The principal business address of the seller;

(3) A brief description of the products, equipment, supplies, or services being sold or leased by the seller; and

(4) A statement which explains the manner in which each of the requirements of subsections (a) or (b) of this section are met. (1983, c. 421, s. 1; 1987, c. 325.)

§ 66-95. Required disclosure statement.

At least 48 hours prior to the time the purchaser signs a business opportunity contract, or at least 48 hours prior to the receipt of any consideration by the seller, whichever occurs first, the seller must provide the prospective purchaser a written document, the cover sheet of which is entitled in at least 10-point bold face capital letters "DISCLOSURES REQUIRED BY NORTH CAROLINA LAW." Under this title shall appear the statement in at least 10-point type that "The State of North Carolina has not reviewed and does not approve, recommend, endorse or sponsor any business opportunity. The information contained in this disclosure has not been verified by the State. If you have any questions about this investment, see an attorney before you sign a contract or agreement."

Nothing except the title and required statement shall appear on the cover sheet. The disclosure document shall contain the following information:

(1) The name of the seller, whether the seller is doing business as an individual, partnership, or corporation, the names under which the seller has done, is doing or intends to do business, and the name of any parent or affiliated company that will engage in business transactions with purchasers or who takes responsibility for statements made by the seller.

(2) The names and addresses and titles of the seller's officers, directors, trustees, general partners, general managers, principal executives, and any other persons charged with responsibility for the seller's business activities relating to the sale of business opportunities. The disclosure document shall additionally contain a statement disclosing who, if any, of the above persons:

a. Has been the subject of any legal or administrative proceeding alleging the violation of any business opportunity or franchise law, or fraud, embezzlement, fraudulent conversion, restraint of trade, unfair or deceptive practices, misappropriation of property or comparable allegations;

b. Has been the subject of any bankruptcy, reorganization or receivership proceeding, or was an owner, a principal officer or a general partner of any entity which has been subject to such proceeding.

The disclosure document shall set forth the name of the person, the penalties or damages assessed and/or terms of settlement, and nature of and the parties to the action or proceeding, the court or other forum, the date, the current status of the action or proceeding, the terms and conditions of any order of decree, the any other information to enable the purchaser to assess the prior business activities of the seller.

(3) The prior business experience of the seller relating to business opportunities including:

a. The name, address, and a description of any business opportunity previously offered by the seller;

b. The length of time the seller has offered each such business opportunity;

c. The length of time the seller has conducted the business opportunity currently being offered to the purchaser.

(4) A full and detailed description of the actual services that the business opportunity seller undertakes to perform for the purchaser.

(5) A copy of a current (not older than 13 months) financial statement of the seller, updated to reflect any material changes in the seller's financial condition.

(6) If training of any type is promised by the seller, the disclosure statement must set forth a complete description of the training and the length of the training.

(7) If the seller promises services to be performed in connection with the placement of the equipment, product(s) or supplies at various location(s), the disclosure statement must set forth the full nature of those services as well as the nature of the agreements to be made with the owners or managers of these location(s) where the purchaser's equipment, product(s) or supplies will be placed.

(8) If the business opportunity seller is required to secure a bond or establish a trust deposit pursuant to G.S. 66-96, the document shall state either:

a.____ "As required by North Carolina law, the seller has secured a bond issued by

(name and address of surety company)

a surety company authorized to do business in this State. Before signing a contract to purchase this business opportunity, you should check with the surety company to determine the bond's current status," or

b.____ "As required by North Carolina law, the seller has established a trust account

(number of account)

_____ with _____

(name and address of bank or savings institution)

Before signing a contract to purchase this business opportunity, you should check with the bank or savings institution to determine the current status of the trust account."

(9) The following statement:

"If the seller fails to deliver the product(s), equipment or supplies necessary to begin substantial operation of the business within 45 days of the delivery date stated in your contract, you may notify the seller in writing and demand that the contract be cancelled."

(10) If the seller makes any statement concerning sales or earnings, or range of sales or earnings that may be made through this business opportunity, the document must disclose:

a. The total number of purchasers of business opportunities involving the product(s), equipment, supplies or services being offered who to the seller's knowledge have actually received earnings in the amount or range specified, within three years prior to the date of the disclosure statement.

b. The total number of purchasers of business opportunities involving the product(s), equipment, supplies or services being offered within three years prior to the date of the disclosure statement. (1977, c. 884, s. 1; 1981, c. 817, s. 2.)

§ 66-96. Bond or trust account required.

If the business opportunity seller makes any of the representations set forth in G.S. 66-94(3), the seller must either have obtained a surety bond issued by a surety company authorized to do business in this State or have established a trust account with a licensed and insured bank or savings institution located in the State of North Carolina. The amount of the bond or trust account shall be an amount not less than fifty thousand dollars ($50,000). The bond or trust account shall be in favor of the State of North Carolina. Any person who is damaged by any violation of this Article, or by the seller's breach of the contract for the business opportunity sale or of any obligation arising therefrom may bring an action against the bond or trust account to recover damages suffered; provided, however, that the aggregate liability of the surety or trustee shall be only for actual damages and in no event shall exceed the amount of the bond or trust account. (1977, c. 884, s. 1.)

§ 66-97. Filing with Secretary of State.

(a) The seller of every business opportunity shall file with the Secretary of State two copies of the disclosure statement required by G.S. 66-95, accompanied by a fee in the amount of two hundred fifty dollars ($250.00) made payable to the Secretary of State, prior to placing any advertisement or making any other representations to prospective purchasers in this State. The seller shall update this filing as any material change in the required information occurs, but no less than annually.

(b) Every seller shall file, in such form as the Secretary of State may prescribe, an irrevocable consent appointing the Secretary of State or his successors in office to be his attorney to receive service of any lawful process in any noncriminal suit, action or proceeding against the seller or his successor, executor or administrator which arises under this Article after the consent has been filed, with the same force and validity as if served personally on the person filing the consent. Service may be made by leaving a copy of the process in the office of the Secretary of State, but is not effective unless (i) the plaintiff, who may be the Attorney General in a suit, action or proceeding instituted by him, forthwith sends notice of the service and a copy of the process by registered mail to the defendant or respondent at his address on file with the Secretary of State, and (ii) the plaintiff's affidavit of compliance with this section is filed in the case on or before the return date of the process, if any, or within such further time as the court allows.

(c) If the seller of a business opportunity is required by G.S. 66-96 to provide a bond or establish a trust account, he shall file with the Secretary of State two copies of the bond or two copies of the formal notification by the depository that the trust account is established contemporaneously with compliance with subsections (a) or (d).

(d) The Secretary of State may accept the Uniform Franchise Offering Circular (UFOC) or the Federal Trade Commission Basic Disclosure Document, provided, that the alternative disclosure document shall be accompanied by a separate sheet setting forth the caption and statement and any other information required by G.S. 66-95.

(e) Failure to so file shall be a Class 1 misdemeanor. (1977, c. 884, s. 1; 1981, c. 817, s. 3; 1993, c. 539, s. 521; 1994, Ex. Sess., c. 24, s. 14(c); 2003-284, s. 35B.3(a).)

§ 66-98. Prohibited acts.

Business opportunity sellers shall not:

(1) Represent that the business opportunity provides income or earning potential of any kind unless the seller has documented data to substantiate the claims of income or earning potential and discloses this data to the prospective purchaser at the time such representations are made;

(2) Use the trademark, service mark, trade names, logotype, advertising or other commercial symbol of any business which does not either control the ownership interest in the seller or accept responsibility for all representations made by the seller in regard to the business opportunity, unless it is clear from the circumstances that the owner of the commercial symbol is not involved in the sale of the business opportunity;

(3) Make or authorize the making of any reference to its compliance with this Article in any advertisement or other contact with prospective purchasers. (1977, c. 884, s. 1.)

§ 66-99. Contracts to be in writing; form; provisions.

(a) Every business opportunity contract shall be in writing and a copy shall be given to the purchaser at the time he signs the contract.

(b) Every contract for a business opportunity shall include the following:

(1) The terms and conditions of payment;

(2) A full and detailed description of the acts or services that the business opportunity seller undertakes to perform for the purchaser;

(3) The seller's principal business address and the name and address of its agent in the State of North Carolina authorized to receive service of process in addition to the Secretary of State as provided in G.S. 66-97(b);

(4) The approximate delivery date of any product(s), equipment or supplies the business opportunity seller is to deliver to the purchaser. (1977, c. 884, s. 1; 1981, c. 817, s. 4; 1983, c. 721, s. 4.)

§ 66-100. Remedies.

(a) If a business opportunity seller uses any untrue or misleading statements in the sale of a business opportunity, or fails to give the proper disclosures in the manner required by G.S. 66-95, or fails to deliver the equipment, supplies or product(s) necessary to begin substantial operation of the business within 45 days of the delivery date stated in the business opportunity contract, or if the contract does not comply with the requirements of G.S. 66-99, then, within one year of the date of the contract, upon written notice to seller, the purchaser may void the contract and shall be entitled to receive from the business opportunity seller all sums paid to the business opportunity seller. Upon receipt of such sums, the purchaser shall make available to the seller at purchaser's address or at the places at which they are located at the time notice is given, all product(s), equipment or supplies received by the purchaser. Provided, that purchaser shall not be entitled to unjust enrichment by exercising the remedies provided in this subsection.

(b) Any purchaser injured by a violation of this Article or by the business opportunity seller's breach of a contract subject to this Article or any obligation arising therefrom may bring an action for recovery of damages, including reasonable attorneys' fees.

(c) Upon complaint of any person that a business opportunity seller has violated the provisions of this Article, the superior court shall have jurisdiction to enjoin the defendant from further such violations.

(d) The remedies provided herein shall be in addition to any other remedies provided for by law or in equity.

(e) The violation of any provisions of this Article shall constitute an unfair practice under G.S. 75-1.1. (1977, c. 884, s. 1.)

§§ 66-101 through 66-105. Reserved for future codification purposes.

Article 20.

Loan Brokers.

§ 66-106. Definitions.

(a) For purposes of this Article the following definitions apply:

(1) A "loan broker" is any person, firm, or corporation who, in return for any consideration from any person, promises to (i) procure for such person, or assist such person in procuring, a loan from any third party; or (ii) consider whether or not it will make a loan to such person.

(2) A "loan" is an agreement to advance money or property in return for the promise to make payments therefor, whether such agreement is styled as a loan, credit card, line of credit, a lease or otherwise.

(b) Except for mortgage loans as defined in G.S. 53-243.01, this Article shall not apply to any party approved as a mortgagee by the Secretary of Housing and Urban Development, the Federal Housing Administration, the Veterans Administration, a National Mortgage Association or any federal agency; nor to any party currently designated and compensated by a North Carolina licensed insurance company as its agent to service loans it makes in this State; nor to any insurance company registered with and licensed by the North Carolina Insurance Commissioner; nor, with respect to residential mortgage loans, to any residential mortgage banker or mortgage broker licensed pursuant to Article 19A of Chapter 53 of the General Statutes or exempt from licensure pursuant to G.S. 53-243.01(12) and G.S. 53-243.02; nor to any attorney-at-law, public accountant, or dealer registered under the North Carolina Securities Act, acting in the professional capacity for which such attorney-at-law, public accountant, or dealer is registered or licensed under the laws of the State of North Carolina. Provided further that subdivision (1)(ii) above shall not apply to any lender whose loans or advances to any person, firm or corporation in North Carolina aggregate more than one million dollars

($1,000,000) in the preceding calendar year. (1979, c. 705, s. 1; 1981, c. 785, s. 1; 1993, c. 339, s. 2; 2001-393, s. 4; 2008-228, s. 17.)

§ 66-107. Required disclosure statement.

At least seven days prior to the time any person signs a contract for the services of a loan broker, or the time of the receipt of any consideration by the loan broker, whichever occurs first, the broker must provide to the party with whom he contracts a written document, the cover sheet of which is entitled in at least 10-point bold face capital letters "DISCLOSURES REQUIRED BY NORTH CAROLINA LAW." Under this title shall appear the statement in at least 10-point type that "The State of North Carolina has not reviewed and does not approve, recommend, endorse or sponsor any loan brokerage contract. The information contained in this disclosure has not been verified by the State. If you have any questions see an attorney before you sign a contract or agreement." Nothing except the title and required statement shall appear on the cover sheet. The disclosure document shall contain the following information:

(1) The name of the broker; whether the broker is doing business as an individual, partnership, or corporation; the names under which the broker has done, is doing or intends to do business; and the name of any parent or affiliated companies;

(2) The names, addresses and titles of the broker's officers, directors, trustees, general partners, general managers, principal executives, and any other persons charged with responsibility for the broker's business activities; and all the broker's employees located in North Carolina;

(3) The length of time the broker has conducted business as a loan broker;

(4) The total number of loan brokerage contracts the broker has entered within the past 12 months;

(5) The number of loan brokerage contracts in which the broker has successfully obtained a loan for the prospective borrower within the past 12 months;

(6) A copy of a current (not older than 13 months) financial statement of the broker, updated to reflect any material changes in the broker's financial condition;

(7) A full and detailed description of the actual services that the broker undertakes to perform for the prospective borrower;

(8) A specific statement of the circumstances in which the broker will be entitled to obtain or retain consideration from the party with whom he contracts;

(9) One of the following statements, whichever is appropriate:

a.____ "As required by North Carolina law, this loan broker has secured a bond by

(name and address of surety company)

a surety authorized to do business in this State. Before signing a contract with this loan broker, you should check with the surety company to determine the bond's current status," or

b.____ "As required by North Carolina law, this loan broker has established a trust account

(number of account)

with _____

(name/address of bank or savings institution).

Before signing a contract with this loan broker you should check with the bank or savings institution to determine the current status of the trust account." (1979, c. 705, s. 1.)

§ 66-108. Bond or trust account required.

(a) Every loan broker must obtain a surety bond issued by a surety company authorized to do business in this State, or establish a trust account with a licensed and insured bank or savings institution located in the State of

North Carolina. The amount of the bond or trust account shall be ten thousand dollars ($10,000). The bond or trust account shall be in favor of the State of North Carolina. Any person damaged by the loan broker's breach of contract or of any obligation arising therefrom, or by any violation of this Article, may bring an action against the bond or trust account to recover damages suffered. The aggregate liability of the surety or trustee shall be only for actual damages and in no event shall exceed the amount of the bond or trust account.

(b) Failure to comply with subsection (a) shall be a Class 1 misdemeanor.

(c) No loan broker shall collect any advance fee or other valuable consideration from a borrower prior to the closing of the loan. This prohibition shall not preclude the loan broker from collecting reasonable and necessary fees payable to third parties for appraisal, property survey, title examination, and credit reports. (1979, c. 705, s. 1; 1993, c. 339, s. 3, c. 539, s. 522; 1994, Ex. Sess., c. 24, s. 14(c).)

§ 66-109. Filing with Secretary of State.

(a) Prior to placing any advertisement or making any other representations to prospective borrowers in this State, every loan broker shall file with the Secretary of State two copies of the disclosure statement required by G.S. 66-107, and either a copy of the bond required by G.S. 66-108, or a copy of the formal notification by the depository that the trust account required by G.S. 66-108 is established. These filings shall be updated as any material changes in the required information or the status of the bond or trust account occur, but no less than annually.

(b) Failure to comply with subsection (a) shall be a Class 1 misdemeanor. (1979, c. 705, s. 1; 1981, c. 785, s. 2; 1993, c. 539, s. 523; 1994, Ex. Sess., c. 24, s. 14(c).)

§ 66-110. Contracts to be in writing.

Every loan brokerage contract shall be in writing, and signed by all contracting parties. A copy of the contract shall be given to the prospective borrower at the time he signs the contract. (1979, c. 705, s. 1.)

§ 66-111. Remedies.

(a) If a loan broker uses any untrue or misleading statements in connection with a loan brokerage contract, fails to fully comply with the requirements of this Article, fails to comply with the terms of the contract or any obligation arising therefrom, or fails to make diligent effort to grant a loan to or procure a loan on behalf of the prospective borrower, then, upon written notice to the broker, the prospective borrower may void the contract, and shall be entitled to receive from the broker all sums paid to the broker, and recover any additional damages including attorney's fees.

(b) Upon complaint of any person that a loan broker has violated the provisions of this Article, the superior court shall have jurisdiction to enjoin that defendant from further such violations.

(c) The remedies provided herein shall be in addition to any other remedies provided for by law or in equity.

(d) The violation of any provisions of this Article shall constitute an unfair practice under G.S. 75-1.1. (1979, c. 705, s. 1.)

§ 66-112. Scope.

The provisions of this Article shall apply in all circumstances in which any party to the contract conducted any contractual activity (including but not limited to solicitation, discussion, negotiation, offer, acceptance, signing, or performance) in this State. (1979, c. 705, s. 1.)

§§ 66-113 through 66-117. Reserved for future codification purposes.

Article 21.

Prepaid Entertainment Contracts.

§ 66-118. Definitions.

As used in this Article, unless the context clearly requires otherwise:

(1)   "Contract cost" means the total consideration paid by a buyer pursuant to a contract including but not limited to:

a.   Any initiation or nonrecurring fee charged;

b.   All periodic fees required by the contract;

c.   All dues or maintenance fees; and

d.   All finance charges, time-price differentials, interest, and other similar fees and charges.

(2)   "Contract duration" means the total period of use allowed by a buyer's contract, including months or time periods that are called "free" or "bonus" or that are described in any other terms suggesting that they are provided free of charge.

(3)   "Prepaid entertainment contract" means any contract in which:

a.   The buyer of a service pays for or is obligated to pay for service prior to the buyer's receipt of or enjoyment of any or all of the services;

b.   The seller is other than a licensed nonprofit school, college, or university; the State or any subdivision thereof; or a nonprofit religious, ethnic, or community organization; and

c.   The services to be performed are related to any one of the following:

1.   Dance lessons or facilities, or any related services or events;

2.   Matching, dating, or social club services or facilities, including any service represented as providing names of, introduction to, or opportunity to meet members of the opposite sex;

3.   Martial arts training;

4. Health or athletic club services or facilities. (1979, c. 833, s. 1; 1991 (Reg. Sess., 1992), c. 1009, s. 1.)

§ 66-119. Contract requirements.

Every prepaid entertainment contract shall:

(1) Be in writing, fully completed, dated and signed by all contracting parties. A copy of the contract shall be given to the buyer at the time he signs the contract;

(2) Have a duration of service that is a precisely measured period of years or any definite part of a year;

(3) Contain a full statement of the buyer's rights under G.S. 66-120;

(4) Contain, in immediate proximity to the space reserved for the signature of the buyer, in bold face type of a minimum size of 10 points, a statement of the buyer's rights under G.S. 66-121, in substantially the following form:

"You the buyer, may cancel this contract at any time prior to midnight of the third business day after the date of this contract. To cancel, you must notify the seller in writing not later than midnight of

_____

(Date)."

(1979, c. 833, s. 1.)

§ 66-120. Buyer's rights.

Every seller of a prepaid entertainment contract must:

(1) Deliver to the buyer all information of a personal or private nature, including but not limited to answers to tests or questionnaires, photographs, evaluations, and background information, within 30 days after request therefor;

(2) Refund to the buyer at least ninety percent (90%) of the pro rata cost of any unused services, within 30 days after request therefor, if:

a. The buyer is unable to receive benefits from the seller's services by reason of death or disability; or

b. The buyer relocates more than eight miles from his present location, and more than 30 miles from the seller's facility and any substantially similar facility that will accept the seller's obligation under the contract and this Article; or

c. The seller relocates his facility more than eight miles from its present location, or the services provided by the seller are materially impaired.

(3) Refund to the buyer the pro rata cost of any unused services under all contracts between the parties, within 30 days after request therefor, if the aggregate price of all contracts in force between the parties exceeds one thousand five hundred dollars ($1,500). Provided, if the contract so provides, the seller may retain a cancellation fee of not more than 25 percent (25%) of the pro rata cost of unused services on all contracts, not to exceed five hundred dollars ($500.00). (1979, c. 833, s. 1.)

§ 66-121. Buyer's right to cancel.

(a) In addition to any right otherwise to revoke an offer or cancel a sale or contract, the buyer has the right to cancel a prepaid entertainment contract sale until midnight of the third business day after the buyer signs a contract which complies with G.S. 66-119(4).

(b) Cancellation occurs when the buyer gives written notice of cancellation to the seller at the address stated in the contract.

(c) Notice of cancellation, if given by mail, is given when it is deposited in the United States mail properly addressed and postage prepaid.

(d) Notice of cancellation need not take a particular form and is sufficient if it indicates by any form of written expression the intention of the buyer not to be bound by the contract.

(e) For purposes of this Article, business days are all days other than Saturdays, Sundays, holidays, and days on which the seller's facility is not open to the buyer. (1979, c. 833, s. 1.)

§ 66-122. Rights and responsibilities after cancellation.

Within 30 days after a prepaid entertainment contract has been cancelled in accordance with G.S. 66-121, the seller must tender to the buyer any payments made by the buyer and any note or other evidence of indebtedness. (1979, c. 833, s. 1.)

§ 66-123. Prohibited practices.

(a) No person shall sell any prepaid entertainment contract or contracts which, when taken together with all other contracts in force between the parties have an aggregate duration of service in excess of three years.

(b) No person shall sell any prepaid entertainment contract unless performance of that contract is to begin within 180 days. (1979, c. 833, s. 1.)

§ 66-124. Bond or escrow account required.

(a) Prior to the sale of any prepaid entertainment contract for services which are available on the day of sale, the seller shall purchase a surety bond issued by a surety company authorized to do business in this State, as follows:

(1) The amount of the surety bond shall be equal to the aggregate value of outstanding liabilities to buyers, or ten thousand dollars ($10,000), whichever is greater. For purposes of this section, "liabilities" means the moneys actually received in advance from the buyer on or after January 1, 1993, for contract costs, less the prorated value of services rendered by the seller. The bond shall

be in favor of the State of North Carolina and in a form approved by the Attorney General. The surety company shall have a duty to disclose the amount and status of the bond to the public upon request. Any person who is damaged by reason of the closing of a facility or bankruptcy of the seller, may bring an action against the bond to recover damages suffered; provided, however, that the aggregate liability of the surety shall be only for actual damages and in no event shall exceed the amount of the bond.

(2)   The amount of the bond shall be based upon a written sworn statement by the seller under penalty of perjury stating the seller's outstanding liabilities to buyers. A corporate seller's statement shall be signed by the president of the corporation; the statement of a partnership shall be signed by a general partner; and the statement of a sole proprietorship shall be signed by the sole proprietor. The statement and a copy of the bond shall be filed with the Attorney General within 90 days after the first contract is sold and at 180-day intervals thereafter.

(3)   The amount of the bond shall be increased or may be decreased, as necessary, to take into account changes in the seller's outstanding liabilities to buyers on a semiannual basis.

(4)   The bonding requirement of this section applies to each location of the seller in any case where a seller operates or plans to operate more than one facility in the State. A separate bond for each separately located facility shall be filed with the Attorney General.

(5)   Notwithstanding any other provision of this section, no seller is required to purchase a bond in excess of two hundred fifty thousand dollars ($250,000) per facility.

(6)   A change in ownership shall not release, cancel, or terminate liability under any bond previously established unless the Attorney General agrees in writing to the release, cancellation, or termination because the new owner has established a new bond for the benefit of the previous owner's members, or because the former owner has paid the required funds to its members.

(7)   In lieu of purchasing the bond required by subdivision (1), an irrevocable letter of credit from a bank insured by the Federal Deposit Insurance Corporation, in a form acceptable to the Attorney General, may be filed with the Attorney General.

(8) Claims and actions by a buyer of prepaid entertainment contract services:

a. A buyer of prepaid entertainment contract services who suffers or sustains any loss or damage by reason of the closing of a facility or bankruptcy of the seller shall file a claim with the surety, and, if the claim is not paid, may bring an action based on the bond and recover against the surety. In the case of a letter of credit that has been filed with the Attorney General, the buyer may file a claim with the Attorney General;

b. Any claim under paragraph a. of this subdivision shall be filed no later than one year from the date on which the facility closed or bankruptcy was filed;

c. The Attorney General may file a claim with the surety on behalf of any buyer in paragraph a. of this subdivision. The surety shall pay the amount of the claims to the Attorney General for distribution to claimants entitled to restitution and shall be relieved of liability to that extent;

d. The liability of the surety under any bond may not exceed the aggregate amount of the bond, regardless of the number or amount of claims filed;

e. If the claims filed should exceed the amount of the bond, the surety shall pay the amount of the bond to the Attorney General for distribution to claimants entitled to restitution and shall be relieved of all liability under the bond.

(9) The seller shall be exempt from the bonding requirement if all of its unexpired contracts and present membership plans meet the following criteria: (i) no initiation fee or similar nonrecurring fee is charged, and (ii) at no time is any member charged to pay for the use of facilities or services more than 31 days in advance.

(b) If, for any reason, services under a prepaid entertainment contract are not available to the buyer on the date of sale, then:

(1) The seller shall establish a surety bond issued by a surety company authorized to do business in the State or shall establish an escrow account with a licensed and insured bank or savings institution located in this State. The surety bond or escrow account shall be in the amount of ten thousand dollars ($10,000) per location or in an amount equal to all contract costs received from the buyer, whichever is greater. The bond or escrow account shall be in favor of the State of North Carolina and a copy of the bond or escrow agreement shall

be filed with the Attorney General prior to the sale of any prepaid entertainment contracts. The bond or escrow account shall remain in force until 60 days after all services of the seller are available to the buyer, at which time the seller shall comply with the bonding requirement of subsection (a) of this section. The escrow account shall be established and maintained only in a financial institution which agrees in writing with the Attorney General to hold all funds deposited and not to release such funds until receipt of written authorization from the Attorney General. The funds deposited will be eligible for withdrawal by the depositor after the facility has been open and providing services for 60 days and the Attorney General gives written authorization for withdrawal. Any person who is damaged by any violation of this Article, or by the seller's breach of the contract for sale or any obligation arising therefrom may bring an action against the bond or escrow account to recover damages suffered; provided, however, that the aggregate liability of the surety or escrow agent shall be for actual damages only and in no event shall exceed the amount of the bond or escrow account.

(2) The buyer's right to cancel the contract pursuant to G.S. 66-121 shall be extended until midnight of the third business day after the date upon which the services become available and the buyer is notified that the services are available. (1979, c. 833, s. 1; 1991 (Reg. Sess., 1992), c. 1009, s. 2.)

§ 66-124.1. Record keeping; provision of records to the Attorney General.

(a) Any person or business bonded under this Article shall maintain accurate records of the bond and of premium payments on it. These records shall be open to inspection by the Attorney General at any time during normal business hours.

(b) Any person who sells prepaid entertainment contracts shall maintain accurate records, updated as necessary, of the name, address, contract terms, and payments of each buyer of services. These records shall be open to inspection by the Attorney General, upon reasonable notice not to exceed 72 hours, at any time during normal business hours.

(c) On the permanent closing of a facility, the seller of the services shall provide the following information to the Attorney General within 15 business days:

(1) A list of the names and addresses of all buyers holding unexpired contracts;

(2) The original or a copy of all buyers' contracts; and

(3) A record of all payments received under buyers' agreements. (1991 (Reg. Sess., 1992), c. 1009, s. 3.)

§ 66-125. Remedies.

(a) Any buyer injured by any violation of this Article may bring an action for recovery of damages, including reasonable attorney's fees.

(b) The remedies herein shall be in addition to any other remedies provided for by law or in equity, but the damages assessed shall not exceed the largest amount of damages available by any single remedy.

(c) The violation of any provisions of this Article shall constitute an unfair practice under G.S. 75-1.1. (1979, c. 833, s. 1.)

§§ 66-126 through 66-130. Reserved for future codification purposes.

Article 22.

Discount Buying Clubs.

§ 66-131. Definition.

For the purpose of this Article, a "discount buying club" is any person, firm or corporation, which in exchange for any valuable consideration offers to sell or to arrange the sale of goods or services to its customers at prices represented to be lower than are generally available. "Discount buying club" shall not include any cooperative buying association or other group in which no person is intended to profit or actually profits beyond the benefit that all members receive from buying at a discount; nor shall any person, firm or corporation be deemed "a discount buying club" solely by virtue of the fact that (i) for fifty dollars ($50.00) or less it sells tickets or coupons valid for use in obtaining goods or services from a retail merchant, or (ii) as a service collateral to its principal business, and for no additional charge it arranges for its members or customers to purchase or lease directly from particular merchants at a specified discount. (1981, c. 594, s. 1.)

§ 66-132. Contracts to be in writing.

(a) Every contract between a discount buying club and its customers shall be in writing, fully completed, dated and signed by all contracting parties. A copy of the completed contract shall be given to the buyer at the time he signs it. The contract shall in clear, conspicuous and simple language:

(1) State the duration of the contract in a definite period of years or months. If the contract may be periodically renewed, the contract shall state specifically the terms under which it may be renewed; and the amount of any renewal fees must be stated unless the contract meets the requirements of subsection (b) of this section.

(2) State that the buying club will maintain a trust account and bond in compliance with G.S. 66-135, and identify the location of the trust account and the name and address of the surety company.

(3) Contain, immediately above the customer's signature in boldface type of not less than 10 points size, a statement substantially as follows:

"You, the customer, may cancel this contract at any time prior to midnight of the third business day after the date of this contract. To cancel you must notify the company in writing of your intent to cancel."

(4) List the categories of goods and services the buying club contracts to make available.

(5) State the procedures by which the customer can select, order, and pay for merchandise or services and state the time and manner of delivery.

(6) State the method the discount buying club will use in setting the price customers will pay for goods or services.

(7)   List any charges, however denominated, which are incidental to the purchase of goods or services and which must be paid by the customer.

(8)   State the discount buying club's obligations with respect to warranties on goods or services ordered.

(9)   State the customer's rights and obligations with respect to the cancellation or return of ordered goods.

(b)   The written contract required by subsection (a) above need not be signed or dated by the customer if the following requirements are met:

(1)   The total consideration paid by each member or customer does not exceed a one-time or annual fee of one hundred dollars ($100.00);

(2)   The member or customer has the unconditional right to cancel the contract at any time and receive within 10 days a full refund of the one-time membership fee, or the annual membership fee covering the current membership period, whichever the case may be;

(3)   Instead of the notice required in subsection (a)(3), above, the written contract contains on its first page in boldface type of not less than 10 points size, or not less than the point size of the contract terms or information printed immediately adjacent thereto, whichever point size shall be larger, a statement substantially as follows:

"You, the customer, may cancel this contract at any time and receive a total refund of any fees or consideration already paid for the current membership period. To cancel you must notify the company in writing of your intent to cancel."; and

(4)   The written contract is mailed to the buyer on or before the date the membership is first charged or billed. (1981, c. 594, s. 1; 1989, c. 495, s. 1.)

§ 66-133. Customer's right to cancel.

(a)   In addition to any other right to revoke an offer or cancel a sale or contract, the customer has the right to cancel a contract for the services of a discount buying club until midnight of the third business day after the buyer signs a contract which complies with G.S. 66-132.

(b)   Cancellation occurs when the customer gives written notice of cancellation to the discount buying club at the address stated in the contract.

(c)   Notice of cancellation, if given by mail, is given when it is deposited in the United States mail properly addressed with postage prepaid.

(d)   Notice of cancellation need not take any particular form and is sufficient if it indicates by any form of written expression that the customer intends or wishes not to be bound by the contract.

(e)   For purposes of this Article, business days are all days other than Saturdays, Sundays, holidays, and days on which the discount buying club is not open for business. (1981, c. 594, s. 1.)

§ 66-134. Prohibited acts.

Discount buying clubs shall not:

(1)   Represent to any potential customer that his opportunity to join is limited in time or that his delay in joining may subject him to an increased price. This shall not preclude reference to a general price increase that will take effect on a specified date.

(2)   Discourage or refuse to allow potential customers to inspect all of their current merchandise catalogs and price lists during normal business hours at their place of business.

(3)   Compare their prices for goods or services with other prices unless the comparison prices are prices at which substantial sales of the same goods or services were made in the same area within the past 90 days, and unless a written copy of the comparison is given to the buyer to keep.

(4)   Fail upon the customer's request to cancel without charge any purchase order for:

a.   Services, if such services have not been substantially performed;

b. Goods to be specially manufactured, if such manufacture has not been substantially performed; or

c. Any other goods, if they have not been delivered to the customer or consigned to a certified public carrier for delivery;

within 90 days after the purchase order was received by the buying club. This provision shall not be construed to limit a customer's right to earlier performance created by contract or by any other applicable law or regulation.

(5) Charge any amount in excess of demonstrable actual damages upon a customer's cancellation of an order. (1981, c. 594, s. 1.)

§ 66-135. Bond and trust account required.

(a) Every discount buying club shall obtain and maintain a bond from a surety company licensed to do business in North Carolina. Such bond shall be in an amount not less than one hundred times the one-time or annual membership fee, or fifty thousand dollars ($50,000), whichever is greater.

(b) Every discount buying club shall hold advance payments for goods and services in trust in a separate account used solely for that purpose. The funds in such account shall be held free from all liens. Records of such account shall be kept by the buying club in the regular course of its business sufficient to identify the amount held for each customer, the dates of the receipt and withdrawal of funds, and the purpose of withdrawal. Such records must be retained for a period not less than four years following withdrawal. Funds may not be withdrawn from the trust account unless and until (i) the ordered goods have been actually delivered to the customer or consigned to a certified public carrier, or (ii) ordered services have been provided in full, or (iii) the buying club has refunded the customer's payment. Provided, the discount buying club shall not be required to comply with the foregoing trust account requirements if the discount buying club meets the requirements of G.S. 66-132(b), bills its customers through a credit card account and obtains and maintains an additional bond in the amount of fifty thousand dollars ($50,000) from a surety company licensed to do business in North Carolina.

(c) Any person who is damaged by any violation of this Article, or by any breach by the discount buying club of its contract, may bring an action against the bond, provided that the aggregate liability of the surety shall not exceed the amount of the bond.

(d) Violations of subsections (a) or (b) of this section shall constitute a Class I felony. (1981, c. 594, s. 1; 1989, c. 495, ss. 2, 3; 1993, c. 539, s. 1282; 1994, Ex. Sess., c. 24, s. 14(c).)

§ 66-136. Remedies.

(a) Any person injured by a violation of this Article, or breach of any obligation created by this Article or contract subject thereto, may bring an action for recovery of damages, including reasonable attorneys' fees.

(b) The violation of any provision of this Article shall constitute an unfair act or practice under G.S. 75-1.1.

(c) The remedies provided herein shall be in addition to any other remedies provided by law or equity. (1981, c. 594, s. 1.)

§ 66-137. Taxes.

Discount buying clubs must pay North Carolina sales taxes and other applicable North Carolina taxes. (1989, c. 495, s. 4.)

§§ 66-138 through 66-141: Reserved for future codification purposes.

Article 23.

Rental Referral Agencies.

§ 66-142. Definition.

For the purposes of this Article, a "rental referral agency" is a person or business which offers to assist any person in locating residential rental property in return for any consideration from a prospective tenant. (1981, c. 610, s. 1.)

§ 66-143. Fees and deposits.

(a) A rental referral agency shall not charge or attempt to collect any fees or other consideration from any prospective tenant except where rental housing is in fact obtained by such person through the assistance of that agency. For the purposes of this Article, such housing is obtained when the prospective tenant has contracted to rent the property.

(b) Deposits to be applied toward fees may be required by a rental referral agency pursuant to a written contract which includes provisions stating:

(1) The specifications of housing sought by the prospective tenant, including maximum rent, desired lease period, geographic area, number of bedrooms required, number of children to be housed, and number and type of pets;

(2) That the deposit will be refunded within 10 days of the prospective tenant's request should the specified housing not be obtained through the agency's assistance within 30 days of the date of the contract;

(3) That the rental referral agency will maintain a trust account or bond in compliance with G.S. 66-145, and identifying the depository institution or bonding company by name and address.

(c) Notwithstanding subsections (a) and (b) of this section, a rental referral agency may charge or retain from any deposit a fee, not to exceed twenty dollars ($20.00), even if the prospective tenant fails to obtain rental housing through its assistance, provided that the following conditions are met:

(1) Any and all advertising for the rental referral agency discloses in a clear and conspicuous manner the agency's name, the fact that it is a "rental referral agency" using that term, and the fact that it charges a fee; and

(2) If a prospective tenant contacts the rental referral agency in response to an advertisement for a specific property listed by the agency and inquires about that property, the rental referral agency shall neither collect a fee nor obtain the prospective tenant's signature on a contract without first verifying that the advertised property remains available and disclosing to the prospective tenant whether or not it is still available.

(d) Prospective tenants shall apply in writing for a refund no sooner than 30 days after the date of the contract and no later than one year after the date of the contract. If the prospective tenant does not apply for a refund before one year has elapsed, the fee shall be deemed earned by the rental referral agency and may be removed from the trust account. (1981, c. 610, s. 1; 1991, c. 737, s. 1.)

§ 66-144. Representations of availability.

(a) A rental referral agency shall not make any representation that any property is available for rent unless availability has been verified by the agency within 48 hours prior to the representation. The availability of property described in media advertisements shall be verified within eight hours before being submitted to the advertising medium and in no event earlier than 96 hours prior to publication of the advertisement.

(b) Notations of the time and date of verification and the verifier's identity shall be recorded by the agency and made available for inspection by any person from whom the agency has received a deposit or a fee. (1981, c. 610, s. 1; 1991, c. 737, s. 2.)

§ 66-145. Bond or trust account required.

(a) Every rental referral agency before beginning business shall establish a trust account with a licensed and insured bank or savings institution located in the State of North Carolina. Each deposit to be applied towards a fee collected under G.S. 66-143(b) shall be placed in the trust account and shall be withdrawn only to refund the deposit to the applicant pursuant to G.S. 66-143(b)(2) or when a fee is earned by the agency as provided in G.S. 66-143(a).

(b) A rental referral agency may elect to post a bond in lieu of the trust account required by this section. The amount of the bond shall at no time be less than the amount that would be required by this section to be held in trust. In no event, however, shall the bond be less than five thousand dollars ($5,000). The rental referral agency shall file the bond with the clerk of the superior court of the county in which its principal place of business is located.

(c) Any person who is damaged by any violation of this Article, or by any breach by the rental referral agency of its contract, may bring an action for the remedies referred to and provided in G.S. 66-146 against the bond or trust account; provided that the aggregate liability of the surety or trustee shall not exceed the amount of the bond or trust account.

(d) Violation of subsections (a) or (b) of this section shall constitute a Class 1 misdemeanor. (1981, c. 610, s. 1; 1993, c. 539, s. 524; 1994, Ex. Sess., c. 24, s. 14(c).)

§ 66-146. Remedies.

(a) Any person injured by a violation of this Article, or breach of any obligation created by this Article or contract subject thereto, may bring an action for recovery of damages, including reasonable attorneys' fees.

(b) The violation of any provision of this Article shall constitute an unfair act or practice under G.S. 75-1.1.

(c) The remedies provided herein shall be in addition to any other remedies provided by law or equity. (1981, c. 610, s. 1.)

§§ 66-147 through 66-151. Reserved for future codification purposes.

Article 24.

Trade Secrets Protection Act.

§ 66-152. Definitions.

As used in this Article, unless the context requires otherwise:

(1) "Misappropriation" means acquisition, disclosure, or use of a trade secret of another without express or implied authority or consent, unless such trade secret was arrived at by independent development, reverse engineering, or was obtained from another person with a right to disclose the trade secret.

(2) "Person" means an individual, corporation, government, governmental subdivision or agency, business trust, estate, trust, partnership, association, joint venture, or any other legal or commercial entity.

(3) "Trade secret" means business or technical information, including but not limited to a formula, pattern, program, device, compilation of information, method, technique, or process that:

a. Derives independent actual or potential commercial value from not being generally known or readily ascertainable through independent development or reverse engineering by persons who can obtain economic value from its disclosure or use; and

b. Is the subject of efforts that are reasonable under the circumstances to maintain its secrecy.

The existence of a trade secret shall not be negated merely because the information comprising the trade secret has also been developed, used, or owned independently by more than one person, or licensed to other persons. (1981, c. 890, s. 1.)

§ 66-153. Action for misappropriation.

The owner of a trade secret shall have remedy by civil action for misappropriation of his trade secret. (1981, c. 890, s. 1.)

§ 66-154. Remedies.

(a) Except as provided herein, actual or threatened misappropriation of a trade secret may be preliminarily enjoined during the pendency of the action and shall be permanently enjoined upon judgment finding misappropriation for the period that the trade secret exists plus an additional period as the court may deem necessary under the circumstances to eliminate any inequitable or unjust advantage arising from the misappropriation.

(1) If the court determines that it would be unreasonable to enjoin use after a judgment finding misappropriation, an injunction may condition such use upon payment of a reasonable royalty for any period the court may deem just. In appropriate circumstances, affirmative acts to protect the trade secret may be compelled by order of the court.

(2) A person who in good faith derives knowledge of a trade secret from or through misappropriation or by mistake, or any other person subsequently acquiring the trade secret therefrom or thereby, shall be enjoined from disclosing the trade secret, but no damages shall be awarded against any person for any misappropriation prior to the time the person knows or has reason to know that it is a trade secret. If the person has substantially changed his position in good faith reliance upon the availability of the trade secret for future use, he shall not be enjoined from using the trade secret but may be required to pay a reasonable royalty as deemed just by the court. If the person has acquired inventory through such knowledge or use of a trade secret, he can dispose of the inventory without payment of royalty. If his use of the trade secret has no adverse economic effect upon the owner of the trade secret, the only available remedy shall be an injunction against disclosure.

(b) In addition to the relief authorized by subsection (a), actual damages may be recovered, measured by the economic loss or the unjust enrichment caused by misappropriation of a trade secret, whichever is greater.

(c) If willful and malicious misappropriation exists, the trier of fact also may award punitive damages in its discretion.

(d) If a claim of misappropriation is made in bad faith or if willful and malicious misappropriation exists, the court may award reasonable attorneys' fees to the prevailing party. (1981, c. 890, s. 1.)

§ 66-155. Burden of proof.

Misappropriation of a trade secret is prima facie established by the introduction of substantial evidence that the person against whom relief is sought both:

(1)   Knows or should have known of the trade secret; and

(2)   Has had a specific opportunity to acquire it for disclosure or use or has acquired, disclosed, or used it without the express or implied consent or authority of the owner.

This prima facie evidence is rebutted by the introduction of substantial evidence that the person against whom relief is sought acquired the information comprising the trade secret by independent development, reverse engineering, or it was obtained from another person with a right to disclose the trade secret. This section shall not be construed to deprive the person against whom relief is sought of any other defenses provided under the law. (1981, c. 890, s. 1.)

§ 66-156. Preservation of secrecy.

In an action under this Article, a court shall protect an alleged trade secret by reasonable steps which may include granting protective orders in connection with discovery proceedings, holding in-camera hearings, sealing the records of the action subject to further court order, and ordering any person who gains access to an alleged trade secret during the litigation not to disclose such alleged trade secret without prior court approval. (1981, c. 890, s. 1.)

§ 66-157. Statute of limitations.

An action for misappropriation of a trade secret must be commenced within three years after the misappropriation complained of is or reasonably should have been discovered. (1981, c. 890, s. 1.)

§§ 66-158 through 66-162. Reserved for future codification purposes.

Article 25.

Regulation of Precious Metal Businesses.

§ 66-163: Recodified as Part 2 of Article 45 of Chapter 66, G.S. 66-405 through 66-414, by Session Laws 2012-46, s. 15, effective October 1, 2012, and applicable to offenses committed on or after that date.

§ 66-164: Recodified as Part 2 of Article 45 of Chapter 66, G.S. 66-405 through 66-414, by Session Laws 2012-46, s. 15, effective October 1, 2012, and applicable to offenses committed on or after that date.

§ 66-165: Recodified as Part 2 of Article 45 of Chapter 66, G.S. 66-405 through 66-414, by Session Laws 2012-46, s. 15, effective October 1, 2012, and applicable to offenses committed on or after that date.

§ 66-166: Repealed by Session Laws 2009-482, § 3, effective October 1, 2009.

§ 66-167: Recodified as Part 2 of Article 45 of Chapter 66, G.S. 66-405 through 66-414, by Session Laws 2012-46, s. 15, effective October 1, 2012, and applicable to offenses committed on or after that date.

§ 66-168: Recodified as Part 2 of Article 45 of Chapter 66, G.S. 66-405 through 66-414, by Session Laws 2012-46, s. 15, effective October 1, 2012, and applicable to offenses committed on or after that date.

§ 66-169: Recodified as Part 2 of Article 45 of Chapter 66, G.S. 66-405 through 66-414, by Session Laws 2012-46, s. 15, effective October 1, 2012, and applicable to offenses committed on or after that date.

§ 66-170: Recodified as Part 2 of Article 45 of Chapter 66, G.S. 66-405 through 66-414, by Session Laws 2012-46, s. 15, effective October 1, 2012, and applicable to offenses committed on or after that date.

§ 66-171: Recodified as Part 2 of Article 45 of Chapter 66, G.S. 66-405 through 66-414, by Session Laws 2012-46, s. 15, effective October 1, 2012, and applicable to offenses committed on or after that date.

§ 66-172: Recodified as Part 2 of Article 45 of Chapter 66, G.S. 66-405 through 66-414, by Session Laws 2012-46, s. 15, effective October 1, 2012, and applicable to offenses committed on or after that date.

§ 66-173: Recodified as Part 2 of Article 45 of Chapter 66, G.S. 66-405 through 66-414, by Session Laws 2012-46, s. 15, effective October 1, 2012, and applicable to offenses committed on or after that date.

§ 66-174: Reserved for future codification purposes.

§ 66-175: Reserved for future codification purposes.

§ 66-176: Reserved for future codification purposes.

§ 66-177: Reserved for future codification purposes.

§ 66-178: Reserved for future codification purposes.

§ 66-179: Reserved for future codification purposes.

Article 26.

Farm Machinery Agreements.

§ 66-180. Definitions.

As used in this Article, unless the context requires otherwise:

(1)   "Agreement" means a written or oral contract or agreement between a dealer and a wholesaler, manufacturer, or distributor by which the dealer is granted one or more of the following rights:

a.   To sell or distribute goods or services.

b.   To use a trade name, trademark, service mark, logo type, or advertising or other commercial symbol.

(2)   "Current model" means a model listed in the wholesaler's, manufacturer's, or distributor's current sales manual or any supplements.

(3)   "Current net price" means the price listed in the supplier's price list or catalog in effect at the time the agreement is terminated, less any applicable discounts allowed.

(4) "Dealer" means a person engaged in the business of selling at retail farm, construction, utility or industrial, equipment, implements, machinery, attachments, outdoor power equipment, or repair parts.

(5) "Family member" means a spouse, brother, sister, parent, grandparent, child, grandchild, mother-in-law, father-in-law, daughter-in-law, son-in-law, stepparent, or stepchild, or a lineal descendant of the dealer or principal owner of the dealership.

(6) "Good cause" means failure by a dealer to comply with requirements imposed upon the dealer by the agreement if the requirements are not different from those imposed on other dealers similarly situated in this State. In addition, good cause exists in any of the following circumstances:

a. A petition under bankruptcy or receivership law has been filed against the dealer.

b. The dealer has made an intentional misrepresentation with the intent to defraud supplier.

c. Default by the dealer under a chattel mortgage or other security agreement between the dealer and the supplier or a revocation or discontinuance of a guarantee of a present or future obligation of the retailer to the supplier.

d. Closeout or sale of a substantial part of the dealer's business related to the handling of goods; the commencement or dissolution or liquidation of the dealer if the dealer is a partnership or corporation; or a change, without the prior written approval of the supplier, which shall not be unreasonably withheld, in the location of the dealer's principal place of business or additional locations set forth in the agreement.

e. Withdrawal of an individual proprietor, partner, major shareholder, or manager of the dealership, or a substantial reduction in interest of a partner or major shareholder, without the prior written consent of the supplier.

f. Revocation or discontinuance of any guarantee of the dealer's present or future obligations to the supplier.

g. The dealer has failed to operate in the normal course of business for seven consecutive business days or has otherwise abandoned the business.

h. The dealer has pleaded guilty to or has been convicted of a felony affecting the relationship between the dealer and the supplier.

i. The dealer transfers an interest in the dealership, or a person with a substantial interest in the ownership or control of the dealership, including an individual proprietor, partner, or major shareholder, withdraws from the dealership or dies, or a substantial reduction occurs in the interest of a partner or major shareholder in the dealership.

(7) "Inventory" means farm implements and machinery, construction, utility and industrial equipment, consumer products, outdoor power equipment, attachments, or repair parts.

(8) "Net cost" means the price the dealer paid the supplier for the inventory, less all applicable discounts allowed, plus the amount the dealer paid for freight costs from the supplier's location to the dealer's location, plus reasonable cost of assembly or disassembly performed by the dealer.

(9) "Supplier" means a wholesaler, manufacturer, distributor, or any purchaser of assets or stock of any surviving corporation resulting from a merger or liquidation, any receiver or assignee, or any trustee of the original manufacturer, wholesaler, or distributor who enters into an agreement with a dealer.

(10) "Superseded part" means any part that will provide the same function as a currently available part as of the date of cancellation.

(11) "Termination" of an agreement means the termination, cancellation, nonrenewal, or noncontinuance of the agreement. (1985, c. 441, s. 1; 2001-343, s. 1.)

§ 66-181. Usage of trade.

The terms "utility" and "industrial," when used to refer to equipment, implements, machinery, attachments, or repair parts, shall have the meaning commonly used and understood among dealers and suppliers of farm equipment as a usage of trade in accordance with G.S. 25-1-303(c). (1985, c. 441, s. 1; 2006-112, s. 22.)

§ 66-182. Notice of termination of agreements.

(a) Notwithstanding any agreement to the contrary, a supplier who terminates or otherwise fails to renew or substantially changes the competitive circumstances of an agreement with a dealer without good cause shall notify the dealer of the termination not less than 90 days prior to the effective date of the termination and shall provide a 60-day right-to-cure the deficiency. If the deficiency is cured within the allotted time, the notice is void. In the case where cancellation is enacted due to market penetration, a reasonable period of time shall have existed where the supplier has worked with the dealer to gain the desired market share. If there is any reason constituting good cause for action, the notice shall state that reason.

(a1) Notwithstanding any agreement to the contrary, a supplier who terminates or otherwise fails to renew or substantially changes the competitive circumstances of an agreement with a dealer for good cause is not required to notify the dealer of the termination or to provide a right-to-cure the deficiency.

(b) Notwithstanding any agreement to the contrary, a dealer who terminates an agreement with a supplier shall notify the supplier of the termination not less than 90 days prior to the effective date of the termination.

(b1) Repealed by Session Laws 2003-195, s. 1, effective October 1, 2003.

(c) Notification under this section shall be in writing and shall be by certified mail or personally delivered to the recipient. It shall contain all of the following:

(1) A statement of intention to terminate the dealership.

(2) A statement of the reasons for the termination.

(3) The date on which the termination takes effect. (1985, c. 441, s. 1; 2001-343, s. 1; 2003-195, s. 1.)

§ 66-183. Supplier's duty to repurchase.

(a) Whenever a dealer enters into an agreement evidenced by a written or oral contract in which the dealer agrees to maintain an inventory, and the agreement is terminated by either party, the supplier shall repurchase the dealer's inventory as provided in this Article unless the dealer chooses to keep the inventory. If the dealer has any outstanding debts to the supplier, then the repurchase amount may be set off or credited to the retailer's account.

(b)   Whenever a dealer enters into an agreement in which the dealer agrees to maintain an inventory, and the dealer or the majority stockholder of the dealer, if the dealer is a corporation, dies or becomes incompetent, the supplier shall, at the option of the heir, personal representative, or guardian of the dealer, or the person who succeeds to the stock of the majority stockholder, repurchase the inventory as if the agreement had been terminated. The heir, personal representative, guardian, or succeeding stockholder has one year from the date of the death of the dealer or majority stockholder to exercise the option under this Article. (1985, c. 441, s. 1; 2001-343, s. 1.)

§ 66-184. Repurchase terms.

(a)   The supplier shall repurchase from the dealer within 90 days after termination of the agreement all inventory previously purchased from the supplier that remains unsold on the date of termination of the agreement.

(b)   The supplier shall pay the dealer:

(1)   One hundred percent (100%) of the current net price of all new, unused, unsold, undamaged, and complete farm, construction, utility, and industrial equipment, implements, machinery, outdoor power equipment, and attachments.

(2)   Ninety percent (90%) of the current net price of all new, unused, and undamaged repair and superseded parts.

(3)   Seventy-five percent (75%) of the net cost of all specialized repair tools purchased in the previous three years and fifty percent (50%) of the net cost of all specialized repair tools purchased in the previous four through six years pursuant to the requirements of the supplier and held by the dealer on the date of termination. Such specialized repair tools shall be unique to the supplier's product line and shall be in complete and resalable condition. Farm implements, machinery, utility and industrial equipment, and outdoor power equipment used in demonstrations, including equipment leased primarily for demonstration or lease, shall also be subject to repurchase under this section at its agreed

depreciated value, provided the equipment is in new condition and has not been damaged.

(4)   At its amortized value, the price of any specific data processing hardware and software and telecommunications equipment that the supplier required the dealer to purchase within the past five years.

(c)   Repealed by Session Laws 2001-343, s. 1.

(d)   The supplier shall pay the cost of shipping the inventory from the dealer's location and shall pay the dealer ten percent (10%) of the current net price of all new, unused, undamaged repair parts returned, to cover the cost of handling, packing, and loading. The supplier may perform the handling, packing, and loading instead of paying the ten percent (10%) for the services. The dealer and the supplier may each furnish a representative to inspect all parts and certify their acceptability when packed for shipment.

(e)   The supplier shall pay the full repurchase amount to the dealer not later than 30 days after receipt of the inventory. If the dealer has any outstanding debts to the supplier, then the repurchase amount may be credited to the dealer's account.

(f)   Upon payment of the repurchase amount to the dealer, the title and right of possession to the repurchased inventory shall transfer to the supplier. Annually, at the end of each calendar year, or after termination or cancellation of the agreement, the dealer's reserve account for recourse, retail sale, or lease contracts shall not be debited by a supplier or lender for any deficiency unless the dealer or the heirs of the dealer have been given at least seven business days' notice by certified or registered United States mail, return receipt requested, of any proposed sale of the equipment financed and an opportunity to purchase the equipment. The former dealer or the heirs of the dealer shall be given quarterly status reports on any remaining outstanding recourse contracts. As the recourse contracts are reduced, any reserve account funds shall be returned to the dealer or the heirs of the dealer in direct proportion to the liabilities outstanding.

(g)   In the event of the death of the dealer or the majority stockholder of a corporation operating as a dealer, the supplier shall, at the option of the heir, repurchase the inventory from the heir of the dealer or majority stockholder as if the supplier had terminated the agreement. The heir shall have one year from the date of the death of the dealer or majority stockholder to exercise the heir's options under this section. Nothing in this section shall require the repurchase of any inventory if the heir and the supplier enter into a new agreement to operate the retail dealership.

(h) A supplier shall have 90 days in which to consider and make a determination upon a request by a family member to enter into a new agreement to operate the dealership. In the event the supplier determines that the requesting family member is not acceptable, the supplier shall provide the family member with a written notice of its determination with the stated reasons for nonacceptance. This section does not entitle an heir, personal representative, or family member to operate a dealership without the specific written consent of the supplier.

(i) Notwithstanding the provisions of this section, in the event that a supplier and a dealer have executed an agreement concerning succession rights prior to the dealer's death, and if the agreement has not been revoked, that agreement shall be enforced even if it designates someone other than the surviving spouse or heir of the decedent as the successor. (1985, c. 441, s. 1; 2001-343, s. 1.)

§ 66-185. Exceptions to repurchase requirement.

This Article does not require the repurchase from a dealer of:

(1) A repair part with a limited storage life or otherwise subject to deterioration, such as gaskets or batteries, except for industrial "press on" or industrial pneumatic tires.

(2) A single repair part that is priced as a set of two or more items.

(3) A repair part that, because of its condition, is not resalable as a new part without repackaging or reconditioning.

(3a) Any repair part that is not in new, unused, undamaged condition.

(4) An item of inventory for which the dealer does not have title free of all claims, liens, and encumbrances other than those of the supplier.

(5) Any inventory that the dealer chooses to keep.

(6) Any inventory that was ordered by the dealer after either party's receipt of notice of termination of the agreement.

(6a) Any farm implements and machinery, construction, utility and industrial equipment, outdoor power equipment, and attachments that are not current models or that are not in new, unused, undamaged, complete condition, provided that the equipment used in demonstrations or leased, as provided in G.S. 66-184, shall be considered new and unused.

(6b) Any farm implements and machinery, construction, utility and industrial equipment, outdoor power equipment, and attachments that were purchased more than 36 months prior to notice of termination of the agreement.

(7) Any inventory that was acquired by the dealer from a source other than the supplier. (1985, c. 441, s. 1; 2001-343, s. 1.)

§ 66-186. Uniform commercial practice.

(a) This Article does not affect a security interest of the supplier in the inventory of the dealer.

(b) Repealed by Session Laws 2004-190, s. 4, effective January 1, 2005.

(c) The dealer and supplier shall furnish representatives to inspect all parts and certify their acceptability when packed for shipment. Failure of the supplier to provide a representative within 60 days shall result in automatic acceptance by the supplier of all returned items. (1985, c. 441, s. 1; 2001-343, s. 1; 2004-190, s. 4.)

§ 66-187. Warranty obligations.

(a) Whenever a supplier and a dealer enter into an agreement, the supplier shall pay any warranty claim made by the dealer for warranty parts or service within 30 days after its approval. The supplier shall approve or disapprove a warranty claim within 30 days after its receipt. If a claim is disapproved, the manufacturer, wholesaler, or distributor shall notify the dealer within 30 days stating the specific grounds upon which the disapproval is based. If a claim is not specifically disapproved in writing within 30 days after its receipt it is approved and payment must follow within 30 days.

(b)   Whenever a supplier and a dealer enter into an agreement, the supplier shall indemnify and hold harmless the dealer against any judgment for damages or any settlement agreed to by the supplier, including court costs and a reasonable attorney's fee, arising out of a complaint, claim, or lawsuit including negligence, strict liability, misrepresentation, breach of warranty, or rescission of the sale, to the extent the judgment or settlement relates to the manufacture, assembly, or design of inventory, or other conduct of the supplier beyond the dealer's control.

(c)   If, after termination of an agreement, the dealer submits a claim to the manufacturer, wholesaler, or distributor for warranty work performed prior to the effective date of the termination, the manufacturer, wholesaler, or distributor shall accept or reject the claim within 30 days of receipt.

(d)   If a claim is not paid within the time allowed under this section, interest shall accrue at the maximum lawful interest rate.

(e)   Warranty work performed by the dealer shall be compensated in accordance with the reasonable and customary amount of time required to complete the work, expressed in hours and fractions thereof. The cost of the work shall be computed by multiplying the time required to complete the work by the dealer's established customer hourly retail labor rate. The dealer shall inform the manufacturer, wholesaler, or distributor for whom the dealer is performing warranty work of the dealer's established customer hourly retail labor rate before the dealer performs any work.

(f)   Expenses expressly excluded under the warranty of the manufacturer, wholesaler, or distributor to the customer shall neither be included nor required to be paid for warranty work performed, even if the dealer requests compensation for the work performed.

(g)   The dealer shall be paid for all parts used by the dealer in performing warranty work. Payment shall be in an amount equal to the dealer's net price for the parts, plus a minimum of fifteen percent (15%).

(h)   The manufacturer, wholesaler, or distributor has a right to adjust compensation for errors discovered during an audit and, if necessary, to adjust claims paid in error.

(i)   The dealer shall have the right to accept the reimbursement terms and conditions of the manufacturer, wholesaler, or distributor in lieu of the terms and conditions of this section. (1985, c. 441, s. 1; 2001-343, s. 1.)

§ 66-187.1. Prohibited acts.

No supplier shall do any of the following:

(1)   Coerce any dealer to accept delivery of equipment, parts, or accessories which the dealer has not ordered voluntarily, except as required by any applicable law, or unless the parts or accessories are safety parts or accessories required by the supplier.

(2)   Condition the sale of additional equipment to a dealer upon a requirement that the dealer also purchase other goods or services, except that a supplier may require the dealer to purchase those parts reasonably necessary to maintain the quality of operation in the field of the equipment used in the trade area.

(3)   Coerce a dealer into refusing to purchase equipment manufactured by another supplier.

(4)   Terminate, cancel, or fail to renew or substantially change the competitive circumstances of the retail agreement based on the results of any circumstance beyond the dealer's control, including a natural disaster such as a sustained drought, high unemployment in the dealership market area, or a labor dispute. (2001-343, s. 1.)

§ 66-188. Failure to repurchase; civil remedy.

(a)   If a supplier fails or refuses to repurchase any inventory covered under the provisions of this Article within the time periods established in G.S. 66-184, the supplier is civilly liable for one hundred percent (100%) of the current net price of the inventory, any freight charges paid by the dealer, the dealer's reasonable attorney's fee and court costs, and interest on the current net price of the inventory computed at the legal rate of interest from the 91st day after termination of the agreement.

(b) Notwithstanding any agreement to the contrary, and in addition to any other legal remedies available, any person who suffers monetary loss due to a violation of this Article or because he refuses to accede to a proposal for an arrangement that, if consummated, is in violation of this Article, may bring a civil action to enjoin further violations and to recover damages sustained by him together with the costs of the suit, including a reasonable attorney's fee.

(b1) The provisions of G.S. 66-182 through G.S. 66-187.1 shall not be waivable in any contract or agreement, and any such attempted waiver shall be null and void.

(c) A civil action commenced under the provisions of this Article shall be brought within four years after the violation complained of is or reasonably should have been discovered, whichever occurs first. (1985, c. 441, s. 1; 2001-343, s. 1.)

§ 66-189. Reserved for future codification purposes.

Article 27.

Sales Representative Commissions.

§ 66-190. Definitions.

The following definitions apply in this Article:

(1) "Commission" means compensation accruing to a sales representative for payment by a principal, the rate of which is expressed as a percentage of the amount of orders, sales, or profits or as a specified amount per order or per sale.

(2) "Person" means an individual, corporation, limited liability company, partnership, unincorporated association, estate, trust, or other entity.

(3) "Principal" means a person who:

a. Manufactures, produces, imports, or distributes a product or service;

b. Contracts with a sales representative to solicit orders for the product or service; and

c. Compensates the sales representative, in whole or in part, by commission.

(4) "Sales representative" means a person who:

a. Contracts with a principal to solicit orders for products or services;

b. Is compensated, in whole or in part, by commission;

c. Is not a seller who complies with:

1. G.S. 25A-39 and G.S. 25A-40; or

2. Part 429 of 16 Code of Federal Regulations (January 1, 2003);

d. Repealed by Session Laws 2003-331, s. 1, effective October 1, 2003.

e. Is not an employee of the principal;

f. Does not sell or take orders for the sale of advertising services; and

g. Is not a person requiring a real estate broker's or sales agent's license under Chapter 93A of the General Statutes.

(5) "Terminate" and "termination" mean the end of the business relationship between the sales representative and the principal, whether by agreement, by expiration of time, or by exercise of a right of termination of either party. (1989, c. 506, s. 1; 2003-331, s. 1.)

§ 66-190.1. Written contracts.

The agreement or contract between a sales representative and a principal shall be in writing. The absence of a written agreement or contract shall not bar a cause of action by, or any remedy available to, a party. (2003-331, s. 1.)

§ 66-191. Payment of commissions; termination.

When a contract between a sales representative and a principal is terminated for any reason other than malfeasance on the part of the sales representative, the principal shall pay the sales representative all commissions due under the contract within 30 days after the effective date of the termination and all commissions that become due after the effective date of termination within 15 days after they become due. If the principal does not make payment as required by this section, the sales representative shall make a written demand upon the principal, sent by certified mail, for the commissions then due. The principal shall respond in writing to the demand within 15 days after the principal receives the written demand. (1989, c. 506, s. 1; 2003-331, s. 1.)

§ 66-192. Civil liability.

(a)   A principal who fails to comply with the provisions of G.S. 66-191 or is shown to have wrongfully revoked an offer of commission under G.S. 66-192.1 is liable to the sales representative in a civil action for (i) all amounts due the sales representative plus exemplary damages in an amount not to exceed two times the amount of commissions due the sales representative, (ii) attorney's fees actually and reasonably incurred by the sales representative in the action, and (iii) court costs.

(b)   Where the court determines that an action brought by a sales representative against a principal under this Article is frivolous, the sales representative is liable to the principal for court costs and for attorney's fees actually and reasonably incurred by the principal in defending the action.

(c)   A principal who is not a resident of this State who contracts with a sales representative to solicit orders in this State shall be subject to personal jurisdiction as provided in G.S. 1-75.4.

(d) Nothing in this Article shall invalidate or restrict any other or additional right or remedy available to a sales representative or preclude a sales representative from seeking to recover in one action on all claims against a principal. (1989, c. 506, s. 1; 2003-331, s. 1.)

§ 66-192.1. Revocable offers of commission; entitlement.

If a principal makes a revocable offer of a commission to a sales representative, the sales representative is entitled to the commission agreed upon if:

(1) The principal revokes the offer of commission;

(2) The sales representative establishes that the revocation was for the purpose of avoiding payment of the commission;

(3) The revocation occurs after the principal has obtained a written order for the principal's product or service because of the efforts of the sales representative; and

(4) The principal's product or service that is the subject of the order is provided to and paid for by a customer. (2003-331, s. 1.)

§ 66-193. Contracts void.

A provision in any contract between a sales representative and a principal purporting to waive any provision of this Article, whether by expressed waiver or by a contract subject to the laws of another state, is void. (1989, c. 506, s. 1; 2003-331, s. 1.)

§§ 66-194 through 66-199. Reserved for future codification purposes.

Article 28.

Rental Car Advertising and Sales Practices.

§ 66-200. Scope.

This Article applies to all persons renting vehicles from locations within this State. (1989, c. 631, s. 2, c. 770, s. 62.)

§ 66-201. Definitions.

As used in this Article:

(1)   "Collision damage waiver" means any contract or contractual provision, whether separate from or a part of a rental agreement, whereby the rental car company agrees for a charge to waive any and all claims against the renter for any damages to the rented vehicle during the term of the rental agreement.

(2)   "Damage" means any damage or loss to the rented vehicle, including loss of use and any costs and expenses incident to the damage or loss.

(3)   "Person" includes an individual, aggregation of individuals, corporation, company, association, or partnership.

(4)   "Rental agreement" means any written agreement setting forth the terms and the conditions governing the use of a vehicle provided by the rental car company.

(5)   "Rental car company" means any person in the business of providing vehicles to the public.

(6)   "Renter" means any person obtaining the use of a vehicle from a rental car company under the terms of a rental agreement.

(7)   "Vehicle" means a motor vehicle of the private passenger type including passenger vans and minivans that are primarily intended for transport of persons.

(8)   "Vehicle license and registration fees" means charges that may be imposed upon any rental transaction originating in this State to recoup the costs

incurred by a rental car company to license, title, inspect, and register rental vehicles. Rental car companies shall make a good faith effort to ensure that any vehicle license and registration fees collected do not exceed the actual costs incurred by the rental car company to license, title, inspect, and register rental vehicles. Any amounts collected by the rental car company in excess of the actual amount of its costs incurred shall be retained by the rental car company and applied to the costs incurred in the next calendar year for licensing, titling, inspecting, and registering rental vehicles. In that event, the good faith estimate of any vehicle license and registration fees to be charged by the company in the next calendar year shall be reduced to take into account the excess amount collected from the prior year. (1989, c. 631, s. 2; c. 770, s. 62; 2007-235, s. 1.)

§ 66-202. Rental car advertising.

(a)   Except as set forth in subsections (d) and (e) of this section and G.S. 66-204(a), a rental car company shall only advertise and charge a rental rate that includes the entire amount, except taxes and a mileage charge, if any, that a renter must pay to hire or lease a vehicle for the period of time to which the rental rate applies.

(b)   If a rental car company states a rental rate in a print advertisement or in an in-person or computer-transmitted quotation contained in the rental car company's proprietary computer reservation system, the rental car company shall clearly disclose or cause to be disclosed in that advertisement or quotation the terms of any mileage conditions relating to the advertised or quoted rental rate, including, but not limited to: To the extent applicable, the amount of mileage and fuel charges; the number of miles for which no charge will be imposed; and a description of the geographic driving limitations, if any, within the United States and Canada.

(c)   A rental car company shall also include in all price advertising the daily rate it charges for collision damage waivers; shall state in such advertising that collision damage waivers are not required; and shall state that prospective renters should examine or inquire about their automobile insurance policies to see whether such policies will cover damage to rental vehicles.

(d)   For a rental rate stated in an advertisement, quotation, or reservation for an airport location, a rental car company shall clearly and conspicuously disclose the existence and actual amount of the airport charges or fees, if any.

For a rental rate stated in an advertisement, quotation, or reservation involving more than one airport location, a rental car company shall clearly and conspicuously disclose the existence and range of airport charges or fees, if any, or the maximum airport charge or fee. A rental car company, in its discretion, may elect to separate vehicle license and registration fees from its rental rate. For a rental rate stated in an advertisement, quotation, or reservation with a separate vehicle license and registration fee, a rental company shall clearly and conspicuously disclose the existence and range of vehicle license and registration fees or the maximum vehicle license and registration fee. For purposes of this section, advertisements shall include radio, television, other electronic media, and print. For purposes of this section, quotations and reservations shall include in-person or proprietary computer-transmitted reservation systems.

(e) A rental car company shall clearly and conspicuously display the total estimated price, and the amount of the airport charges or fees, if any, and vehicle license and registration fees, if any, in any proprietary computer-assisted reservation system, shown or referenced on the same page on the computer screen viewed by the renter as the displayed rental rate and in a print size not smaller than the print size of the rental rate. When providing a renter a quotation of a rental rate in person or over a voice system, a rental car company shall inform the renter of the total estimated price, inclusive of all taxes, fees, and charges, or shall disclose the amount of airport charges or fees, if any, and vehicle license and registration fees, if any. A rental car company shall separately identify the amount and existence of airport charges or fees and vehicle license and registration fees on the rental agreement. (1989, c. 631, s. 2; c. 770, s. 62; 2001-432, s. 1; 2007-235, s. 2.)

§ 66-203. Prohibited charges.

(a) No rental car company may charge, in addition to the rental rate, taxes, airport charges and fees, if any, vehicle license and registration fees, if any, and mileage charge, if any, any fee that must be paid by the renter as a condition of hiring or leasing a vehicle, such as, but not limited to, required fuel charges or any fee for transporting the renter to the location where the rented vehicle will be delivered to that person.

(b) If a rental car company delivers a vehicle to a person at a location other than the location where the rental car company normally carries on its business, the rental car company shall not charge that person any amount for the rental for the period before the delivery of the vehicle. If a rental car company picks up a rented vehicle from a person at a location other than the location where the rental car company normally carries on its business the rental car company shall not charge to the renter any amount for the rental for the period after the rented vehicle is available for pickup in accordance with the notification given to the rental car company to pick up the rented vehicle. (1989, c. 631, s. 2; c. 770, s. 62; 2001-432, s. 2; 2007-235, s. 3.)

§ 66-204. Permitted charges.

(a)   In addition to the rental rate, taxes, airport charges and fees, if any, vehicle license and registration fees, if any, and mileage charge, if any, a rental car company may charge a renter for an item or service provided in connection with a particular rental transaction if the renter can avoid incurring that charge by choosing not to obtain or utilize the optional item or service. Items and services for which a rental car company may impose an additional charge include, but are not limited to: Optional insurance and accessories requested by the renter unless otherwise prohibited by law; service charges incident to a person's optional return of the vehicle to a location other than the location where the vehicle was hired or leased; optional collision damage waivers; and charges for refueling the vehicle at the conclusion of the rental transaction in the event the rented vehicle is not returned with as much fuel as was in its fuel tank at the beginning of the rental.

(b)   A rental car company may also impose an additional charge based on reasonable driving experience criteria established by the rental car company. (1989, c. 631, s. 2; c. 770, s. 62; 2001-432, s. 3; 2007-235, s. 4.)

§ 66-205. Agent licenses required.

No employee or other representative of a rental car company shall solicit or sell any kind of insurance in connection with a rental agreement unless he is duly licensed under Article 33 of Chapter 58 of the General Statutes. (1989, c. 631, s. 2, c. 770, s. 62.)

§ 66-206. Effects of violations.

Any violation of the provisions of this Article constitutes an unfair trade practice under G.S. 75-1.1. (1989, c. 631, s. 2, c. 770, s. 62.)

§ 66-207. Rental car companies assist in publicizing law.

(a)   A rental car company shall notify renters of the law requiring motorists to stop for and not pass stopped school buses that are properly marked and designated and that are receiving or discharging passengers. The Division of Motor Vehicles shall design a written notification in English, French, German, Japanese, and Spanish and the notification shall be no more than one side of a page. The Division of Motor Vehicles shall also develop a design for use on placards under subdivisions (b)(2) and (b)(3) of this section. The design may be used or adapted by the rental car company. The placards shall consist of the words "It is unlawful in North Carolina to pass a school bus that is stopped and receiving or discharging passengers.", or a visual symbol indicating passing a stopped school bus is unlawful in North Carolina, or both. The Division of Motor Vehicles shall publish the written notification and the design for placards on the Internet and rental car companies shall obtain both by downloading and printing them from that source.

(b)   The notification required under subsection (a) of this section may be made either:

(1)   By handing each renter who presents an International Driver Permit with a copy of the written notification prepared by the Division of Motor Vehicles under subsection (a) of this section;

(2)   If the rental car company operates airport shuttle buses to transport renters to pick up vehicles, by posting on each bus at least one placard containing a written notification or visual symbol, or both; or

(3)   If the rental car company operates a counter at which renters pick up documentation, by posting on that counter or at a place easily visible from the counter at least one placard containing a written notification or visual symbol, or both.

Each placard that contains a written notification shall provide that information in all the languages listed in subsection (a) of this section.

(c) There shall be no civil or criminal liability in negligence nor shall an action under G.S. 66-206 apply for any car rental company that fails to provide the information or post the placard required by this section. (2001-331, s. 2.)

§ 66-208. Reserved for future codification purposes.

Article 29.

Invention Development Services.

§ 66-209. Definitions.

As used in this Article, the following terms shall have the meanings given:

(1) "Contract" or "contract for invention development services" means a contract by which an invention developer undertakes invention development services for a customer for a stated payment or consideration, whether or not the payment or consideration has yet been made.

(2) "Customer" means any natural person who is solicited by, inquires about, seeks the services of, or enters into a contract with an invention developer for invention development services.

(3) "Invention development services" means any act done by or for an invention developer for the procurement or attempted procurement by the invention developer of a licensee or buyer of an intellectual property right in an invention. The term includes the evaluation, perfecting, marketing, brokering, or promoting of an invention, a patent search, and preparation or prosecution of a patent application by a person not registered to practice before the United States Patent and Trademark Office.

(4) "Invention" means any discovery, process, machine, design, formulation, composition of matter, product, concept, or idea, or any combination of these.

(5) "Invention developer" is an individual, firm, partnership, or corporation, or an agent, employee, officer, partner, or independent contractor of one of those entities, that offers to perform or performs invention development services for a customer and that is not:

a. A department or agency of the federal, State, or local government;

b. A charitable, scientific, educational, religious, or other organization qualified under G.S. 105-130.9 or described in Section 170(b)(1)(A) of the Internal Revenue Code of 1986, as amended;

c. A person registered before the United States Patent and Trademark Office acting solely within the scope of that person's professional license;

d. A person, firm, corporation, association, or other entity that does not charge a fee, including reimbursement for expenditures made or costs incurred by the entity, for invention development services other than payment made from a portion of the income received by a customer by virtue of the acts performed by the entity; or

e. An attorney licensed to practice law in North Carolina acting solely within the scope of that person's professional license.

(6) "Business day" means any day other than a Saturday, Sunday, or legal holiday. (1989, c. 746, s. 1; c. 770, s. 62.1(1), (2); 1991, c. 235, s. 1.)

§ 66-210. Disclosures made prior to contract.

In either the first written communication from the invention developer to a specific customer, or at the first personal meeting between the invention developer and a customer whichever may first occur, the invention developer shall make a written disclosure to the customer of the information required in this section which includes:

(1) The median fee charged to all of the invention developer's customers who have signed contracts with the developer in the preceding six months, excluding customers who have signed in the preceding 30 days;

(2)   A single statement setting forth (i) the total number of customers who have contracted with the invention developer, except that the number need not reflect those customers who have contracted within the preceding 30 days, and (ii) the number of customers who have received, by virtue of the invention developer's performance of invention development services, an amount of money in excess of the amount of money paid by those customers to the invention developer pursuant to a contract for invention development services;

(3)   The following statement: "Unless the invention developer is a lawyer or person registered before the United States Patent and Trademark Office, he is NOT permitted to give you legal advice concerning patent, copyright, trademark law, or the law of unfair competition or to advise you of whether your idea or invention may be patentable or may be protected under the patent, copyright, or trademark laws of the United States, or any other law. No patent, copyright, or trademark protection will be acquired for you by the invention developer. Your failure to inquire into the law governing patent, trademark, or copyright matters may jeopardize your rights in your idea or invention, both in the United States and in foreign countries. Your failure to identify and investigate existing patents, trademarks, or registered copyrights may place you in jeopardy of infringing the copyrights, patent, or trademark rights of other persons if you proceed to make, use, distribute, or sell your idea or invention." (1989, c. 746, s. 1; c. 770, s. 62.1(1), (2); 1991, c. 235, s. 1.)

§ 66-211. Standard provisions for cover notice.

(a)   A contract for invention development services must have a conspicuous and legible cover sheet attached. The cover sheet must set forth:

(1)   The name, home address, office address, and local address of the invention developer; and

(2)   The following notice printed in bold-faced type of not less than 10-point size:

THIS CONTRACT BETWEEN YOU AND AN INVENTION DEVELOPER IS REGULATED BY ARTICLE 29 OF CHAPTER 66 OF THE GENERAL STATUTES OF THE STATE OF NORTH CAROLINA. YOU ARE NOT PERMITTED OR REQUIRED TO MAKE ANY PAYMENTS UNDER THIS

CONTRACT UNTIL FOUR WORKING DAYS AFTER YOU SIGN THIS CONTRACT AND RECEIVE A COMPLETED COPY OF IT.

YOU CAN TERMINATE THIS CONTRACT AT ANY TIME BEFORE YOU MAKE PAYMENT. YOU CAN TERMINATE THIS CONTRACT SIMPLY BY NOT SUBMITTING PAYMENT.

IF YOU ASSIGN EVEN A PARTIAL INTEREST IN THE INVENTION TO THE INVENTION DEVELOPER, THE INVENTION DEVELOPER MAY HAVE THE RIGHT TO SELL OR DISPOSE OF THE INVENTION WITHOUT YOUR CONSENT AND MAY NOT HAVE TO SHARE THE PROFITS WITH YOU.

THE TOTAL NUMBER OF CUSTOMERS WHO HAVE CONTRACTED WITH THE INVENTION DEVELOPER SINCE ___(year)___ IS _(number)___. THE TOTAL NUMBER OF CUSTOMERS KNOWN BY THIS INVENTION DEVELOPER TO HAVE RECEIVED BY VIRTUE OF THIS INVENTION DEVELOPER'S PERFORMANCE, AN AMOUNT OF MONEY IN EXCESS OF THE AMOUNT PAID BY THE CUSTOMER TO THIS INVENTION DEVELOPER IS __(number)____.

YOU ARE ENCOURAGED TO CONSULT WITH A QUALIFIED ATTORNEY BEFORE SIGNING THIS CONTRACT. BY PROCEEDING WITHOUT THE ADVICE OF A QUALIFIED ATTORNEY YOU COULD LOSE ANY RIGHTS YOU MIGHT HAVE IN YOUR IDEA OR INVENTION.

(b)   The invention developer shall complete the cover sheet with the proper information to be provided in the blanks. In the first blank the invention developer shall enter the year that the invention developer began business, or January 1, 1990, whichever is earlier. The numbers entered in the last two blanks need not include those who have contracted with the invention developer during the 30 days immediately preceding the date of the contract. If the number to be inserted in the third blank is zero, it must be so stated.

(c)   The cover notice may not contain anything in addition to the information required by subsection (a) of this section. (1989, c. 746, s. 1; c. 770, s. 62.1(1)-(3); 1991, c. 235, s. 1.)

§ 66-212. Contracting requirements.

(a) Each contract for invention development services by which an invention developer undertakes invention development services for a customer is subject to this act. The contract must be in writing and the invention developer shall give a copy of the contract to the customer at the time the customer signs the contract.

(b) If it is the invention developer's normal practice to seek more than one contract in connection with an invention, or if the invention developer normally seeks to perform services in connection with an invention in more than one phase with the performance of each phase covered in one or more subsequent contracts, the invention developer shall give to the customer at the time the customer signs the first contract:

(1) A written statement describing that practice; and

(2) A written summary of the developer's normal terms, if any, of subsequent contracts, including the approximate amount of the developer's normal fees or other consideration, if any, that may be required from the customer.

(c) For the purposes of this section, delivery of a promissory note, check, bill of exchange, or negotiable instrument of any kind to the invention developer or to a third party for the benefit of the invention developer irrespective of the date or dates appearing in that instrument is payment.

(d) Notwithstanding any contractual provisions of [to] the contrary, payment for invention development services may not be required, made, or received before the fourth business day after the day on which the customer receives a copy of the contract for invention development services signed by the invention developer and the customer.

(e) Until the payment for invention development services is made, the parties during the contract for invention development services have the option to terminate the contract. The customer may exercise the option by refraining from making payment to the invention developer. The invention developer may exercise the option to terminate by giving to the customer written notice of its exercise of the option. The written notice becomes effective on receipt by the customer. (1989, c. 746, s. 1; c. 770, s. 62.1(1), (2); 1991, c. 235, s. 1.)

§ 66-213. Mandatory contract terms.

(a) A contract for invention development services shall set forth the information required in this section in at least 10-point type or equivalent size if handwritten.

(b) The contract shall describe fully and in detail the acts or services that the invention developer contracts to perform for the customer.

(c) The contract shall include the terms and conditions of payment and contract termination rights required by G.S. 66-212(e).

(d) The contract shall state whether the invention developer contracts to construct one or more prototypes, models, or devices embodying the customer's invention, the number of such prototypes to be constructed, and whether the invention developer contracts to sell or distribute such prototypes, models, or devices.

(e) If an oral or written estimate of projected customer sales, profits, earnings and/or royalties is made by the invention developer, the contract shall state the estimate and the data upon which it is based.

(f) The contract shall state the expected date of completion of the invention development services, whether or not time is of the essence, and whether or not the terms include provisions in case of delay past the expected date of completion.

(g) The contract shall explain that the invention developer is required to maintain all records and correspondence relating to performance of the invention development services for that customer for a period not less than three years after expiration of the term of the contract for invention development services. Further, such records and correspondence will be made available to the customer or his representative for review and copying at the customer's expense on the invention developer's premises during normal business hours upon seven days' written notice, the time period to begin from the date the notice is placed in the United States mail properly addressed and first class postage prepaid.

(h) The contract shall state the name of the person or firm contracting to perform the invention development services, all names under which said person or firm is doing or has done business as an invention developer for the previous 10 years, the names of all parent and subsidiary companies to the firm, and the names of all companies that have a contractual obligation to the firm to perform invention development services.

(i) The contract shall state the invention developer's principal business address and the name and address of its agent in this State who is authorized to receive service of process in North Carolina. (1989, c. 746, s. 1; c. 770, ss. 62.1(1), (2), (4); 1991, c. 235, s. 1.)

§ 66-214. Financial requirements.

(a) Except as provided by subsection (c) of this section, each invention developer doing business in this State as defined by the North Carolina General Statutes shall maintain a bond issued by a surety company authorized to do business in this State. The principal sum of the bond must be at least five percent (5%) of the invention developer's gross income from the invention development business in this State during the invention developer's last fiscal year or twenty-five thousand dollars ($25,000), whichever is greater. The invention developer shall file a copy of the bond with the Secretary of State before the day on which the invention developer begins business in this State. The invention developer shall have 90 days after the end of each fiscal year within which to change the bond as may be necessary to conform to the requirement of this subdivision.

(b) The bond required by subsection (a) of this section must be in favor of the State of North Carolina for the benefit of any person who, after entering into a contract for invention development services with an invention developer is damaged by fraud, dishonesty, or failure to provide the services of the invention developer in performance of the contract. Any person claiming against the bond may maintain an action at law against the invention developer and surety. The aggregate liability of the surety to all persons for all breaches of conditions of the bond required by the subsection is limited to the amount of the bond.

(c) Instead of furnishing the bond required by subsection (a) of this section, the invention developer may deposit with the Secretary of State a cash deposit equal to the amount of the bond required by this section. The cash deposit may be satisfied by:

(1) Certificates of deposit payable to the Secretary of State issued by banks doing business in this State and insured by the Federal Deposit Insurance Corporation;

(2) Investment certificates of share accounts assigned to the Secretary of State and issued by a savings and loan association doing business in this State, and insured by the Federal Savings and Loan Insurance Corporation;

(3) Bearer bonds issued by the United States government or by this State; or

(4) Cash deposit with the Secretary of State. (1989, c. 746, s. 1; c. 770, s. 62.1(1), (2); 1991, c. 235, s. 1.)

§ 66-215. Remedies.

(a) Any contract for invention development services that does not substantially comply with this Article is voidable at the option of the customer. A contract for invention development services entered into in reliance on any false, fraudulent, or misleading information, representation, notice, or advertisement of the invention developer is voidable at the option of the customer. Any waiver by the customer of any provision of this act shall be deemed contrary to public policy and shall be void and unenforceable.

(b) Any customer or person who has been injured by a violation of this Article by an invention developer, by a false or fraudulent statement, representation, or omission of material fact by an invention developer, or by failure of an invention developer to make all disclosures required by this Article may recover in a civil action against the invention developer:

(1) Court costs;

(2) Attorneys['] fees; and

(3) The amount of actual damages, if any, sustained by the customer, which damages may be increased to an amount not to exceed three times the

damages sustained. (1989, c. 746, s. 1; c. 770, s. 62.1(1), (2); 1991, c. 235, s. 1.)

§ 66-216. Enforcement.

The Attorney General shall enforce this Article and may recover a civil penalty not to exceed twenty-five thousand dollars ($25,000) for each violation of this Article and may seek equitable relief to restrain the violation of this Article. The clear proceeds of civil penalties provided for in this section shall be remitted to the Civil Penalty and Forfeiture Fund in accordance with G.S. 115C-457.2. (1989, c. 746, s. 1; c. 770, s. 62.1(1), (2); 1991, c. 235, s. 1; 1998-215, s. 97.)

§§ 66-217 through 66-219. Reserved for future codification purposes.

Article 30.

Credit Repair Services Act.

§ 66-220. Short title and purpose.

(a)   This Article shall be known and may be cited as the Credit Repair Services Act.

(b)   The General Assembly recognizes that many of its citizens rely heavily on favorable credit ratings in order to obtain goods and services, and that some of these citizens are unable to secure credit because of unfavorable credit histories. The General Assembly further recognizes that consumers sometimes need assistance in obtaining credit or in correcting erroneous credit histories, and that this need has given rise to the establishment of businesses organized for the purpose of providing credit repair services. The purpose of this Article is to ensure that businesses offering credit repair services are providing these services in a manner that is fair and reasonable to the consuming public. (1991, c. 327, s. 1.)

§ 66-221. Definitions.

As used in this Article, unless the context requires otherwise:

(1) "Credit repair business" means any person who, with respect to the extension of credit by others, sells, provides, or performs, or represents that such person can or will sell, provide, or perform any of the following services in return for the payment of money or other valuable consideration:

a. Improving, repairing, or correcting a consumer's credit record, history, or rating;

b. Obtaining revolving charge card credit or retail installment credit;

c. Providing advice or assistance to a consumer with regard to either sub-subdivision a. or b. above.

(2) "Credit repair business" does not include:

a. Any bank, credit union, or savings institution organized and chartered under the laws of this State or the United States, or any consumer finance lender licensed pursuant to Article 15 of Chapter 53 of the General Statutes;

b. Any nonprofit organization exempt from taxation under section 501(c)(3) of the Internal Revenue Code (26 U.S.C. § 501(c)(3));

c. Any person licensed as a real estate broker or real estate salesman by this State where the person is acting within the course and scope of the license;

d. Any person licensed to practice law in this State where the person renders services within the course and scope of that person's practice as a lawyer;

e. Any broker-dealer registered with the Securities and Exchange Commission or the Commodities Future Trading Commission where the broker-dealer is acting within the course and scope of that regulation; or

f.   Any consumer reporting agency as defined in the Federal Fair Credit Reporting Act.

(3)   "Consumer" means any individual who is solicited to purchase or who purchases the services of a credit repair business. (1991, c. 327, s. 1.)

§ 66-222. Bond or trust account required.

Every credit repair business shall obtain a surety bond issued by a surety company authorized to do business in this State, or shall establish a trust account with a licensed and insured bank or savings institution located in the State of North Carolina. The amount of the bond or trust account shall be ten thousand dollars ($10,000). The bond or trust account shall be in favor of the State of North Carolina. Any person damaged by the credit repair business' breach of contract or of any obligation arising therefrom, or by any violation of this Article, may bring an action against the bond or trust account to recover damages suffered. The aggregate liability of the surety or trustee shall be only for actual damages and in no event shall exceed the amount of the bond or trust account. (1991, c. 327, s. 1.)

§ 66-223. Prohibited acts.

A credit repair business and its salespersons, agents, and representatives, and independent contractors who sell or attempt to sell the services of a credit repair business, shall not do any of the following:

(1)   Charge or receive any money or other valuable consideration prior to full and complete performance of the services that the credit repair business has agreed to perform for or on behalf of the consumer;

(2)   Charge or receive any money or other valuable consideration solely for referral of the consumer to a retail seller or to any other credit grantor who will or may extend credit to the consumer, if the credit that is or will be extended to the consumer is upon substantially the same terms as those available to the general public;

(3) Represent that it can directly or indirectly arrange for the removal of derogatory credit information from the consumer's credit report or otherwise improve the consumer's credit report or credit standing, provided, this shall not prevent truthful, unexaggerated statements about the consumer's rights under existing law regarding his credit history or regarding access to his credit file;

(4) Make, or counsel or advise any consumer to make, any statement that is untrue or misleading and which is known or which by the exercise of reasonable care should be known, to be untrue or misleading, to a consumer reporting agency or to any person who has extended credit to a consumer or to whom a consumer is applying for an extension of credit, with respect to a consumer's creditworthiness, credit standing, or credit capacity; or

(5) Make or use any untrue or misleading representations in the offer or sale of the services of a credit repair business or engage, directly or indirectly, in any act, practice, or course of business which operates or would operate as a fraud or deception upon any person in connection with the offer or sale of the services of a credit repair business. (1991, c. 327, s. 1.)

§ 66-224. Contractual requirements.

(a) Effective October 1, 1991, every contract between a consumer and a credit repair business for the purchase of the services of the credit repair business shall be in writing, dated, signed by the consumer, and shall include the following:

(1) A conspicuous statement in size equal to at least 10-point boldface type, in immediate proximity to the space reserved for the signature of the consumer, as follows:

"YOU, THE BUYER, MAY CANCEL THIS CONTRACT AT ANY TIME PRIOR TO MIDNIGHT OF THE THIRD BUSINESS DAY AFTER THE DATE OF THE TRANSACTION. SEE THE ATTACHED NOTICE OF CANCELLATION FORM FOR AN EXPLANATION OF THIS RIGHT."

(2) The terms and conditions of payment, including the total of all payments to be made by the consumer, whether to the credit repair business or to some other person;

(3) A complete and detailed description of the services to be performed and the results to be achieved by the credit repair business for or on behalf of the consumer, including all guarantees and all promises of full or partial refunds and a list of the adverse information appearing on the consumer's credit report that the credit repair business expects to have modified;

(4) The principal business address of the credit repair business and the name and address of its agent in this State authorized to receive service of process; and

(5) One of the following statements, as appropriate, in substantially the following form:

a. "As required by North Carolina law, this credit repair business has secured a bond by _____(name and address of surety company), a surety authorized to do business in this State. Before signing a contract with this business, you should check with the surety company to determine the bond's current status.", or

b. "As required by North Carolina law, this credit repair business has established an escrow account _____(number) with _____(name and address of bank or savings institution). Before signing a contract with this business, you should check with the bank or savings institution to determine the current status of the account."

(b) The contract shall be accompanied by a completed form in duplicate, captioned "NOTICE OF CANCELLATION", which shall be attached to the contract and easily detachable, and which shall contain in at least 10-point boldface type the following statement:

"NOTICE OF CANCELLATION

YOU MAY CANCEL THIS CONTRACT, WITHOUT ANY PENALTY OR OBLIGATION, AT ANY TIME PRIOR TO MIDNIGHT OF THE THIRD BUSINESS DAY AFTER THE DATE THE CONTRACT IS SIGNED.

IF YOU CANCEL, ANY PAYMENT MADE BY YOU UNDER THIS CONTRACT WILL BE RETURNED WITHIN 10 DAYS FOLLOWING RECEIPT BY THE SELLER OF YOUR CANCELLATION NOTICE.

TO CANCEL THIS CONTRACT, MAIL OR DELIVER A SIGNED AND DATED COPY OF THIS CANCELLATION NOTICE, OR ANY OTHER WRITTEN NOTICE, TO

_____ (Name of Seller)

AT _____
(Address of Seller)

_____ (Place of Business) NOT LATER

THAN MIDNIGHT
_____ (Date).

I HEREBY CANCEL THIS TRANSACTION.

_____
___

Date　　　　　　　　　Buyer's Signature".

A copy of the fully completed contract and all other documents the credit repair business requires the consumer to sign shall be given by the credit repair business to the consumer at the time they are signed. (1991, c. 327, s. 1; 1991 (Reg. Sess., 1992), c. 1030, s. 19.)

§ 66-225. Violations.

(a) If a credit repair business uses any untrue or misleading statements in connection with a credit repair contract, fails to fully comply with the requirements of this Article, or fails to comply with the terms of the contract or any obligation arising therefrom, then, upon written notice to the credit repair business, the consumer may void the contract, and shall be entitled to receive from the credit repair business all sums paid to the credit repair business, and recover any additional damages including reasonable attorneys' fees.

(b) Any waiver by a consumer of any of the provisions of this Article shall be deemed void and unenforceable by a credit repair business.

(c) Upon complaint of any person that a credit repair business has violated the provisions of this Article, the superior court shall have jurisdiction to enjoin that defendant from further such violations.

(d) In a proceeding involving this Article, the burden of proving an exemption or an exception from the definition of a credit repair business shall be borne by the person claiming the exemption or exception.

(e) The remedies provided herein shall be in addition to any other remedies provided for by law or in equity.

(f) The violation of any provision of this Article shall constitute an unfair trade practice under G.S. 75-1.1 and the violation of any provision of this Article shall constitute a Class I felony. (1991, c. 327; 1993, c. 539, s. 1283; 1994, Ex. Sess., c. 24, s. 14(c).)

§ 66-226. Scope.

The provisions of this Article shall apply in all circumstances in which any party to the contract conducted any contractual activity, including but not limited to solicitation, discussion, negotiation, offer, acceptance, signing, or performance in this State. (1991, c. 327.)

§§ 66-227 through 66-229. Reserved for future codification purposes.

Article 31.

Membership Camping Act.

§ 66-230. Title.

This Article shall be known and may be cited as the "Membership Camping Act". (1991 (Reg. Sess., 1992), c. 1009, s. 4.)

§ 66-231. Applicability.

This Article shall apply to each membership camping contract executed at least in part in this State after January 1, 1993, regardless of the location of the membership camping operator's principal office or his campground or recreational facilities. (1991 (Reg. Sess., 1992), c. 1009, s. 4.)

§ 66-232. Definitions.

For purposes of this Article the following definitions apply:

(1)   "Agreement" means a membership camping agreement.

(2)   "Blanket encumbrance" means any mortgage, deed of trust, option to purchase, vendor's lien or interest under a contract or agreement of sale, judgment lien, federal or State tax lien, or other material lien or encumbrance which secures or evidences the obligation to pay money or to sell or convey all or part of a campground located in this State, made available to purchasers by the membership camping operator and which authorizes, permits, or requires the foreclosure or other disposition of the campground. Blanket encumbrance shall include the lessor's interest in a lease of all or part of a campground which is located in this State and which is made available to purchasers by a membership camping operator. Blanket encumbrance shall not include a lien for taxes or assessments levied by a public body which are not yet due and payable.

(3)   "Business day" means any day except Sunday or a legal holiday.

(4)   "Camping site" means a space designed and promoted for the purpose of locating a trailer, tent, tent trailer, recreational vehicle, pickup camper, van or other similar device used for camping.

(5)   "Campground" means any single tract or parcel of real property within the State on which there are at least 10 camping sites.

(6)   "Contract" means a membership camping contract.

(7)   "Contract cost" means the total consideration paid by a purchaser pursuant to a contract including but not limited to:

a.   Any initiation or nonrecurring fee charged;

b.   All periodic fees required by the contract;

c.   All dues or maintenance fees; and

d.   All finance charges, time-price differentials, interest, and other similar fees and charges.

(8)   "Facility" means an amenity within a campground set aside or otherwise made available to purchasers for their use and enjoyment of the campground, and may include campsites, swimming pools, tennis courts, recreational buildings, boat docks, restrooms, showers, laundry rooms, and trading posts or grocery stores.

(9)   "Membership camping contract" or "membership camping agreement" means any written agreement of more than one year's duration, executed in whole or in part within this State, which grants to a purchaser a right or license to use the campground of a membership camping operator or any portion thereof. Any agreement which constitutes a "time share instrument" as defined in G.S. 93A-41 is excluded from this definition.

(10)   "Membership camping operator" means any person who owns or operates a campground and offers or sells membership camping contracts. A membership camping operator shall not include:

a.   An enterprise that is exempt from federal income tax under § 501(c) of the Internal Revenue Code;

b. An enterprise that is exempt from State income tax under Article 4 of Chapter 105 of the General Statutes; or

c. Mobile home parks wherein the residents occupy the premises as their primary homes or have leased or purchased a lot for their exclusive use.

(11) "Offer," "offer to sell," "offer to execute" or "offering" means any offer, solicitation, advertisement, or inducement to execute a membership camping agreement.

(12) "Person" means any individual, corporation, partnership, company, unincorporated association, or any other legal entity other than a government or agency or a subdivision thereof.

(13) "Purchaser" means a person who enters into a membership camping contract with the membership camping operator.

(14) "Purchase money" means any money, currency, note, security, or other consideration paid by the purchaser for a membership camping agreement.

(15) "Reciprocal program" means any arrangement under which a purchaser is permitted to use camping sites or facilities at one or more campgrounds not owned or operated by the membership camping operator with whom the purchaser has entered into a membership camping contract.

(16) "Salesperson" means an individual, other than a membership camping operator, who offers to sell a membership camping contract by means of a direct sales presentation, but does not include a person who merely refers a prospective purchaser to a salesperson without making any direct sales presentation. (1991 (Reg. Sess., 1992), c. 1009, s. 4.)

§ 66-233. Administration; unlawful offer or execution of membership camping contract.

(a) This Article shall be administered by the Secretary of State of North Carolina or his designee, and shall be enforced by the Attorney General of North Carolina or his designee.

(b) It shall be unlawful for any membership camping operator to offer to sell any membership camping contract in this State unless he is registered with the Secretary of State. (1991 (Reg. Sess., 1992), c. 1009, s. 4.)

§ 66-234. Registration of membership camping operator.

(a) The application for registration shall be on a form prescribed by the Secretary of State and shall include the following:

(1) The applicant's name, address, and the organizational form of the business, including the date, and jurisdiction under which the business was organized; the address of each of its offices in this State; and the name and address of each campground located in this State, which is owned or operated, in whole or in part, by the applicant;

(2) The name, address, and principal occupation for the past five years of every officer of the applicant, including its principal managers, and the extent and nature of the interest of each person at the time the application is filed;

(3) A list of all owners of ten percent (10%) or more of the capital stock of the applicant, except that this list is not required if the applicant is a company required to report under the Securities and Exchange Act of 1934;

(4) A brief description of and a certified copy of the instrument which creates the applicant's ownership of, or other right to use the campground and the facilities at the campground which are to be available for use by purchasers, and a brief description of any material encumbrance, together with a copy of any lease, license, franchise, reciprocal agreement or other agreement entitling the applicant to use such campground and facilities, and any material provision of the agreement which restricts a purchaser's use of such campground or facilities;

(5) A sample copy of each instrument which will be delivered to a purchaser to evidence his membership in the campground and a sample copy of each agreement which a purchaser will be required to execute;

(6) A list of special taxes or assessments, whether current or proposed, which affect the campground;

(7) A copy of the disclosure statement required by this Article;

(8) A narrative description of the promotional plan for the sale of the membership camping contracts;

(9) A statement of the relationship, if any, between the applicant and other parties owning, controlling or managing the campground and the expected duration of that relationship. If the relationship is a contractual one, a statement of the methods and conditions under which the relationship can be terminated prior to the expected termination of the relationship;

(10) A complete list of locations and addresses of any and all sales offices located within the State;

(11) The names of any other states or foreign countries in which an application for registration of the membership camping operator or the membership camping contract or any similar document has been filed; and

(12) A brief description of the membership camping operator's experience in the membership camping business, including the length of time such operator has been in the membership camping business; and a statement detailing whether the applicant within the past five years has been convicted of any misdemeanor or felony involving theft, fraud, dishonesty, or moral turpitude, or whether the applicant has been enjoined from, had any civil penalty assessed for, or been found to have engaged in any violation of any law designed to protect consumers. If the applicant is a corporation, this statement shall be provided for each officer of the corporation.

(b) The application shall be signed by the membership camping operator, an officer or general partner thereof or by another person holding a power of attorney for this purpose from the membership camping operator. If the application is signed pursuant to a power of attorney, a copy of the power of attorney shall be included with the application.

(c) The application shall be submitted along with the appropriate application fee.

(d) The registration of the membership camping operator shall be renewed annually with the fee required in G.S. 66-236 not later than 30 days prior to the anniversary of the current registration. The application shall include all changes which have occurred in the information included in the application previously filed.

(e) Registration with the Secretary of State shall not be deemed to be an approval or endorsement by the Secretary of State of the membership camping operator, his membership camping contract, or his campground, and any attempt by the membership camping operator to indicate that registration constitutes such approval or endorsement shall be unlawful. (1991 (Reg. Sess., 1992), c. 1009, s. 4; 1995 (Reg. Sess., 1996), c. 742, s. 34.)

§ 66-235. Time of effect of registration.

Upon receipt of the original application for registration in proper form, the Secretary of State shall, within 10 business days, issue a notice to the applicant that the Secretary of State has received the registration. Within 30 days thereafter, the Secretary of State shall notify the operator that the registration has been accepted or rejected, and if rejected, a brief statement explaining the reason. Registration shall be effective upon notice of acceptance by the Secretary of State. Renewal of registration shall be effective upon the anniversary of the current registration or 30 days after receipt, whichever date occurs last, unless otherwise rejected. (1991 (Reg. Sess., 1992), c. 1009, s. 4.)

§ 66-236. Registration fees.

An applicant for registration under this Article must include the fee set out in the following table with the application for registration:

Application
Amount

Initial registration as a membership camping operator
$1,500

Renewal of registration as a membership camping operator
1,000

Initial registration as a salesperson
10

Renewal of registration as a salesperson
10

Fees collected under this section shall be applied to the cost of administering this Article. (1991 (Reg. Sess., 1992), c. 1009, s. 4.)

§ 66-237. Registration of salespersons.

(a) It shall be unlawful for any salesperson to offer to sell any membership camping contract in this State unless he is registered with the Secretary of State. The application of a salesperson for registration shall be on a form prescribed by the Secretary of State and shall include the following:

(1) A statement detailing whether the applicant within the past five years has been convicted of any misdemeanor or felony involving theft, fraud, dishonesty, or moral turpitude, or whether the applicant has been enjoined from, had any civil penalty assessed for, or been found to have engaged in any violation of any law designed to protect consumers, and

(2) A statement describing the applicant's employment history for the past five years and whether any termination of employment during the last five years was occasioned by any theft, fraud, or act of dishonesty.

(b) Registration shall be effective for a period of one year. Registration shall be renewed annually by the filing of a form prescribed by the Secretary of State for such purpose. The registration application or the renewal application shall automatically become effective upon the expiration of seven business days following the filing with the Secretary of State. (1991 (Reg. Sess., 1992), c. 1009, s. 4.)

§ 66-238. Membership camping operator's disclosure statement.

(a) Every membership camping operator, salesperson, or other person who is in the business of offering for sale or transfer the rights under existing membership camping contracts for a fee shall disclose the following information to a purchaser before the purchaser signs a contract or gives any money or thing of value for the purchase of a contract. The disclosures shall be delivered to the purchaser prior to the time the contract is signed and must be presented in a clear, legible format prescribed by the Secretary of State.

(b) The disclosures shall consist of the following:

(1) A cover page containing only the following in the order stated:

a. The words "MEMBERSHIP CAMPING OPERATOR'S DISCLOSURE STATEMENT": printed in boldface type of a minimum size of 10 points, followed by;

b. The name and principal business address of the membership camping operator, followed by;

c. A statement that the membership camping operator is in the business of offering for sale membership camping contracts, followed by;

d. The following, printed in boldface type of a minimum size of 10 points: IMPORTANT! READ THIS DISCLOSURE STATEMENT BEFORE YOU SIGN ANYTHING. THE LAW REQUIRES THAT YOU GET A COPY OF THIS DISCLOSURE STATEMENT BEFORE YOU SIGN. IF YOUR SALESPERSON TELLS YOU ANYTHING DIFFERENT FROM WHAT IS WRITTEN, THEN DO NOT SIGN. DO NOT BUY THIS MEMBERSHIP ASSUMING THAT YOU WILL BE ABLE TO RESELL IT, followed by;

e. The following language, printed in boldface type of a minimum size of 10 points:

YOU HAVE A 3-DAY RIGHT TO CANCEL A CAMPING MEMBERSHIP CONTRACT. THIS RIGHT OF CANCELLATION CANNOT BE WAIVED. YOUR RIGHT TO CANCEL ENDS AT MIDNIGHT ON THE 3RD BUSINESS DAY FOLLOWING THE DATE ON WHICH THE CONTRACT WAS SIGNED. IF YOU HAVE ANY QUESTIONS ABOUT YOUR RIGHTS, CONTACT THE NORTH CAROLINA ATTORNEY GENERAL'S OFFICE.

(2) The following pages of the disclosure statement shall contain all of the following:

a. The name of the operator and the address of the operator's principal place of business in North Carolina, or if the operator has no place of business in North Carolina, the operator's principal place of business;

b. A brief description of the nature of the purchaser's right or license to use the campground and the facilities which are to be available for use by purchasers;

c. A brief description of the membership camping operator's experience in the membership camping business, including the length of time such operator has been in the membership camping business;

d. The location of each of the campgrounds which is to be available for use by purchasers, excluding campgrounds which will be available to a purchaser only if he is a member in good standing of a reciprocal program; and a description of the facilities at each campground then available for use by purchasers and those which are represented to purchasers as being planned, together with a brief description of any facilities that are or will be available to nonpurchasers or nonmembers;

e. As to all memberships offered by the membership camping operator at each campground:

1. The form of membership offered;

2. The types of duration of membership along with a summary of the major privileges, restrictions, and limitations applicable to each type;

3. Provisions, if any, that have been made for public utilities at each campsite including water, electricity, telephone, and sewage facilities; and

4. The maximum number of current memberships to be sold per site at that campground.

f. Any initial, additional, or special fee due from the purchaser together with a description of the purpose and method of calculating the fee;

g. A general description of any financing offered or available through the membership camping operator;

h. Any schedule of fees or charges that purchasers are or may be required to pay for use of the campground or any facilities or reciprocal program;

i. The extent to which financial arrangements, if any, have been provided for the completion of facilities, together with a statement of the membership camping operator's obligation to complete planned facilities. The statement shall include a description of any restrictions or limitations on the membership camping operator's obligation to begin or to complete the facilities;

j. Any services which the membership camping operator currently provides or expenses he pays which are expected to become the responsibility of the purchasers, including the projected liability which each such service or expense may impose on each purchaser;

k. A summary or copy, whether by way of supplement or otherwise, of the rules, restrictions, or covenants regulating the purchaser's use of the campground and the facilities which are to be available for use by the purchasers, including a statement of whether and how the rules, restrictions, or covenants may be changed;

l. A description of any restraints on the transfer of the membership camping contract;

m. A statement of the policies covering the availability of campsites, the availability of reservations, and the conditions under which they are made;

n. A statement of any grounds for forfeiture of a purchaser's membership camping contract;

o. A statement describing the material terms and conditions of any reciprocal program to be available to the purchaser including a statement concerning whether the purchaser's participation in any reciprocal program is dependent upon the continued affiliation of the membership camping operator with that reciprocal program and whether the membership camping operator reserves the right to terminate such affiliation.

(3) The membership camping operator shall promptly amend his membership camping operator's disclosure statement to reflect any material change in the campground or its facilities. He shall also file within 30 days any such amendments with the Secretary of State. Each disclosure statement

provided to a prospective purchaser must contain the most recent date when the statement was revised. (1991 (Reg. Sess., 1992), c. 1009, s. 4.)

§ 66-239. Contract terms.

(a) The membership camping operator shall deliver to the purchaser a fully executed copy of a membership camping contract in writing, which contract shall include at least the following information:

(1) The name of the membership camping operator and the address of its principal place of business;

(2) The actual date the membership camping contract was executed by the purchaser;

(3) The total financial obligation imposed on the purchaser by the contract, including the initial purchase price and any additional charge the purchaser may be required to pay;

(4) A description of the nature and duration of the membership being purchased;

(5) A statement that the membership camping operator is required by law to provide each purchaser with a copy of the membership camping operator's disclosure statement prior to execution of the contract and that failure to do so is a violation of the law;

(6) The full name of each salesperson involved in the promotion and sale of the membership camping contract; and

(7) In immediate proximity to the space reserved in the contract for the signature of the purchaser and in boldface type of a minimum size of 10 points, a statement in substantially the following form: "You the buyer, may cancel this contract at any time prior to midnight of the third business day after the date of this contract. See the attached notice of cancellation form for an explanation of this right." (1991 (Reg. Sess., 1992), c. 1009, s. 4.)

§ 66-240. Cancellation.

In addition to any other right to revoke an offer or cancel a sale or contract, the purchaser has the right to cancel a membership camping contract sale until midnight of the third business day after the purchaser signs the contract.

(1) The membership camping operator must furnish the purchaser, at the time the purchaser signs the membership camping contract or otherwise agrees to buy services from the membership camping operator, a completed form in duplicate, captioned "NOTICE OF CANCELLATION" which shall contain in 10 point boldface type the following information and statements in the same language, e.g., Spanish, as that used in the contract:

"NOTICE OF CANCELLATION

_____ (Enter date of transaction)_____

                                                     (date)

      You, the purchaser, may cancel this transaction, without any penalty or obligation, within three business days from the date above. Business days are all days other than Sundays and legal holidays. You must cancel in writing. If given by mail, notice of cancellation is given when it is deposited in the United States mail properly addressed and postage prepaid.

      If you cancel, any payments made by you under the contract or sale, and any negotiable instrument executed by you will be returned within 30 days following receipt by the seller of your cancellation notice, and any security interest arising out of the transaction will be cancelled.

      To cancel this transaction, mail or deliver a signed and dated copy of this cancellation notice or any other written notice to

_____

_____

(Name of membership camping operator)

_____ at

_____

(Membership camping operator's mailing and physical address)

not later than midnight of

_____

(date)

I hereby cancel this transaction.

_____

(date)

_____

(Purchaser's signature)"

(2)   The membership camping operator shall, before furnishing copies of the "Notice of Cancellation" to the purchaser, complete both copies by entering the name of the membership camping operator, the address of the membership camping operator's place of business, the date of the transaction, and the date, not earlier than the third business day following the day of the transaction, by which the purchaser may give notice of cancellation.

(3)   The membership camping operator shall orally inform each purchaser, at the time he signs a contract or purchases the services, of his three-day right to cancel; provided, that no oral notice is required in any case in which the membership camping operator does not solicit the purchaser's business in person and the purchaser signs the contract outside the presence of the membership camping operator and returns the signed contract to the membership camping operator by mail.

(4) Cancellation occurs when the purchaser gives written notice of cancellation to the membership camping operator at the address stated in the contract or in the notice of cancellation.

(5) Notice of cancellation, if given by mail, is given when it is deposited in the United States mail properly addressed and postage prepaid.

(6) Notice of cancellation by the purchaser is sufficient if it indicates by any form of written expression the intention of the purchaser not to be bound by the contract.

(7) Upon cancellation, the membership camping operator shall refund to the purchaser all payments made pursuant to the canceled membership camping contract and any notes or security instruments. The refund shall be made within 30 days and where payment has been made by credit card, may be made by an appropriate credit to the purchaser's account.

(8) Failure of the membership camping operator to honor a purchaser's cancellation is a violation of this Article. (1991 (Reg. Sess., 1992), c. 1009, s. 4.)

§ 66-241. Escrow account.

(a) All purchase money received from or on behalf of a purchaser in connection with the execution of a membership camping contract shall be deposited in an escrow account designated solely for that purpose, which may be the membership camping operator's own escrow or trust account or that of his attorney's, until 10 calendar days after the date the contract was executed, unless a later time is provided in the membership camping contract. If the membership camping operator has not received notice of the purchaser's cancellation within 10 calendar days after the execution of the contract, any purchase money may be released to the membership camping operator upon the conveyance, in writing, to the purchaser of the right or license to use the campground and facilities as required in the membership camping contract.

(b) A copy of the escrow agreement creating the escrow account shall be filed with the Secretary of State prior to the sale of membership camping contracts. (1991 (Reg. Sess., 1992), c. 1009, s. 4.)

§ 66-242. Advertising, solicitations.

A membership camping operator shall disclose in all advertising programs which seek to induce prospective purchasers to visit the campground that the program is conducted by a membership camping operator and the purpose of any requested visit. (1991 (Reg. Sess., 1992), c. 1009, s. 4.)

§ 66-243. Provision of records to the Secretary of State.

Any membership camping operator shall maintain accurate records of the escrow account. These records shall be open to inspection to the Secretary of State at any time during normal business hours. (1991 (Reg. Sess., 1992), c. 1009, s. 4.)

§ 66-244. Limitation on duration of contract term.

A membership camping contract shall clearly state the duration of the contract. A contract shall either have a duration of no more than 30 years or give the purchaser the right to cancel the contract at any time after 30 years without further obligation and without a refund of any of the contract cost. (1991 (Reg. Sess., 1992), c. 1009, s. 4.)

§ 66-245. Prohibited practices.

It shall be unlawful for any membership camping operator or salesperson to state or imply in attempting to sell a membership or to persuade a member to make payment that the purchaser will be able to sell the contract and thereby eliminate his obligation or recoup all or a substantial part of his purchase price. (1991 (Reg. Sess., 1992), c. 1009, s. 4.)

§ 66-246. Nondisturbance provisions.

(a) With respect to any property in this State acquired and put into operation by a membership camping operator on or after January 1, 1993, the membership camping operator shall not offer or execute a membership camping contract in this State granting the right to use the property until the following requirements are met:

(1) Each person holding an interest in a voluntary blanket encumbrance has executed and delivered to the Secretary of State a nondisturbance agreement and recorded the agreement in the real estate records of the county in which the campground is located. The agreement shall include all of the following:

a. That the rights of the holder or holders of the blanket encumbrance in the affected campground are subordinate to the rights of purchasers;

b. That any person who acquires the affected campground or any portion of the campground by the exercise of any right of sale or foreclosure contained in the blanket encumbrance takes the campground subject to the rights of purchasers; and

c. That the holder or holders of the blanket encumbrance shall not use or cause the campground to be used in a manner which interferes with the right of purchasers to use the campground and its facilities in accordance with the terms and conditions of the membership camping contract; and

(2) Each hypothecation lender which has a lien on or security interest in the membership camping operator's ownership interest in the campground has executed and delivered to the Secretary of State a nondisturbance agreement and recorded the agreement in the real estate records of the county in which the campground is located. In addition, each person holding an interest in a blanket encumbrance superior to the interest held by the hypothecation lender has executed, delivered, and recorded an instrument stating that such person will give the hypothecation lender notice of, and at least 30 days to cure, any default under the blanket encumbrance before the person commences any foreclosure action affecting the campground. For the purposes of this section:

a. Hypothecation lender shall mean a financial institution which provides a major hypothecation loan to a membership camping operator;

b. Major hypothecation loan shall mean a loan or line of credit secured by substantially all of the contracts receivable arising from the membership camping operator's sale of membership camping contracts; and

c. Nondisturbance agreement shall mean an instrument by which a hypothecation lender agrees to conditions substantially the same as those set forth in subdivision (1) of this subsection.

(b) In lieu of compliance with subsection (a) of this section, a surety bond or letter of credit satisfying the requirements of this subsection may be delivered and accepted by the Secretary of State. The surety bond or letter of credit shall be issued to the Secretary of State for the benefit of purchasers and shall be in an amount which is not less than one hundred five percent (105%) of the remaining principal balance of every indebtedness secured by a blanket encumbrance affecting the campground. The bond shall be issued by a surety which is authorized to do business in this State and which has sufficient net worth to satisfy the indebtedness. The aggregate liability of the surety for all damages shall not exceed the amount of the bond. The letter of credit shall be irrevocable, shall be drawn upon an insured bank, savings and loan association, or other financial institution, and shall be in a form and content acceptable to the Secretary of State. The bond or letter of credit shall provide for payment of all amounts secured by the blanket encumbrance, including costs, expenses, and legal fees of the lienholder, if for any reason the blanket encumbrance is enforced. (1991 (Reg. Sess., 1992), c. 1009, s. 4.)

§ 66-247. Remedies.

(a) Any purchaser injured by any violation of this Article may bring an action for rescission and restitution or for recovery of damages and for reasonable attorney's fees.

(b) The remedies herein shall be in addition to any other remedies provided for by law or in equity, but the damages assessed shall not exceed the largest amount of damages available by any single remedy.

(c) In addition to any other remedies provided for by law or in equity, the Secretary of State may bring an action to:

(1) Revoke the registration of a membership camping operator or a salesperson and seek an injunction to enjoin him from engaging in the business of offering for sale or selling camping membership contracts in this State, or

(2) Enforce a final court order from any state or federal jurisdiction restricting or enjoining the acts or practices of a membership camping operator or a salesperson pertaining to the business of offering or selling membership camping contracts.

(d) The violation of any provisions of this Article shall constitute an unfair practice under G.S. 75-1.1. (1991 (Reg. Sess., 1992), c. 1009, s. 4.)

§ 66-248. Reserved for future codification purposes.

§ 66-249. Reserved for future codification purposes.

Article 32.

Peddlers, Itinerant Merchants, and Specialty Markets.

§ 66-250. Definitions.

The following definitions apply in this Article:

(1) Itinerant merchant. - A person, other than a merchant with an established retail store in the county, who transports an inventory of goods to a building, vacant lot, or other location in a county and who, at that location, displays the goods for sale and sells the goods at retail or offers the goods for sale at retail.

(2) Peddler. - A person who travels from place to place with an inventory of goods, who sells the goods at retail or offers the goods for sale at retail, and who delivers the identical goods.

(3) Person. - An individual, a firm, an association, a partnership, a limited liability company, a corporation, a unit of government, or another group acting as a unit.

(4) Specialty market. - A location, other than a permanent retail store, where space is rented to others for the purpose of selling goods at retail or offering goods for sale at retail.

(5) Specialty market operator. - A person, other than the State or a unit of local government, who rents space, at a location other than a permanent retail store, to others for the purpose of selling goods at retail or offering goods for sale at retail.

(6) Specialty market vendor. - A person, other than a merchant with an established retail store in the county, who transports an inventory of goods to a specialty market and, at that location, displays the goods for sale and sells the goods at retail or offers the goods for sale at retail. (1996, 2nd Ex. Sess., c. 14, s. 24.)

§ 66-251. Itinerant merchant and peddler must have permission of property owner.

An itinerant merchant or a peddler who travels from place to place by vehicle must obtain a written statement signed by the owner or lessee of any property upon which the itinerant merchant or peddler offers goods for sale giving the owner's or lessee's permission to offer goods for sale upon the property of the owner or lessee. This statement must clearly state the name of the owner or lessee, the location of the premises for which the permission is granted, and the dates during which the permission is valid. The statement must be conspicuously and prominently displayed, so as to be visible for inspection by patrons of the itinerant merchant or peddler, at the places or locations at which the goods are to be sold or offered for sale. (1996, 2nd Ex. Sess., c. 14, s. 24.)

§ 66-252. Display and possession of certificate of registration.

(a) When Required. - A person who sells tangible personal property at a specialty market, other than the person's own household personal property, is considered a retailer under G.S. 105-164.4 and must obtain a certificate of registration from the Department of Revenue before the person may engage in business. An itinerant merchant must keep the merchant's certificate of registration conspicuously and prominently displayed, so as to be visible for inspection by patrons of the itinerant merchant at the places or locations at which the goods are to be sold or offered for sale. A peddler must carry the peddler's certificate of registration when the peddler offers goods for sale and must produce the certificate upon the request of any customer, State or local revenue agent, or law enforcement agent. A specialty market vendor must keep the certificate of registration conspicuously and prominently displayed, so as to be visible for inspection by patrons of the specialty market vendor at the places or locations at which the goods are to be sold or offered for sale. A specialty market operator must have its certificate of registration, if any, available for inspection during all times that the specialty market is open and must produce it upon the request of any customer, State or local revenue agent, or law enforcement agent.

(b) Compliance. - The requirement that a certificate of registration be displayed is satisfied if the vendor displays either of the following:

(1) A copy of the certificate.

(2) Evidence that the certificate has been applied for and the applicable registration fee has been paid within 30 days before the date the certificate was required to be displayed. (1996, 2nd Ex. Sess., c. 14, s. 24; 1998-121, s. 6.)

§ 66-253. Display of identification upon request.

Upon the request of any customer, State or local revenue agent, or law enforcement agent, a peddler, an itinerant merchant, a specialty market operator, or a specialty market vendor must provide its name and permanent address. A peddler, itinerant merchant, specialty market operator, or specialty market vendor who is an individual must, upon the request of any customer, State or local revenue agent, or law enforcement agent, provide a valid drivers license, a special identification card issued under G.S. 20-37.7, a military identification, or a passport bearing a physical description of the person named reasonably describing the peddler, itinerant merchant, specialty market operator, or specialty market vendor. A peddler, itinerant merchant, specialty market operator, or specialty market vendor that is a corporation must, upon the request of any customer, State or local revenue agent, or law enforcement agent, give the name and registered agent of the corporation and the address of the registered office of the corporation, as filed with the Secretary of State. (1996, 2nd Ex. Sess., c. 14, s. 24.)

§ 66-254. Records of source of new merchandise.

(a) Record Required. - Each peddler, itinerant merchant, and specialty market vendor must keep a written record of the source of new merchandise the merchant offers for sale. The record must be a receipt or an invoice from the person who sold the merchandise to the merchant. The receipt or invoice must specifically identify the product being sold by product name and quantity purchased and must contain the complete business name of the seller and a description of the type of business. If the seller was an individual, the receipt or invoice must contain the seller's drivers license number, its state of issuance and expiration date, and the seller's date of birth. The merchant must verify this information by comparing the seller's drivers license to the receipt or invoice and signing the receipt or invoice. A special identification card issued by the Division of Motor Vehicles may be used in place of the seller's drivers license for the purposes of providing and verifying information required under this section. If the seller was a corporation, the receipt or invoice must contain the corporation's federal tax identification number, the state of incorporation, the name and address of the corporation's registered agent in this State, if any, and the corporation's principal office address.

(b) Keeping the Record. - Each peddler, itinerant merchant, and specialty market vendor must keep the record required by subsection (a) of this section with the new merchandise being offered for sale. Once the new merchandise is sold, the merchant must keep the record for a period of three years after the date of the sale.

(c) Displaying Record or Affidavit. - A peddler, an itinerant merchant, or a specialty market vendor must produce either of the following upon the request of a law enforcement agent:

(1) The record required by subsection (a) of this section of the source of new merchandise the merchant offers for sale.

(2) An affidavit under oath or affirmation identifying the source of new merchandise the merchant offers for sale, including the name and address of the seller, the license number of any auctioneer seller, and the date and place of purchase of the merchandise.

A merchant's failure to produce the requested record or an affidavit within a reasonable time of request by a law enforcement agent is prima facie evidence of possession of stolen property. Pending the production of the requested record or affidavit, the agent may take the merchandise into custody as evidence at the time the request is made. Merchandise impounded under this subsection must be disposed of in accordance with G.S. 15-11.1.

(d) Posted Notice. - A specialty market operator must conspicuously post in plain view of all specialty market vendors a sign informing all vendors that failure to produce, upon the request of a law enforcement agent, either the records or affidavit required under this section is prima facie evidence of possession of stolen property. (1996, 2nd Ex. Sess., c. 14, s. 24.)

§ 66-254.1. Certain sales prohibited.

No person who is described by G.S. 66-250(1), (2), (5), or (6) shall sell or offer to sell any product that meets any of the following criteria:

(1) The product contains pseudoephedrine as the sole active ingredient or in combination with other active ingredients.

(2) The product is a drug as defined by G.S. 106-121(6).

Any person who violates this section shall be guilty of a Class 1 misdemeanor for the first offense, a Class A1 misdemeanor for a second offense, and a Class I felony for a third or subsequent offense. (2005-434, s. 5.)

§ 66-255. Specialty market or operator of an event registration list.

A specialty market operator or operator of an event where space is provided to a vendor must maintain a daily registration list of all specialty market or other vendors selling or offering goods for sale at the specialty market or other event. The registration list must clearly and legibly show each vendor's name, permanent address, and certificate of registration number. The specialty market operator or other event operator must require each vendor to exhibit a valid certificate of registration for visual inspection by the specialty market operator or other event operator at the time of registration, and must require each vendor to keep the certificate of registration conspicuously and prominently displayed, so as to be visible for inspection by patrons of the vendor at the places or locations at which the goods are offered for sale. Each daily registration list maintained pursuant to this section must be retained by the specialty market operator or other event operator for no less than two years and must at any time be made available upon request to any law enforcement officer or the Secretary of Revenue or the Secretary's duly authorized agent. For purposes of the registration list, the exemptions in G.S. 66-256 do not apply. (1996, 2nd Ex. Sess., c. 14, s. 24; 1998-121, s. 7; 2013-414, s. 31.)

§ 66-256. Exemptions from Article.

This Article does not apply to the following:

(1)   A peddler or an itinerant merchant who sells only one or more of the following types of merchandise:

a.   Farm or nursery products produced by the merchant.

b.   Crafts or goods made by the merchant.

c.   The merchant's own household personal property.

d.   Printed material.

e.   Wood for fuel.

f.   Ice, seafood, meat, poultry, livestock, eggs, dairy products, bread, cakes, or pies.

(2)   A peddler or an itinerant merchant who is an authorized automobile dealer licensed pursuant to Chapter 20 of the General Statutes.

(3)   A peddler or an itinerant merchant who is a nonprofit charitable, educational, religious, scientific, or civic organization.

(4)   A peddler who maintains a fixed permanent location from which at least ninety percent (90%) of the peddler's sales are made but who sells some goods in the county of the fixed location by peddling.

(5) An itinerant merchant who meets any of the following descriptions:

a. Locates at a farmer's market.

b. Is part of the State Fair or an agriculture fair that is licensed by the Commissioner of Agriculture pursuant to G.S. 106-520.3.

c. Sells goods at an auction conducted by an auctioneer licensed pursuant to Chapter 85B of the General Statutes.

(6) A peddler who complies with the requirements of G.S. 25A-38 through G.S. 25A-42, or who complies with the requirements of G.S. 14-401.13. (1996, 2nd Ex. Sess., c. 14, s. 24.)

§ 66-257. Misdemeanor violations.

(a) Class 1 Misdemeanors. - A person who does any of the following commits a Class 1 misdemeanor:

(1) Fails to keep a record of new merchandise and fails to produce a record or an affidavit pursuant to G.S. 66-254.

(2) Falsifies a record of new merchandise required by G.S. 66-254.

(b) Class 2 Misdemeanors. - A person who does any of the following commits a Class 2 misdemeanor:

(1) If the person is an itinerant merchant or a specialty market vendor, fails to display the certificate of registration as required by G.S. 66-252.

(2) If the person is a specialty market operator, fails to maintain the daily registration list as required by G.S. 66-255.

(c) Class 3 Misdemeanors. - A person who does any of the following commits a Class 3 misdemeanor:

(1) If the person is a peddler or an itinerant merchant, fails to obtain the permission of the property owner as required by G.S. 66-251.

(2) If the person is a peddler or a specialty market operator, fails to produce the certificate of registration as required by G.S. 66-252.

(3) Fails to provide name, address, or identification upon request as required by G.S. 66-253 or provides false information in response to the request.

(4) Knowingly gives false information when registering pursuant to G.S. 66-255.

(d) Defense. - Whenever satisfactory evidence is presented in any court of the fact that permission to use property was not displayed as required by G.S. 66-251 or that a certificate of registration was not displayed or produced as required by G.S. 66-252, the person charged may not be found guilty of that violation if the person produces in court a valid permission or a valid certificate of registration, respectively, that had been issued prior to the time the person was charged. (1996, 2nd Ex. Sess., c. 14, s. 24; 1998-121, s. 8.)

§ 66-258. Local regulation not affected.

This Article does not affect the authority of a county or city to impose additional requirements on peddlers, itinerant merchants, specialty market vendors, or specialty market operators by an ordinance adopted under G.S. 153A-125 or G.S. 160A-178. (1996, 2nd Ex. Sess., c. 14, s. 24.)

§ 66-259. Reserved for future codification purposes.

Article 33.

Telephonic Seller Registration and Bond Requirement.

§ 66-260. Definitions.

As used in this Article, unless the context requires otherwise:

(1) "Gift or prize" means any premium, bonus, award, or any other thing of value.

(2) "Item" means any good or any service. "Item" includes coupon books, vouchers, or certificates that are to be used with businesses other than the seller's business.

(3) "Owner" means a person who owns or controls ten percent (10%) or more of the equity of, or otherwise has a claim to ten percent (10%) or more of the net income of, a telephonic seller.

(4) "Person" includes any individual, firm, association, corporation, partnership, joint venture, or any other business entity.

(5) "Principal" means an owner, an executive officer of a corporation, a general partner of a partnership, a sole proprietor of a sole proprietorship, a trustee of a trust, or any other individual with similar supervisory functions with respect to any person.

(6) "Purchaser" or "prospective purchaser" means a person who is solicited to become obligated to a telephonic seller or to make any donation or gift to any person represented by the telephonic seller.

(7) "Room operator" means any principal, employee, or agent responsible for the operational management and supervision of facilities from which telephonic sales calls are made or received.

(8) "Salesperson" means any individual employed, appointed, or authorized by a telephonic seller, whether referred to by the telephonic seller as an agency, representative, or independent contractor, who attempts to solicit or solicits a sale on behalf of the telephonic seller.

(9) "Secretary" means the Office of the Secretary of State.

(10) "Telephone solicitation" or "attempted telephone solicitation" means any telephonic communication designed to persuade any person to purchase goods or services, to enter a contest, or to contribute to a charity or a person represented to be a charity, regardless of whether the telephone call initiating

the solicitation is placed by the (i) telephonic seller or (ii) a person responding to any unsolicited notice or notices sent or provided by or on behalf of the seller, which notice or notices represent to the recipient that he or she has won a gift or prize, that the recipient may obtain or qualify for credit by contacting the seller, or that the seller has buyers interested in purchasing the recipient's property.

(11) "Telephonic seller" or "seller" means a person who, directly or through salespersons, causes a telephone solicitation or attempted telephone solicitation to occur. "Telephonic seller" and "seller" do not include any of the following:

a. A securities "dealer" within the meaning of G.S. 78A-2(2) or a person excluded from the definition of "dealer" by that provision: a "salesman" within the meaning of G.S. 78A-2(9); an "investment adviser" within the meaning of G.S. 78C-2(1) or a person excluded from the definition of "investment adviser" by that provision; or an "investment adviser representative" within the meaning of G.S. 78C-2(3); provided that such persons shall be excluded from the terms "telephonic seller" and "seller" only with respect to activities regulated by Chapters 78A and 78C.

b. Any person conducting sales or solicitations on behalf of a licensee of the Federal Communications Commission or holder of a franchise or certificate of public convenience and necessity from the North Carolina Utilities Commission.

c. Any insurance agent or broker who is properly licensed by the Department of Insurance and who is soliciting within the scope of the agent's or broker's license or any employee or independent contractor of an insurance company licensed by the Department of Insurance conducting sales or solicitations on behalf of that company.

d. Any federally chartered bank, savings institution, or credit union or any bank, savings institution, or credit union properly licensed by the State or subject to federal regulating authorities.

e. Any organization that is exempt under section 501(c)(3) of the Internal Revenue Code of 1986 or any successor section, or that is organized exclusively for one or more of the purposes specified in section 501(c)(3) of the Internal Revenue Code of 1986 or any successor section and that upon dissolution shall distribute its assets to an entity that is exempt under section 501(c)(3) of the Internal Revenue Code of 1986 or any successor section, the

United States, or a state; any "charitable solicitor" properly licensed under Article 2 of Chapter 131F of the General Statutes, or any person exempt from Chapter 131F of the General Statutes under G.S. 131F-3.

f. A person who periodically issues and delivers catalogs to potential purchasers and the catalog:

1. Includes a written description or illustration and the sales price of each item offered for sale;

2. Includes at least 24 full pages of written material or illustrations;

3. Is distributed in more than one state; and

4. Has an annual circulation of not less than 250,000 customers.

g. A person engaging in a commercial telephone solicitation where the solicitation is an isolated transaction and not done in the course of a pattern of repeated transactions of a like nature.

h. A person primarily soliciting the sale of a newspaper of general circulation, a publisher of a magazine or other periodical of general circulation, or an agent of such a publisher acting pursuant to a written agency agreement.

i. A person soliciting the sale of services provided by a cable television system operating under the authority of a local franchise.

j. Any passenger airline licensed by the Federal Aviation Administration.

k. Any person holding a real estate broker's or sales agent's license under Chapter 93A of the General Statutes and who is soliciting within the scope of the broker's or agent's license.

l. Any person soliciting a transaction regulated by the Commodities Futures Trading Commission, provided the person is registered or temporarily licensed by the Commodities Futures Trading Commission under the Commodity Exchange Act, 7 U.S.C. § 1, et seq.

m. Any person soliciting a purchase from a business, provided the person soliciting makes reasonable efforts to ensure that the person solicited has actual authority to bind the business to a purchase agreement.

n. A foreign corporation, limited liability company, or limited partnership that has obtained and maintained a certificate of authority to transact business or conduct affairs in this State pursuant to Chapter 55, 55A, or 57D or Article 5 of Chapter 59 of the General Statutes and that only transacts business or conducts affairs in this State using the name set forth in the certificate of authority.

o. An issuer or a subsidiary of an issuer that has a class of securities which is subject to section 12 of the Securities Exchange Act of 1934 (15 U.S.C. § 781) and which is either registered or exempt from registration under paragraph (A), paragraph (B), paragraph (C), paragraph (E), paragraph (F), paragraph (G), or paragraph (H) of subsection (g)(2) of that section.

p. A person soliciting the sale of food, seeds, or plants when a sale does not involve an amount in excess of one hundred dollars ($100.00) directed to a single address.

q. A person soliciting:

1. Without intent to complete or obtain provisional acceptance of a sale during the telephone solicitation;

2. Who does not make the major sales presentation during the telephone solicitation but arranges for the major sales presentation to be made at a later face-to-face meeting between the salesperson and the purchaser;

3. Who does not cause an individual to go to the prospective purchaser to collect payment for the purchase or to deliver any item purchased directly following the telephone solicitation; or

4. Who offers to send the purchaser descriptive literature and does not require payment prior to the purchaser's review of the descriptive literature.

r. A person soliciting the purchase of contracts for the maintenance or repair of items previously purchased from the person making the solicitation or on whose behalf the solicitation is made.

s. A book, video, recording, or multimedia club or contractual plan or arrangement:

1. Under which the seller provides the consumer with a form with which the consumer can instruct the seller not to ship the offered merchandise.

2. Which is regulated by the Federal Trade Commission trade regulation concerning "use of negative option plans by sellers in commerce".

3. Which provides for the sale of books, recordings, multimedia products or goods, or videos which are not covered under paragraphs 1. or 2. of this sub-subdivision, including continuity plans, subscription arrangements, standing order arrangements, supplements, and series arrangements under which the seller periodically ships merchandise to a consumer who has consented in advance to receive such merchandise on a periodic basis.

t. A person who for at least two years has been operating under the same name as that used in connection with its telemarketing operations and retail establishment in North Carolina where consumer goods are displayed and offered for sale on a continuing basis if a majority of the person's business involves the buyers obtaining services or products at the person's retail establishment.

u. A person:

1. Who provides telephone solicitation services under contract to sellers;

2. Who has been operating continuously for at least three years under the same business name; and

3. For whom at least seventy-five percent (75%) of the person's contracts are performed on behalf of other persons exempt under this section.

v. A person soliciting political contributions in accordance with Article 22A of Chapter 163 of the General Statutes.

w. The seller of a "business opportunity" as defined in G.S. 66-94, while engaged in activities subject to regulation under Article 19 of Chapter 66 of the General Statutes, provided that such seller has complied with the provisions of G.S. 66-97.

x. A "loan broker" as defined in G.S. 66-106, while engaged in activities subject to regulation under Article 20 of Chapter 66 of the General Statutes, provided that such loan broker has complied with the provisions of G.S. 66-109.

y.   A "membership camping operator" as defined in G.S. 66-232(10) or a "salesperson" as defined in G.S. 66-232(16), while engaged in activities subject to regulation under Article 31 of Chapter 66 of the General Statutes, provided that such persons have complied with the provisions of G.S. 66-234 and 66-237, as applicable. (1997-482, s. 1; 2013-157, s. 17.)

§ 66-261. Registration of telephonic sellers.

(a)   Not less than 10 days before commencing telephone solicitations in this State, a telephonic seller shall register with the Secretary by filing the information required in G.S. 66-262 and paying a filing fee of one hundred dollars ($100.00). A telephonic seller is doing business in this State if it solicits or attempts to solicit prospective purchasers from locations in this State or solicits or attempts to solicit prospective purchasers who are located in this State.

(b)   The information required in G.S. 66-262 shall be submitted on a form provided by the Secretary and shall contain the notarized signatures of each principal of the telephonic seller.

(c)   Registration of a telephonic seller shall be valid for one year from the effective date thereof and may be annually renewed by making the filing required in G.S. 66-262 and paying the filing fee of one hundred dollars ($100.00). Registration shall not be deemed effective unless all required information is provided and any deficiencies or errors noted by the Secretary have been corrected to the satisfaction of the Secretary.

(d)   Whenever, prior to expiration of a seller's annual registration, there is a change in the information required by G.S. 66-262, the seller shall, within 10 days after the change, file an addendum with the Secretary updating the information. (1997-482, s. 1.)

§ 66-262. Filing information.

(a)   Each filing submitted to the Secretary shall contain all of the following information:

(1)   The name or names, including any assumed names, under which the telephonic seller is doing or intends to do business in this State.

(2)   The telephonic seller's business form and place of organization and, if the seller is a corporation, copies of its articles of incorporation and bylaws and amendments thereto, or if a partnership, a copy of the partnership agreement.

(3)   Complete street address of the telephonic seller's principal place of business.

(4)   The complete street address of each location from which telephone solicitations are placed by the telephonic seller.

(5)   A listing of all telephone numbers to be used by the telephonic seller, including area codes, and the complete street address of the business premises served by each number.

(6)   The name and title of each principal.

(7)   The complete street address of the residence, the date of birth, and the social security number of each principal.

(8)   The true name, street address, date of birth, and the social security number of each room operator, together with the room operator's full employment history during the preceding two years.

(9)   The name and address of all banks or savings institutions where the telephonic seller maintains deposit accounts.

(10)   The name and address of each long-distance telephone carrier used by the telephonic seller.

(11)   A summary of each civil or criminal proceeding brought against the telephonic seller, any of its principals, or any of its room operators during the preceding five years by federal, State, or local officials relating to telephonic sales practices of each. The summary shall include the date each action was commenced, the criminal or civil charges alleged, the case caption, the court file number, the court venue, and the disposition of the action. For purposes of this section, a "civil proceeding includes" means assurances of voluntary

compliance, assurances of discontinuance, consent judgments, and similar agreements executed with federal, State, or local officials.

(b)   For purposes of this section, "street address" does not include a private mail service address. (1997-482, s. 1.)

§ 66-263. Bond requirement; prizes and gifts.

(a)   At least 10 days before the commencement of any promotion offering any gift or prize with an actual or represented market value of five hundred dollars ($500.00) or more, the telephonic seller shall notify the Secretary in writing of the details of the promotion, fully describing the nature and number of all gifts or prizes and their current market value, the seller's rules and regulations governing the promotion, and the date the gifts or prizes are to be awarded. All gifts or prizes offered shall be awarded. Concurrent with notifying the Secretary under this subsection, the telephonic seller shall post a bond with the Secretary for the market value or the represented value, whichever is greater, of all gifts or prizes represented as available under the promotion. The bond must be issued by a surety company authorized to do business in this State. The bond shall be in favor of the State of North Carolina for the benefit of any person entitled to receive a gift or prize under the promotion who did not receive it within 30 days of the specified date of award. The amount recoverable by any person under the bond shall not exceed the market value, the represented value of the gift or prize, or the amount of any consideration or contribution paid by that person in response to the telephone solicitation, whichever is greatest.

(b)   Within 45 days after the specified date of the award of the gift or prize, the seller shall provide, in writing, to the Secretary, proof that the gifts or prizes were awarded. The writing shall include the name, address, and telephone number of all persons receiving awards or prizes. The bond shall be maintained until the Secretary receives reliable proof that the gifts or prizes have been delivered to the intended recipients.

(c)   The Attorney General, on behalf of any injured purchaser, or any purchaser who is injured by the bankruptcy of the telephonic seller or its breach of any agreement entered into in its capacity as a telephonic seller, may initiate a civil action to recover against the bond. (1997-482, s. 1.)

§ 66-264. Calls made to minors.

A telephonic seller must inquire as to whether the prospective purchaser it is contacting is under 18 years of age. If the prospective purchaser purports to be under 18 years of age, the telephonic seller must discontinue the call immediately. (1997-482, s. 1.)

§ 66-265. Offers of gifts or prizes.

(a) It shall be unlawful for any telephonic seller to make a telephone solicitation or attempted telephone solicitation involving any gift or prize when the solicitation or attempted solicitation:

(1) Requests or directs the consumer to further the transaction by calling a 900 number or a pay-per-call number.

(2) Requests or directs the consumer to send any payment or make a donation in order to collect the gift or prize.

(3) Does not comply fully with G.S. 75-30, 75-32, 75-33, or 75-34.

(b) Notwithstanding subsection (a) of this section, a telephonic seller may offer a gift or prize in connection with the bona fide sale of a product or service. (1997-482, s. 1.)

§ 66-266. Penalties.

(a) Any violation of this Article shall constitute an unfair and deceptive trade practice in violation of G.S. 75-1.1.

(b) In an action by the Attorney General against a telephonic seller for violation of this Article, or for any other act or practice by a telephonic seller constituting a violation of G.S. 75-1.1, the court may impose civil penalties of up to twenty-five thousand dollars ($25,000) for each violation involving North

Carolina purchasers or prospective purchasers who are 65 years of age or older.

(c)   The remedies and penalties available under this section shall be supplemental to others available under the law, both civil and criminal.

(d)   Compliance with this Article does not satisfy or substitute for any other requirements for license, registration, or conduct imposed by law.

(e)   In any civil proceeding alleging a violation of this Article, the burden of proving an exemption or an exception from a definition is upon the person claiming it, and in any criminal proceeding alleging a violation of this Article, the burden of producing evidence to support a defense based upon an exemption or an exception from a definition is upon the person claiming it. (1997-482, s. 1.)

§§ 66-267 through 66-269. Reserved for future codification purposes.

Article 34.

Certificates of Authentication.

§ 66-270. Authority of Secretary of State to authenticate documents.

The Secretary, or the Secretary's designee, may sign and issue a certificate of authentication for a document that has been executed or issued in this State so that it can be recognized in a foreign jurisdiction. The certificate may be issued under the seal of the Department of the Secretary of State or under the Great Seal of the State of North Carolina. The Secretary may adopt rules to implement this Article in accordance with Chapter 150B of the General Statutes. (1998-228, s. 14.)

§ 66-271. Definitions.

The following definitions apply in this Article:

(1) Authentication. - Certification of the genuineness of an official's signature, seal, or position within the State of North Carolina so the document can be recognized in a foreign jurisdiction.

(2) Department. - The Department of the Secretary of State.

(3) Foreign jurisdiction. - A jurisdiction outside the State of North Carolina.

(4) Foreign official. - An individual authorized by a foreign jurisdiction to attest to the genuineness of a document or to the position of an individual within that foreign jurisdiction.

(5) Notary public. - Defined in G.S. 10B-3.

(6) Official. - An individual who is a notary public, an individual who is elected or appointed to hold an office in State government, or an individual who is elected or appointed to hold an office in a local governmental unit of this State.

(7) Secretary. - The Secretary of State.

(8) Specimen. - A record of a person's signature, seal, or position as an official within the State maintained in the Department. (1998-228, s. 14; 2005-391, s. 5.)

§ 66-272. Certificate of authentication.

To authenticate a document, the Secretary must compare the official's seal and signature on the document with a specimen of the official's seal and signature on file in the Department. If no specimen is on file in the Department, the Secretary must require that the document be authenticated by an official for whom the Department does have a specimen. The Secretary must also verify the official's authority to perform a particular act when the law of a foreign jurisdiction requires it to be verified before it will recognize the authenticity of the document. When the Secretary is able to authenticate the official's seal, signature, position, and authority, the Secretary shall sign and issue a certificate of authentication. The certificate of authentication shall be appended to the document on a separate sheet. (1998-228, s. 14; 2005-391, s. 6.)

§ 66-273. Prerequisites for authentication.

All of the following conditions must be met before a document can be authenticated:

(1)   All seals and signatures must be originals.

(2)   All dates must follow in chronological order on all certifications.

(3)   All acknowledgments to be authenticated by the Secretary shall be in English and must comply with Chapter 10B of the General Statutes.

(4)   Whenever a copy is used, it must include a statement that it is a true and accurate copy.

(5)   Whenever a document is to be authenticated by the United States Department of State, it must comply with all applicable statutes, rules, and regulations of that office. (1998-228, s. 14; 2000-140, s. 57; 2005-391, s. 7.)

§ 66-274. Limitations on authentication.

(a)   The Secretary shall not issue a certificate of authentication for a document if the Secretary has cause to believe that the certificate is desired for an unlawful or improper purpose. The Secretary may examine not only the document for which a certificate is requested, but also any documents to which the previous seals or other certifications may have been affixed by other authorities. The Secretary may request any additional information that may be necessary to establish that the requested certificate will serve the interests of justice and is not contrary to public policy, including a certified or notarized English translation of document text in a foreign language.

(b)   The Secretary shall not issue a certificate of authentication for any one or more of the following:

(1)   A seal or signature that cannot be authenticated by either the Secretary or another official.

(2)   A seal or signature of a foreign official.

(3)   A facsimile, photostat, photographic, or other reproduction of a signature or seal.

(c)   The Secretary may not include within the certificate of authentication any statement that is not within the Secretary's power or knowledge to authenticate. The Secretary may not certify that a document has been executed or certified in accordance with the law of any particular jurisdiction or that a document is a valid document in a particular jurisdiction. (1998-228, s. 14.)

§ 66-275. Other methods of authentication not precluded.

Nothing in this Article shall preclude or invalidate any other method that is provided by statute or common law for certifying or exemplifying the authenticity of a document or preclude the recognition in a foreign jurisdiction of a document whose authenticity is so certified or exemplified. (1998-228, s. 14.)

§§ 66-276 through 66-279. Reserved for future codification purposes.

Article 35.

Agreements Between North Carolina and Foreign Governments.

§ 66-280. Agreements between North Carolina and foreign governments to be filed.

(a)   A copy of all executed memoranda of understanding and agreements of a noncommercial nature otherwise subject to disclosure under the public record laws of this State, entered into by the State of North Carolina, or any agency of the State, and a foreign government shall be filed by the State agency with the Secretary of State.

(b)   Notwithstanding subsection (a) of this section, the validity or enforceability of any memoranda or agreement subject to this section shall not be affected by the failure to comply with subsection (a) of this section. Documents required to be filed with the Secretary of State under this section shall be indexed and made available to the public in accordance with Chapter 132 of the General Statutes.

(c)   For purposes of this section, "foreign government" means a foreign country's government that is recognized and accredited by the United States Department of State, and includes governmental subdivisions of that country. For purposes of this section, "agency of the State" does not include public educational institutions with respect to their educational, research, or extension activities. (1999-260, s. 1.)

§§ 66-281 through 66-284. Reserved for future codification purposes.

Article 36.

Truthful Advertisements of Costs of Servicing or Repairing Private Passenger Vehicles.

§ 66-285. Advertisements of servicing or repairing private passenger vehicles.

(a)   Any business that services or repairs private passenger vehicles and advertises the cost of a specified service or repair of private passenger vehicles shall disclose in the advertisement all additional charges routinely charged for that service or repair, including shop supplies or charges, except any fees and taxes that are required by law, that a consumer will be charged.

(b)   If a business that services or repairs private passenger vehicles fails to comply with the requirements of this section, then, upon written notice to that business, the consumer is required to pay only those charges disclosed in the advertisement, plus any fees and taxes that are required by law.

(c)   A violation of this section shall constitute an unfair trade practice under G.S. 75-1.1.

(d) For purposes of this section, "private passenger vehicle" has the same meaning as in G.S. 20-4.01. (1999-437, s. 2.)

§§ 66-286 through 66-289. Reserved for future codification purposes.

Article 37.

Tobacco Reserve Fund and Escrow Compliance.

Part 1. Tobacco Reserve Fund.

§ 66-290. Definitions.

As used in this Article:

(1) "Adjusted for inflation" means increased in accordance with the formula for inflation adjustment set forth in Exhibit C to the Master Settlement Agreement.

(2) "Affiliate" means a person who directly or indirectly owns or controls, is owned or controlled by, or is under common ownership or control with, another person. Solely for purposes of this definition, the terms "owns," "is owned," and "ownership" mean ownership of an equity interest, or the equivalent thereof, of ten percent (10%) or more, and the term "person" means an individual, partnership, committee, association, corporation, or any other organization or group of persons.

(3) "Allocable share" means Allocable Share as that term is defined in the Master Settlement Agreement.

(4) "Cigarette" means any product that contains nicotine, is intended to be burned or heated under ordinary conditions of use, and consists of or contains (i) any roll of tobacco wrapped in paper or in any substance not containing tobacco; or (ii) tobacco, in any form, that is functional in the product, which, because of its appearance, the type of tobacco used in the filler, or its packaging and labeling, is likely to be offered to, or purchased by, consumers as

a cigarette; or (iii) any roll of tobacco wrapped in any substance containing tobacco which, because of its appearance, the type of tobacco used in the filler, or its packaging and labeling, is likely to be offered to, or purchased by, consumers as a cigarette described in clause (i) of this definition. The term "cigarette" includes "roll-your-own" (i.e., any tobacco which, because of its appearance, type, packaging, or labeling is suitable for use and likely to be offered to, or purchased by, consumers as tobacco for making cigarettes). For purposes of this definition of "cigarette," 0.09 ounces of "roll-your-own" tobacco shall constitute one individual "cigarette."

(5)   "Master Settlement Agreement" means the settlement agreement (and related documents) entered into on November 23, 1998, by the State and leading United States tobacco product manufacturers.

(6)   "Qualified escrow fund" means an escrow arrangement with a federally or State chartered financial institution having no affiliation with any tobacco product manufacturer and having assets of at least one billion dollars ($1,000,000,000) where such arrangement requires that such financial institution hold the escrowed funds' principal for the benefit of releasing parties and prohibits the tobacco product manufacturer placing the funds into escrow from using, accessing, or directing the use of the funds' principal except as consistent with G.S. 66-291(b).

(7)   "Released claims" means Released Claims as that term is defined in the Master Settlement Agreement.

(8)   "Releasing parties" means Releasing Parties as that term is defined in the Master Settlement Agreement.

(9)   "Tobacco Product Manufacturer" means an entity that after the effective date of this Article directly (and not exclusively through any affiliate):

a.   Manufactures cigarettes anywhere that such manufacturer intends to be sold in the United States, including cigarettes intended to be sold in the United States through an importer (except where such importer is an original participating manufacturer, as that term is defined in the Master Settlement Agreement, that will be responsible for the payments under the Master Settlement Agreement with respect to such cigarettes as a result of the provisions of subsection II(mm) of the Master Settlement Agreement and that pays the taxes specified in subsection II(z) of the Master Settlement Agreement, and provided that the manufacturer of such cigarettes does not market or advertise such cigarettes in the United States);

b. Is the first purchaser anywhere for resale in the United States of cigarettes manufactured anywhere that the manufacturer does not intend to be sold in the United States; or

c. Becomes a successor of an entity described in sub-subdivision a. or b. of this subdivision.

The term "Tobacco Product Manufacturer" shall not include an affiliate of a tobacco product manufacturer unless such affiliate itself falls within any of sub-subdivisions a. through c. of this subdivision.

(10) "Units sold" means the number of individual cigarettes sold in the State by the applicable tobacco product manufacturer (whether directly or through a distributor, retailer, or similar intermediary or intermediaries) during the year in question, as measured by excise taxes collected by the State on packs (or "roll-your-own" tobacco containers). The Secretary of Revenue shall promulgate such rules as are necessary to ascertain the amount of State excise tax paid on the cigarettes of such tobacco product manufacturer for each year. In lieu of adopting rules, the Secretary of Revenue may issue bulletins or directives requiring taxpayers to submit to the Department of Revenue the information necessary to make the required determination under this subdivision. (1999-311, s. 1; 2002-145, s. 2.)

§ 66-291. Requirements.

(a) Any tobacco product manufacturer selling cigarettes to consumers within the State (whether directly or through a distributor, retailer, or similar intermediary or intermediaries) after the effective date of this Article shall do one of the following:

(1) Become a participating manufacturer (as that term is defined in section II(jj) of the Master Settlement Agreement) and generally perform its financial obligations under the Master Settlement Agreement; or

(2) Place into a qualified escrow fund by April 15 of the year following the year in question the following amounts (as such amounts are adjusted for inflation):

a. 1999: $.0094241 per unit sold after the effective date of this Article.

b. 2000: $.0104712 per unit sold.

c. For each of 2001 and 2002: $.0136125 per unit sold.

d. For each of 2003 through 2006: $.0167539 per unit sold.

e. For each of 2007 and each year thereafter: $.0188482 per unit sold.

(b) A tobacco product manufacturer that places funds into escrow pursuant to subdivision (2) of subsection (a) of this section shall receive the interest or other appreciation on such funds as earned. Such funds themselves shall be released from escrow only under the following circumstances:

(1) To pay a judgment or settlement on any released claim brought against such tobacco product manufacturer by the State or any releasing party located or residing in the State. Funds shall be released from escrow under this subdivision (i) in the order in which they were placed into escrow and (ii) only to the extent and at the time necessary to make payments required under such judgment or settlement;

(2) To the extent that a tobacco product manufacturer establishes that the amount it was required to place into escrow on account of units sold in the State in a particular year was greater than the Master Settlement Agreement payments, as determined pursuant to Section IX(i) of that agreement, including after final determination of all adjustments, that the manufacturer would have been required to make on account of the units sold had it been a participating manufacturer, the excess shall be released from escrow and revert back to such tobacco product manufacturer; or

(3) To the extent not released from escrow under subdivisions (1) or (2) of this subsection, funds shall be released from escrow and revert back to such tobacco product manufacturer 25 years after the date on which they were placed into escrow.

(c) Each tobacco product manufacturer that elects to place funds into escrow pursuant to this section shall annually certify to the Attorney General that it is in compliance with this section. The Attorney General may bring a civil action on behalf of the State against any tobacco product manufacturer that fails to place into escrow the funds required under this section. Any tobacco product manufacturer that fails in any year to place into escrow the funds required under this section shall:

(1) Be required within 15 days to place such funds into escrow as shall bring it into compliance with this section. The court, upon a finding of a violation either of subdivision (2) of subsection (a) of this section, of subsection (b) of this section, or of this section, may impose a civil penalty (the clear proceeds of which shall be paid to the Civil Penalty and Forfeiture Fund in accordance with G.S. 115C-457.2) in an amount not to exceed five percent (5%) of the amount improperly withheld from escrow per day of the violation and in a total amount not to exceed one hundred percent (100%) of the original amount improperly withheld from escrow;

(2) In the case of a knowing violation, be required within 15 days to place such funds into escrow as shall bring it into compliance with this section. The court, upon a finding of a knowing violation either of subdivision (2) of subsection (a) of this section, of subsection (b) of this section, or of this section, may impose a civil penalty (the clear proceeds of which shall be paid to the Civil Penalty and Forfeiture Fund in accordance with G.S. 115C-457.2) in an amount not to exceed fifteen percent (15%) of the amount improperly withheld from escrow per day of the violation and in a total amount not to exceed three hundred percent (300%) of the original amount improperly withheld from escrow; and

(3) In the case of a second knowing violation, be prohibited from selling cigarettes to consumers within the State (whether directly or through a distributor, retailer, or similar intermediary) for a period not to exceed two years.

Each failure to make an annual deposit required under this section shall constitute a separate violation. (1999-311, s. 1; 2000-140, s. 58; 2002-145, s. 2; 2005-276, s. 6.12(a); 2005-435, s. 59.1(a).)

Part 2. Tobacco Escrow Compliance.

§ 66-292. Definitions.

The following definitions apply in this Part:

(1) Brand family. - All styles of cigarettes sold under the same trademark and differentiated from one another by means of additional modifiers including, but not limited to, "menthol", "lights", "kings", and "100s".

(2) Escrow agreement. - An agreement by which a qualified escrow fund is created and maintained.

(3) Nonparticipating manufacturer. - A tobacco product manufacturer that is not a participating manufacturer.

(4) Participating manufacturer. - Defined in subsection II(jj) of the Master Settlement Agreement. (2002-145, s. 3.)

§ 66-293. Sale of certain cigarettes prohibited.

(a) Civil Penalty. - It is unlawful for a person required to pay taxes pursuant to Part 2 or 3 of Article 2A of Chapter 105 of the General Statutes to sell or deliver cigarettes belonging to a brand family of a nonparticipating manufacturer if the sale of the cigarettes is subject to such taxes unless the cigarettes are included on the compliant nonparticipating manufacturer's list prepared and made public by the Office of the Attorney General under G.S. 66-294.1 as of the date the person sells or delivers the cigarettes. It is not a violation of this subsection if the brand family was on the compliant nonparticipating manufacturer's list when the person purchased the cigarettes and the person sold or delivered the cigarettes within 60 days of the purchase. The Attorney General may impose a civil penalty on a person that it finds violates this subsection. The amount of the penalty may not exceed the greater of five hundred percent (500%) of the retail value of the cigarettes sold or five thousand dollars ($5,000).

(b) Contraband. - Cigarettes described in subsection (a) of this section are contraband and may be seized by a law enforcement officer. The procedure for seizure and disposition of this contraband is the same as the procedure under G.S. 105-113.31 and G.S. 105-113.32 for non-tax-paid cigarettes. (2002-145, s. 3.)

§ 66-294. Duties of manufacturers.

(a) Participating Manufacturers. - Unless the Office of the Attorney General provides a waiver, a participating manufacturer must submit to the Office of the Attorney General a list of all of the manufacturer's brand families by April 30th of each year. The participating manufacturer must notify the Office of the Attorney General of any changes to the list of brand families it offers for sale 30 days prior to the change.

(b) Nonparticipating Manufacturers. - A nonparticipating manufacturer must:

(1) Appoint and continuously maintain a process service agent within the State of North Carolina to accept service of any notification or enforcement of an action under this Article. The manufacturer shall file a certified copy of each instrument appointing a process service agent with the Secretary of State and the Office of the Attorney General.

(2) Submit an annual application to the Office of the Attorney General for inclusion of the nonparticipating manufacturer's products on the compliant nonparticipating manufacturer's list, in accordance with subsection (c) of this section.

(3) Notify the Office of the Attorney General of any changes to the list of brand families it offers for sale 30 days prior to the change.

(4) Have made the escrow payments required under G.S. 66-291(a)(2) for all cigarettes belonging to the brand families included in the list submitted in the application for inclusion and any brand families added to the list since it was submitted to the Office of the Attorney General.

(5) Submit an escrow agreement to the Office of the Attorney General.

(6) Not deliver cigarettes unless the cigarettes are included on the compliant nonparticipating manufacturer's list in effect on the date of delivery.

(c) Nonparticipating Manufacturer's Application. - A nonparticipating manufacturer must submit an application to the Office of the Attorney General by April 30th of each year for inclusion on the compliant nonparticipating manufacturers' list. The Attorney General may provide a waiver of the deadline for good cause. The application must include a certification that the nonparticipating manufacturer has fulfilled the duties listed in subsection (b) of this section and a list of the brand families of the manufacturer offered for sale in the State during either the current calendar year or the previous calendar year. The certification must be in the form required by the Office of the Attorney General. (2002-145, s. 3.)

§ 66-294.1. Duties of Attorney General.

(a) Annual Lists. - The Office of the Attorney General shall prepare the following lists annually and shall make those lists available for public inspection:

(1) Participating manufacturers. - A list of the participating manufacturers and all brand families of each participating manufacturer that the manufacturer has identified to the Attorney General, in accordance with G.S. 66-294.

(2) Compliant nonparticipating manufacturers. - A list of the nonparticipating manufacturers whose applications for inclusion have been found to be complete and accurate and whose escrow agreements have been approved by the Office of the Attorney General. The list must include those brand families that the manufacturer has identified to the Attorney General, in accordance with G.S. 66-294.

(b) Supplemental Lists. - The Office of the Attorney General must supplement the annual lists as necessary to reflect additions to or deletions of manufacturers and brand families. The Attorney General shall delete a nonparticipating manufacturer and its brand families from the list if it determines that the manufacturer fails to comply with the duties listed in G.S. 66-294. The Attorney General must add a nonparticipating manufacturer and its brand families to the list if it determines all of the following:

(1) The nonparticipating manufacturer has submitted an application under G.S. 66-294, and it is found to be complete and accurate.

(2) The Office of the Attorney General has approved the manufacturer's escrow agreement.

(3) The manufacturer has made any past due payments owed to its escrow account for any of its listed brand families.

(4) The manufacturer has resolved any outstanding penalty demands or adjudicated penalties for its listed brand families.

(c) Quarterly Escrow Installments. - To promote compliance with this Article, the Attorney General shall require a nonparticipating manufacturer to make the escrow deposits required by G.S. 66-291(a)(2) in quarterly installments during the year in which the sales covered by the deposits are made if one or more of the conditions in this subsection apply. A quarterly installment must be made by the last day of the month following the end of the quarter. The Attorney General must notify a nonparticipating manufacturer required to make quarterly escrow deposits under this subsection of its duty to do so by first-class mail sent to the manufacturer's last known address. The Attorney General may require production of information sufficient to enable the Attorney General to determine the adequacy of the amount of any installment escrow payment.

(1) The nonparticipating manufacturer has not previously established and funded a qualified escrow fund in North Carolina.

(2) The nonparticipating manufacturer has not made any escrow deposits for more than one year.

(3) The nonparticipating manufacturer has failed to make a timely and complete escrow deposit in any prior calendar year.

(4) The nonparticipating manufacturer has failed to pay any judgment, including any civil penalty.

(5) The Attorney General has reasonable cause to believe that the nonparticipating manufacturer may not make its full required escrow deposit by April 15 of the year following the year in which the cigarette sales are made. (2002-145, s. 3; 2007-435, s. 1.)

Article 38.

Year 2000 Liability and Damages (Expired December 31, 2004).

§§ 66-295 through 66-299: Expired.

§ 66-300. Reserved for future codification purposes.

§ 66-301: Reserved for future codification purposes.

§ 66-302: Reserved for future codification purposes.

§ 66-303: Reserved for future codification purposes.

§ 66-304: Reserved for future codification purposes.

Article 39.

Self-Service Storage Rental Contracts.

§ 66-305. Contract requirements.

A rental contract for the storage of personal property in a self-service storage business shall state, in bold type of a minimum size of 14 points and conspicuously placed, the terms regarding the imposition of late fees, the terms regarding any consequences of a late payment, and the terms, if any, that pertain to the payment of court costs, attorneys' fees, and any other costs associated with the payment of late fees or with judgment against the consumer for late rental payments or late fees. (1999-416, s. 1.)

§ 66-306. Late fees.

(a) In all rental contracts in which a definite time for the payment of the rent is fixed, the late fee for each rental unit shall not exceed fifteen dollars ($15.00) or fifteen percent (15%) of the rental payment, whichever is greater, and shall not be imposed by the self-service storage business until the rental payment for that rental unit is five days or more late.

(b) A late fee under this section may be imposed only one time for each late rental payment. A late fee for a specific late rental payment shall not be deducted from a subsequent rental payment so as to cause the subsequent rental payment to be in default. (1999-416, s. 1; 2013-239, s. 3.)

§ 66-307. Violations.

(a) Late fees and attorney fees are not recoverable if a self-service storage business violates the provisions of G.S. 66-306.

(b) Any waiver of any of the provisions of this Article shall be deemed void and unenforceable.

(c) The remedies provided in this section are in addition to any other remedies provided for by law or in equity. (1999-416, s. 1.)

§§ 66-308 through 66-310. Reserved for future codification purposes.

Article 40.

Uniform Electronic Transactions Act.

§ 66-311. Short title.

This Article may be cited as the Uniform Electronic Transactions Act. (2000-152, s. 1.)

§ 66-312. Definitions.

As used in this Article, unless the context clearly requires otherwise, the term:

(1)   "Agreement" means the bargain of the parties in fact, as found in their language or inferred from other circumstances and from rules, regulations, and procedures given the effect of agreements under laws otherwise applicable to a particular transaction.

(2)   "Automated transaction" means a transaction conducted or performed, in whole or in part, by electronic means or electronic records, in which the acts or records of one or both parties are not reviewed by an individual in the ordinary course in forming a contract, performing under an existing contract, or fulfilling an obligation required by the transaction.

(3)   "Computer program" means a set of statements or instructions to be used directly or indirectly in an information processing system in order to bring about a certain result.

(4)   "Consumer transaction" means a transaction involving a natural person with respect to or affecting primarily personal, household, or family purposes.

(5)   "Contract" means the total legal obligation resulting from the parties' agreement as affected by this Article and other applicable law.

(6)   "Electronic" means relating to technology having electrical, digital, magnetic, wireless, optical, electromagnetic, or similar capabilities.

(7)   "Electronic agent" means a computer program or an electronic or other automated means used independently to initiate an action or respond to electronic records or performances in whole or in part, without review or action by an individual.

(8)   "Electronic record" means a record created, generated, sent, communicated, received, or stored by electronic means.

(9) "Electronic signature" means an electronic sound, symbol, or process attached to, or logically associated with, a record and executed or adopted by a person with the intent to sign the record.

(10) "Governmental agency" means an executive, legislative, or judicial agency, department, board, commission, authority, institution, or instrumentality of the federal government or of a state or of a county, municipality, or other political subdivision of a state.

(11) "Information" means data, text, images, sounds, codes, computer programs, software, databases, or the like.

(12) "Information processing system" means an electronic system for creating, generating, sending, receiving, storing, displaying, or processing information.

(13) "Person" means an individual, corporation, business trust, estate, trust, partnership, limited liability company, association, joint venture, governmental agency, public corporation, or any other legal or commercial entity.

(14) "Record" means information that is inscribed on a tangible medium or that is stored in an electronic or other medium and is retrievable in perceivable form.

(15) "Security procedure" means a procedure employed for the purpose of verifying that an electronic signature, record, or performance is that of a specific person or for detecting changes or errors in the information in an electronic record. The term includes a procedure that requires the use of algorithms or other codes, identifying words or numbers, encryption, or callback or other acknowledgment procedures.

(16) "State" means a state of the United States, the District of Columbia, Puerto Rico, the United States Virgin Islands, or any territory or insular possession subject to the jurisdiction of the United States. The term includes an Indian tribe or band, or Alaskan native village, which is recognized by federal law or formally acknowledged by a state.

(17) "Transaction" means an action or set of actions occurring between two or more persons relating to the conduct of consumer, business, commercial, or governmental affairs. (2000-152, s. 1; 2001-295, s. 1.)

§ 66-313. Scope.

(a) Except as otherwise provided in subsections (b), (c), and (e) of this section, this Article applies to electronic records and electronic signatures relating to a transaction.

(b) This Article does not apply to a transaction to the extent it is governed by:

(1) A law governing the creation and execution of wills, codicils, or testamentary trusts.

(2) Chapter 25 of the General Statutes other than G.S. 25-1-306, Article 2, and Article 2A.

(3) Article 11A of Chapter 66 of the General Statutes.

(c) This Article applies to an electronic record or electronic signature otherwise excluded from the application of this Article under subsection (b) of this section to the extent it is governed by a law other than those specified in subsection (b) of this section.

(d) A transaction subject to this Article is also subject to other applicable substantive law.

(e) This Article shall not apply to:

(1) Any notice of the cancellation or termination of utility services, including water, heat, and power.

(2) Any notice of default, acceleration, repossession, foreclosure or eviction, or the right to cure, under a credit agreement secured by, or a rental agreement for, a primary residence of an individual.

(3) Any notice of the cancellation or termination of health insurance or benefits, or life insurance or benefits, excluding annuities.

(4) Any notice of the recall of a product, or material failure of a product that risks endangering health or safety.

(5) Any document required to accompany the transportation or handling of hazardous materials, pesticides, or other toxic or dangerous materials. (2000-152, s. 1; 2001-295, s. 2; 2006-112, s. 23.)

§ 66-314. Prospective application.

This Article applies to any electronic record or electronic signature created, generated, sent, communicated, received, or stored on or after the effective date of this Article. (2000-152, s. 1.)

§ 66-315. Use of electronic records and electronic signatures; variation by agreement.

(a) This Article does not require a record or signature to be created, generated, sent, communicated, received, stored, or otherwise processed or used by electronic means or in electronic form.

(b) This Article applies only to transactions between parties each of which has agreed to conduct transactions by electronic means. Whether the parties agree to conduct a transaction by electronic means is determined from the context and surrounding circumstances, including the parties' conduct.

(c) A party that agrees to conduct a transaction by electronic means may refuse to conduct other transactions by electronic means. The right granted by this subsection may not be waived by agreement.

(d) Except as otherwise provided in this Article, the effect of any of its provisions may be varied by agreement. The presence in certain provisions of this Article of the words "unless otherwise agreed", or words of similar import, does not imply that the effect of other provisions may not be varied by agreement.

(e) Whether an electronic record or electronic signature has legal consequences is determined by this Article and other applicable law. (2000-152, s. 1.)

§ 66-316. Construction and application.

This Article must be construed and applied:

(1)   To facilitate electronic transactions consistent with other applicable law;

(2)   To be consistent with reasonable practices concerning electronic transactions and with the continued expansion of those practices; and

(3)   To effectuate its general purpose to make uniform the law with respect to the subject of this act among states enacting it. (2000-152, s. 1.)

§ 66-317. Legal recognition of electronic records, electronic signatures, and electronic contracts.

(a)   A record or signature may not be denied legal effect or enforceability solely because it is in electronic form.

(b)   A contract may not be denied legal effect or enforceability solely because an electronic record was used in its formation.

(c)   If a law requires a record to be in writing, an electronic record satisfies the law provided it complies with the provisions of this Article.

(d)   If a law requires a signature, an electronic signature satisfies the law provided it complies with the provisions of this Article. (2000-152, s. 1.)

§ 66-318. Provision of information in writing; presentation of records.

(a)   If parties have agreed to conduct a transaction by electronic means and a law requires a person to provide, send, or deliver information in writing to another person, the requirement is satisfied if the information is provided, sent, or delivered, as the case may be, in an electronic record capable of retention by the recipient at the time of receipt. An electronic record is not capable of retention by the recipient if:

(1) The sender or its information processing system inhibits the ability of the recipient to print or store the electronic record; or

(2) It is not capable of being accurately reproduced for later reference by all parties or persons who are entitled to retain the contract or other record.

(b) If a law other than this Article requires a record (i) to be posted or displayed in a certain manner, (ii) to be sent, communicated, or transmitted by a specified method, or (iii) to contain information that is formatted in a certain manner, the following rules apply:

(1) The record must be posted or displayed in the manner specified in the other law.

(2) Except as otherwise provided in subdivision (d)(2) of this section, the record must be sent, communicated, or transmitted by the method specified in the other law.

(3) The record must contain the information formatted in the manner specified in the other law.

(c) If a sender inhibits the ability of a recipient to store or print an electronic record, the electronic record is not enforceable against the recipient.

(d) The requirements of this section may not be varied by agreement, but:

(1) To the extent a law other than this act requires information to be provided, sent, or delivered in writing, but permits that requirement to be varied by agreement, the requirement under subsection (a) of this section that the information be in the form of an electronic record capable of retention may also be varied by agreement; and

(2) A requirement under a law other than this Article to send, communicate, or transmit a record by regular United States mail may be varied by agreement to the extent permitted by the other law. (2000-152, s. 1; 2001-295, s. 3.)

§ 66-319. Attribution and effect of electronic record and electronic signature.

(a) An electronic record or electronic signature is attributable to a person if it was the act of the person. The act of the person may be shown in any manner, including a showing of the efficacy of any security procedure applied to determine the person to which the electronic record or electronic signature was attributable.

(b) The effect of an electronic record or electronic signature attributed to a person under subsection (a) of this section is determined from the context and surrounding circumstances at the time of its creation, execution, or adoption, including the parties' agreement, if any, and otherwise as provided by law. (2000-152, s. 1.)

§ 66-320. Effect of change or error.

If a change or error in an electronic record occurs in a transmission between parties to a transaction, the following rules apply:

(1) If the parties have agreed to use a security procedure to detect changes or errors and one party has conformed to the procedure, but the other party has not, and the nonconforming party would have detected the change or error had that party also conformed, the conforming party may avoid the effect of the changed or erroneous electronic record.

(2) In an automated transaction involving an individual, the individual may avoid the effect of an electronic record that resulted from an error made by the individual in dealing with the electronic agent of another person if, at the time the individual learns of the error, the individual:

a. Promptly notifies the other person of the error and that the individual did not intend to be bound by the electronic record received by the other person;

b. Takes reasonable steps, including steps that conform to the other person's reasonable instructions, to return to the other person or, if instructed by the other person, to destroy the consideration received, if any, as a result of the erroneous electronic record; and

c. Has not used or received any benefit or value from the consideration, if any, received from the other person.

(3) If neither subdivision (1) nor subdivision (2) of this section applies, the change or error has the effect provided by other law, including the law of mistake, and the parties' contract, if any.

(4) Subdivisions (2) and (3) of this section may not be varied by agreement. (2000-152, s. 1.)

§ 66-321. Notarization and acknowledgment.

If a law requires a signature or record relating to a transaction to be notarized, acknowledged, verified, or made under oath, the requirement is satisfied if the electronic signature of the person authorized to perform those acts, together with all other information required to be included by other applicable law, is attached to or logically associated with the signature or record. (2000-152, s. 1.)

§ 66-322. Retention of electronic records; originals.

(a) If a law requires that a record be retained, the requirement is satisfied by retaining an electronic record of the information in the record which:

(1) Accurately reflects the information set forth in the record at the time it was first generated in its final form as an electronic record or otherwise; and

(2) Remains accessible for later reference.

(b) A requirement to retain a record in accordance with subsection (a) of this section does not apply to any information the sole purpose of which is to enable the record to be sent, communicated, or received.

(c) A person may satisfy subsection (a) of this section by using the services of another person if the requirements of that subsection are satisfied.

(d) If a law requires a record to be presented or retained in its original form, or provides consequences if the record is not presented or retained in its original form, that law is satisfied by an electronic record retained in accordance with subsection (a) of this section.

(e) If a law requires retention of a check, that requirement is satisfied by retention of an electronic record of the information on the front and back of the check in accordance with subsection (a) of this section.

(f) A record retained as an electronic record in accordance with subsection (a) of this section satisfies a law requiring a person to retain a record for evidentiary, audit, or like purposes, unless a law enacted after the effective date of this Article specifically prohibits the use of an electronic record for the specified purpose.

(g) This section does not preclude a governmental agency of this State from specifying additional requirements for the retention of a record subject to the agency's jurisdiction. (2000-152, s. 1.)

§ 66-323. Admissibility in evidence.

In a proceeding, evidence of a record or signature may not be excluded solely because it is in electronic form. (2000-152, s. 1.)

§ 66-324. Automated transaction.

In an automated transaction, the following rules apply:

(1) A contract may be formed by the interaction of electronic agents of the parties, even if no individual was aware of or reviewed the electronic agents' actions or the resulting terms and agreements.

(2) A contract may be formed by the interaction of an electronic agent and an individual, acting on the individual's own behalf or for another person, including by an interaction in which the individual performs actions that the individual is free to refuse to perform and which the individual knows or has reason to know will cause the electronic agent to complete the transaction or performance.

(3) The terms of the contract are determined by the substantive law applicable to it. (2000-152, s. 1.)

§ 66-325. Time and place of sending and receipt.

(a) Unless otherwise agreed between a sender and a recipient, which in a consumer transaction must be reasonable under the circumstances, an electronic record is sent when it:

(1) Is addressed properly or otherwise directed properly to an information processing system that the recipient has designated or uses for the purpose of receiving electronic records or information of the type sent and from which the recipient is able to retrieve the electronic record;

(2) Is in a form capable of being processed by that system; and

(3) Enters an information processing system outside the control of the sender or of a person that sent the electronic record on behalf of the sender or enters a region of the information processing system designated or used by the recipient which is under the control of the recipient.

(b) Unless otherwise agreed between a sender and a recipient, which in a consumer transaction must be reasonable under the circumstances, an electronic record is received when:

(1) It enters an information processing system that the recipient has designated or uses for the purpose of receiving electronic records or information of the type sent and from which the recipient is able to retrieve the electronic record; and

(2) It is in a form capable of being processed by that system.

(c) Subsection (b) of this section applies even if the place the information processing system is located is different from the place the electronic record is deemed to be received under subsection (d) of this section.

(d) Unless otherwise expressly provided in the electronic record or agreed between the sender and the recipient, an electronic record is deemed to be sent from the sender's place of business and to be received at the recipient's place of business. For purposes of this subsection, the following rules apply:

(1) If the sender or recipient has more than one place of business, the place of business of that person is the place having the closest relationship to the underlying transaction.

(2) If the sender or the recipient does not have a place of business, the place of business is the sender's or recipient's residence, as the case may be.

(e) An electronic record is received under subsection (b) of this section even if no individual is aware of its receipt; provided, however, in a consumer transaction, a record has not been received unless it is received by the intended recipient in a manner in which the sender has a reasonable basis to believe that the record can be opened and read by the recipient.

(f) Receipt of an electronic acknowledgment from an information processing system described in subsection (b) of this section establishes that a record was received but, by itself, does not establish that the content sent corresponds to the content received.

(g) If a person is aware that an electronic record purportedly sent under subsection (a) of this section, or purportedly received under subsection (b) of this section, was not actually sent or received, the legal effect of the sending or receipt is determined by other applicable law. Except to the extent permitted by the other law, the requirements of this subsection may not be varied by agreement. (2000-152, s. 1; 2001-295, s. 4.)

§ 66-326. Transferable records.

(a) In this section, "transferable record" means an electronic record that:

(1) Would be a note under Article 3 of Chapter 25 of the General Statutes or a document under Article 7 of Chapter 25 of the General Statutes if the electronic record were in writing; and

(2) The issuer of the electronic record expressly has agreed is a transferable record.

(b) A person has control of a transferable record if a system employed for evidencing the transfer of interests in the transferable record reliably establishes that person as the person to which the transferable record was issued or transferred.

(c) A system satisfies subsection (b) of this section, and a person is deemed to have control of a transferable record, if the transferable record is created, stored, and assigned in such a manner that:

(1) A single authoritative copy of the transferable record exists which is unique, identifiable, and, except as otherwise provided in subdivisions (4), (5), and (6) of this subsection, unalterable;

(2) The authoritative copy identifies the person asserting control as:

a. The person to which the transferable record was issued; or

b. If the authoritative copy indicates that the transferable record has been transferred, the person to which the transferable record was most recently transferred;

(3) The authoritative copy is communicated to and maintained by the person asserting control or its designated custodian;

(4) Copies or revisions that add or change an identified assignee of the authoritative copy can be made only with the consent of the person asserting control;

(5) Each copy of the authoritative copy and any copy of a copy is readily identifiable as a copy that is not the authoritative copy; and

(6) Any revision of the authoritative copy is readily identifiable as authorized or unauthorized.

(d) Except as otherwise agreed, a person having control of a transferable record is the holder, as defined in G.S. 25-1-201(21), of the transferable record and has the same rights and defenses as a holder of an equivalent record or writing under Chapter 25 of the General Statutes, including, if the applicable statutory requirements under G.S. 25-3-302(a), 25-7-501, or 25-9-330 are satisfied, the rights and defenses of a holder in due course, a holder to which a negotiable document of title has been duly negotiated, or a purchaser, respectively. Delivery, possession, and endorsement are not required to obtain or exercise any of the rights under this subsection.

(e) Except as otherwise agreed, an obligor under a transferable record has the same rights and defenses as an equivalent obligor under equivalent records or writings under Chapter 25 of the General Statutes.

(f) If requested by a person against which enforcement is sought, the person seeking to enforce the transferable record shall provide reasonable proof that the person is in control of the transferable record. Proof may include access to the authoritative copy of the transferable record and related business records sufficient to review the terms of the transferable record and to establish the identity of the person having control of the transferable record. (2000-152, s. 1; 2000-140, s. 97; 2006-112, s. 24.)

§ 66-327. Consumer transactions; alternative procedures for use or acceptance of electronic records or electronic signatures.

(a), (b) Repealed by Session Laws 2001-295, s. 5.

(c) Consent to Electronic Records. - In a consumer transaction in which a statute, regulation, or rule of law of this State requires that information relating to a transaction or transactions in or affecting commerce be made available in writing or be disclosed to a consumer, the consumer's agreement to conduct a transaction by electronic means shall be evidenced as provided in G.S. 66-315, and shall be found only when accomplished in compliance with the following provisions:

(1) The consumer has affirmatively consented to the use of electronic means, and the consumer has not withdrawn consent.

(2) The consumer, prior to consenting to the use of electronic means, is provided with a clear and conspicuous statement:

a. Informing the consumer of any right or option of the consumer to have the record provided or made available on paper or in nonelectronic form.

b. Informing the consumer of the right to withdraw consent to have the record provided or made available in an electronic form and of any conditions or consequences of such withdrawal. Those consequences may include termination of the parties' relationship but may not include the imposition of fees.

c. Informing the consumer of whether the consent to have the record provided or made available in an electronic form applies only to the particular transaction which gave rise to the obligation to provide the record, or to identified categories of records that may be provided or made available during the course of the parties' relationship.

d. Describing the procedures the consumer must use to withdraw consent as provided in sub-subdivision (2)b. of this subsection or to update information needed to contact the consumer electronically.

e. Informing the consumer how, after the consent to have the record provided or made available in an electronic form, the consumer may request and obtain a paper copy of an electronic record.

(3) The consumer, prior to consenting to the use of electronic means, is provided with a statement of the hardware and software requirements for access to and retention of the electronic records; and the consumer consents electronically, or confirms his or her consent electronically, in a manner that reasonably demonstrates that the consumer can access information in the electronic form that will be used to provide the information that is the subject of the consent.

(4) After the consent of a consumer in accordance with subdivision (1) of this subsection, if a change in the hardware or software requirements needed to access or retain electronic records creates a material risk that the consumer will not be able to access or retain a subsequent electronic record that was the subject of the consent, the person providing the electronic record provides the consumer with a statement of the revised hardware and software requirements for access to and retention of the electronic records, provides a statement of the right to withdraw consent without the imposition of any condition or consequence that was not disclosed under sub-subdivision (2)b. of this subsection, and again complies with subdivision (3) of this subsection.

(d) Written Copy Required. - Notwithstanding G.S. 66-315(b), in a consumer transaction in which a statute, regulation, or rule of law of this State requires that information relating to a transaction or transactions be made available in writing or be disclosed to a consumer, where the consumer conducts the transaction on electronic equipment provided by or through the seller, the consumer shall be given a written copy of the contract or disclosure which is not in electronic form. A consumer's consent to receive future notices regarding the transaction in an electronic form is valid only if the consumer confirms electronically, using equipment other than that provided by the seller, that (i) the consumer has the software specified by the seller as necessary to read future notices, and (ii) the consumer agrees to receive the notices in an electronic form.

(e) Oral Communications. - An oral communication or a recording of an oral communication shall not qualify as an electronic record for purposes of this section, except as other provided under applicable law.

(f) Consumer Transaction Entered Into in North Carolina. - If a consumer located in North Carolina enters into a consumer transaction which is created or documented by an electronic record, the transaction shall be deemed to have been entered into in North Carolina for purpose of G.S. 22B-3 which shall apply to the transaction. (2000-152, s. 1; 2001-295, s. 5.)

§ 66-328. Procedures consistent with federal law.

Consistent with the provisions of section 7002(a) of the Electronic Signatures in the Global and National Commerce Act, 15 U.S.C § 7002(a), this Article sets forth alternative procedures or requirements for the use of electronic records to establish the legal effect or validity of records in electronic transactions. (2001-295, s. 6.)

§ 66-329. Choice of law in computer information agreement.

A choice of law provision in a computer information agreement which provides that the contract is to be interpreted pursuant to the laws of a state that has enacted the Uniform Computer Information Transactions Act, as proposed by the National Conference of Commissioners on Uniform State Laws, or any substantially similar law, is voidable and the agreement shall be interpreted pursuant to the laws of this State if the party against whom enforcement of the choice of law provisions is sought is a resident of this State or has its principal place of business located in this State. For purposes of this section, a "computer information agreement" means an agreement that would be governed by the Uniform Computer Information Transactions Act or substantially similar law as enacted in the state specified in the choice of law provisions if that state's law were applied to the agreement. This section may not be varied by agreement of the parties. This section shall remain in force until such time as the North Carolina General Assembly enacts the Uniform Computer Information Transactions Act or any substantially similar law and that law becomes effective. (2001-295, s. 7.)

§ 66-330. Severability clause.

If any provision of this Article or its application to any person or circumstance is held invalid, the invalidity does not affect other provisions or applications of this Article which can be given effect without the invalid provision or application, and to this end the provisions of this Article are severable. (2000-152, s. 1.)

§§ 66-331 through 66-339. Reserved for future codification purposes.

Article 41.

Manufacturing Redevelopment Districts.

§ 66-340: Expired pursuant to Session Laws 2005-462, s. 8, as amended by Session Laws 2006-264, s. 99.5(g), effective September 1, 2008. (2005-462, s. 1.)

§ 66-341: Expired pursuant to Session Laws 2005-462, s. 8, as amended by Session Laws 2006-264, s. 99.5(g), effective September 1, 2008. (2005-462, s. 1.)

§ 66-342: Expired pursuant to Session Laws 2005-462, s. 8, as amended by Session Laws 2006-264, s. 99.5(g), effective September 1, 2008. (2005-462, s. 1.)

§ 66-343: Expired pursuant to Session Laws 2005-462, s. 8, as amended by Session Laws 2006-264, s. 99.5(g), effective September 1, 2008. (2005-462, s. 1.)

§ 66-344: Expired pursuant to Session Laws 2005-462, s. 8, as amended by Session Laws 2006-264, s. 99.5(g), effective September 1, 2008. (2005-462, s. 1.)

§ 66-345: Expired pursuant to Session Laws 2005-462, s. 8, as amended by Session Laws 2006-264, s. 99.5(g), effective September 1, 2008. (2005-462, s. 1.)

§ 66-346: Expired pursuant to Session Laws 2005-462, s. 8, as amended by Session Laws 2006-264, s. 99.5(g), effective September 1, 2008. (2005-462, s. 1.)

§ 66-347. Reserved for future codification purposes.

§ 66-348. Reserved for future codification purposes.

§ 66-349. Reserved for future codification purposes.

Article 42.

State Franchise for Cable Television Service.

§ 66-350. Definitions.

The following definitions apply in this Article:

(1) Cable service. - Defined in G.S. 105-164.3.

(2) Cable system. - Defined in 47 U.S.C. § 522.

(3) Channel. - A portion of the electromagnetic frequency spectrum that is used in a cable system and is capable of delivering a television channel.

(4) Existing agreement. - A local franchise agreement that was awarded under G.S. 153A-137 or G.S. 160A-319 and meets either of the following:

a. Is in effect on January 1, 2007.

b. Expired before January 1, 2007, and the cable service provider under the agreement provides cable service to subscribers in the franchise area on January 1, 2007.

(5) Pass a household. - Make service available to a household, regardless of whether the household subscribes to the service.

(6) PEG channel. - A public, educational, or governmental access channel provided to a county or city.

(7) Secretary. - The Secretary of State.

(8) Video programming. - Defined in G.S. 105-164.3. (2006-151, s. 1.)

§ 66-351. State franchising authority.

(a) Authority. - The Secretary of State is designated the exclusive franchising authority in this State for cable service provided over a cable system. This designation replaces the authorization to counties and cities in former G.S. 153A-137 and G.S. 160A-319 to award a franchise for cable service. This designation is effective January 1, 2007. After this date, a county or city may not award or renew a franchise for cable service.

(b) Award and Scope. - The Secretary is considered to have awarded a franchise to a person who files a notice of franchise under G.S. 66-352. A franchise for cable service authorizes the holder of the franchise to construct and operate a cable system over public rights-of-way within the area to be served. Chapter 160A of the General Statutes governs the regulation of public rights-of-way by a city. (2006-151, s. 1.)

§ 66-352. Award of franchise and commencement of service.

(a) Notice of Franchise. - A person who intends to provide cable service over a cable system in an area must file a notice of franchise with the Secretary before providing the service. A person who files a notice of franchise must pay a fee in the amount set in G.S. 57D-1-22 for filing articles of organization.

A notice of franchise is effective when it is filed with the Secretary. The notice of franchise must include all of the following:

(1) The applicant's name, principal place of business, mailing address, physical address, telephone number, and e-mail address.

(2) A description and map of the area to be served. If the description includes the area within the boundaries of a city, the area to be served is considered to include any area that is subsequently annexed to the city unless the notice limits the area to be served to the boundaries of the city on the effective date of the notice.

(3) A list of each county and city in which the described service area is located, in whole or in part.

(4) A schedule indicating when service is expected to be offered in the service area.

(b) Commencement of Service. - A person who files a notice of franchise under subsection (a) of this section must begin providing cable service in the service area described in the notice within 120 days after the notice is filed. If cable service does not begin within this period, the notice of franchise terminates 130 days after it was filed. If cable service begins within this period, the holder of the State-issued franchise must file a notice of service with the Secretary within 10 days after the cable service begins. Cable service begins when it passes one or more households in the described service area. This subsection does not apply to a cable service provider who terminates an existing agreement whose franchise area includes all of the service area described in a notice of franchise filed by the provider under subsection (a) of this section.

A notice of service for a service area must include all of the following:

(1) The effective date of a notice of franchise for that area.

(2) A description and map of the service area.

(3) A statement that cable service has begun in the service area.

(c) Extension. - A person who intends to provide cable service over a cable system in an area that is contiguous with but outside the service area described in a notice of franchise on file with the Secretary must file a notice of franchise under subsection (a) of this section that includes the proposed area. The initial service requirements in subsection (b) of this section apply to the proposed area. If the map of the area to be served includes any area that is part of the service area of another State-issued franchise, the termination of a notice of franchise for the proposed area for failure to begin service within the required time does not affect the status of the other State-issued franchise.

(d) Withdrawal. - A person may withdraw a notice of franchise by filing a notice of withdrawal with the Secretary. The notice of withdrawal must be filed at least 90 days before the service is withdrawn. (2006-151, s. 1; 2008-148, s. 5; 2013-157, s. 18.)

§ 66-353. Annual service report.

A holder of a State-issued franchise must file an annual service report with the Secretary. The report must be filed on or before July 31 of each year. The report must be accompanied by a fee in the amount set in G.S. 57D-1-22 for filing an annual report. The report must include all of the following:

(1) The effective date of a notice of franchise for that area.

(2) A description and map of the service area.

(3) The approximate number of households in the service area.

(4) A description and a map of the households passed in the service area as of July 1.

(5) The percentage of households passed in the service area as of July 1.

(6) The percentage of households passed in the service area as of July 1 of any preceding year for which a report was required under this section.

(7) A report indicating the extent to which the holder has met the customer service requirements under G.S. 66-356(b).

(8) A schedule indicating when service is expected to be offered in the service area, to the extent the schedule differs from one included in the notice of franchise or in a report previously submitted under this section, and an explanation of the reason for the new schedule. (2006-151, s. 1; 2013-157, s. 19.)

§ 66-354. General filing and report requirements.

(a) General. - A document filed with the Secretary under this Article must be signed by an officer or general partner of the person submitting the document. Within five days after a person files a document with the Secretary under this Article, the person must send a copy of the document to any county or city included in the service area described in the document and to the registered agent of any cable service provider that is providing cable service under an existing agreement in the service area described in the document.

The provisions of Article 2 of Chapter 55D of the General Statutes apply to the submission of a document under this Article. A document filed under this Article is a public record as defined in G.S. 132-1. The Secretary must post a document filed under this Article on its Internet Web site or indicate on its Internet Web site that the document has been filed and is available for inspection.

A successor in interest to a person who has filed a notice of franchise is not required to file another notice of franchise. When a change in ownership occurs, the owner must file a notice of change in ownership with the Secretary within 14 days after the change becomes effective.

(b) Forfeiture. - A person who offers cable service over a cable system without filing a notice of franchise or a notice of service as required by this Article is subject to forfeiture of the revenue received during the period of noncompliance from subscribers to the cable service in the area of noncompliance. Forfeiture does not apply to revenue received from cable service provided over a cable system in an area that is adjacent to a service area described in a notice of franchise and notice of service filed by that cable service provider under G.S. 66-352 if the provider obtains a State-issued franchise and files a notice of service that includes this area within 20 days after a civil action for forfeiture is filed. A forfeiture does not affect the liability of the cable service provider for sales tax due under G.S. 105-164.4 on cable service.

A cable service provider whose area includes the area in which a person is providing cable service without complying with the notice of franchise and notice of service requirements may bring a civil action for forfeiture. The amount required to be forfeited in the action must be remitted to the Civil Penalty and Forfeiture Fund established in G.S. 115C-457.2. (2006-151, s. 1.)

§ 66-355. Effect on existing local franchise agreement.

(a) Existing Agreement. - This Article does not affect an existing agreement except as follows:

(1) Effective January 1, 2007, gross revenue used to calculate the payment of the franchise tax imposed by G.S. 153A-154 or G.S. 160A-214 does not include gross receipts from cable service subject to sales tax under G.S. 105-164.4. This exclusion does not otherwise affect the calculation of gross revenue and the payment to counties and cities of franchise tax revenue under existing agreements that have not been terminated under subsection (b) of this section.

(2) A cable service provider under an existing agreement that is in effect on January 1, 2007, may terminate the agreement in accordance with subsection (b) of this section in any of the following circumstances:

a. A notice of service filed under G.S. 66-352 indicates that one or more households in the franchise area of the existing agreement are passed by both the cable service provider under the existing agreement and the holder of a State-issued franchise.

b. As of January 1, 2007, a county or city has an existing agreement with more than one cable service provider for substantially the same franchise area and at least twenty-five percent (25%) of the households in the franchise areas of the existing agreements are passed by more than one cable service provider.

c. A person provides wireline competition in the franchise area of the existing agreement by offering video programming over wireline facilities to single family households by a method that does not require a franchise under this Article. A notice of termination filed on the basis of wireline competition must include evidence of the competition in providing video programming service, such as an advertisement announcing the availability of the service, the acceptance of an order for the service, and information on the provider's Web site about the availability of the service. A county or city is allowed 60 days to review the evidence. The effective date of the termination is tolled during this review period. At the end of this period, the termination proceeds unless the county or city has obtained an order enjoining the termination based on the cable service provider's failure to establish the existence of wireline competition in its franchise area.

(3) A cable service provider under an existing agreement that expired before January 1, 2007, may obtain a State-issued franchise. The provider does not have to terminate the agreement in accordance with subsection (b) of this section because the agreement has expired.

(b) Termination. - To terminate an existing agreement, a cable service provider must file a notice of termination with the affected county or city and file a notice of franchise with the Secretary. A termination of an existing agreement becomes effective at the end of the month in which the notice of termination is filed with the affected county or city. A termination of an existing agreement ends the obligations under the agreement and under any local cable regulatory ordinance that specifically authorizes the agreement as of the effective date of the termination but does not affect the rights or liabilities of the county or city, a taxpayer, or another person arising under the existing agreement or local ordinance before the effective date of the termination. (2006-151, s. 1.)

§ 66-356. Service standards and requirements.

(a) Discrimination Prohibited. - A person who provides cable service over a cable system may not deny access to the service to any group of potential residential subscribers within the filed service area because of the race or income of the residents. A violation of this subsection is an unfair or deceptive act or practice under G.S. 75-1.1.

In determining whether a cable service provider has violated this subsection with respect to a group of potential residential subscribers in a service area, the following factors must be considered:

(1) The length of time since the provider filed the notice of service for the area. If less than a year has elapsed since the notice of service was filed, it is conclusively presumed that a violation has not occurred.

(2) The cost of providing service to the affected group due to distance from facilities, density, or other factors.

(3) Technological impediments to providing service to the affected group.

(4) Inability to obtain access to property required to provide service to the affected group.

(5) Competitive pressure to respond to service offered by another cable service provider or other provider of video programming.

(b) FCC Standards. - A person who provides cable service over a cable system must comply with the customer service requirements in 47 C.F.R. Part 76 and emergency alert requirements established by the Federal Communications Commission.

(c) Complaints. - The Consumer Protection Division of the Attorney General's Office is designated as the State agency to receive and respond to customer complaints concerning cable services. Persistent or repeated violations of the federal customer service requirements or the terms and conditions of the cable service provider's agreement with customers are unfair or deceptive acts or practices under G.S. 75-1.1.

To facilitate the resolution of customer complaints, the cable service provider must include the following statement on the customer's bill: "If you have a complaint about your cable service, you should first contact customer service at the following telephone number: (insert the cable service provider's customer service telephone number). If the cable service provider does not satisfactorily resolve your complaint, contact the Consumer Protection Division of the Attorney General's Office of the State of North Carolina (insert information on how to contact the Consumer Protection Division of the Attorney General's Office).

(d)   No Build-Out. - No build-out requirements apply to a person who provides cable service under a State-issued franchise.

(e)   [Report to Revenue Laws Study Committee. -] The Consumer Protection Division of the Attorney General's Office must report to the Revenue Laws Study Committee on or before April 1 of each year, beginning April 1, 2008, on the following information concerning cable service complaints the Division has received from cable customers under this section:

(1)   The number of customer complaints.

(2)   The types of customer complaints.

(3)   The different means of resolving customer complaints. (2006-151, ss. 1, 18.)

§ 66-357. Availability and use of PEG channels.

(a)   Application. - This section applies to a person who provides cable service under a State-issued franchise. It does not apply to a person who provides cable service under an existing agreement.

(b)   Local Request. - A county or city must make a written request to a cable service provider for PEG channel capacity. The request must include a statement describing the county's or city's plan to operate and program each channel requested. The cable service provider must provide the requested PEG channel capacity within the later of the following:

(1)   120 days after the cable service provider receives the written request.

(2)   30 days after any interconnection requested under G.S. 66-358(a)(1) is accomplished.

(c) Initial PEG Channels. - A city with a population of at least 50,000 is allowed a minimum of three initial PEG channels plus any channels in excess of this minimum that are activated, as of July 1, 2006, under the terms of an existing franchise agreement whose franchise area includes the city. A city with a population of less than 50,000 is allowed a minimum of two initial PEG channels plus any channels in excess of this minimum that are activated, as of July 1, 2006, under the terms of an existing franchise agreement whose franchise area includes the city. For a city included in the franchise area of an existing agreement, the agreement determines the service tier placement and transmission quality of the initial PEG channels. For a city that is not included in the franchise area of an existing agreement, the initial PEG channels must be on a basic service tier, and the transmission quality of the channels must be equivalent to those of the closest city covered by an existing agreement.

A county is allowed a minimum of two initial PEG channels plus any channels in excess of this minimum that are activated, as of July 1, 2006, under the terms of an existing franchise agreement whose franchise area includes the county. For a county included in the franchise area of an existing agreement, the agreement determines the service tier placement and transmission quality of the initial PEG channels. For a county that is not included in the franchise area of an existing agreement, the initial PEG channels must be on a basic service tier and the transmission quality of the channels must be equivalent to those of any city with PEG channels in the county.

The cable service provider must maintain the same channel designation for a PEG channel unless the service area of the State-issued franchise includes PEG channels that are operated by different counties or cities and those PEG channels have the same channel designation. Each county and city whose PEG channels are served by the same cable system headend must cooperate with each other and with the cable system provider in sharing the capacity needed to provide the PEG channels.

(d) Additional PEG Channels. - A county or city that does not have seven PEG channels, including the initial PEG channels, is eligible for an additional PEG channel if it meets the programming requirements in this subsection. A county or city that has seven PEG channels is not eligible for an additional channel.

A county or city that meets the programming requirements in this subsection may make a written request under subsection (b) of this section for an additional channel. The additional channel may be provided on any service tier. The transmission quality of the additional channel must be at least equivalent to the transmission quality of the other channels provided.

The PEG channels operated by a county or city must meet the following programming requirements for at least 120 continuous days in order for the county or city to obtain an additional channel:

(1)   All of the PEG channels must have scheduled programming for at least eight hours a day.

(2)   The programming content of each of the PEG channels must not repeat more than fifteen percent (15%) of the programming content on any of the other PEG channels.

(3)   No more than fifteen percent (15%) of the programming content on any of the PEG channels may be character-generated programming.

(e)   Use of Channels. - If a county or city no longer provides any programming for transmission over a PEG channel it has activated, the channel may be reprogrammed at the cable service provider's discretion. A cable service provider must give at least a 60-day notice to a county or city before it reprograms a PEG channel that is not used. The cable service provider must restore a previously lost PEG channel within 120 days of the date a county or city certifies to the provider a schedule that demonstrates the channel will be used.

(f)   Operation of Channels. - A cable service provider is responsible only for the transmission of a PEG channel. The county or city to which the PEG channel is provided is responsible for the operation and content of the channel. A county or city that provides content to a cable service provider for transmission on a PEG channel is considered to have authorized the provider to transmit the content throughout the provider's service area, regardless of whether part of the service area is outside the boundaries of the county or city.

All programming on a PEG channel must be noncommercial. A cable service provider may not brand content on a PEG channel with its logo, name, or other identifying marks. A cable service provider is not required to transmit content on a PEG channel that is branded with the logo, name, or other identifying marks of another cable service provider.

(g) Compliance. - A county or city that has not received PEG channel capacity as required by this section may bring an action to compel a cable service provider to comply with this section. (2006-151, s. 1.)

§ 66-358. Transmission of PEG channels.

(a) Service. - A cable service provider operating under a State-issued franchise must transmit a PEG channel by one of the following methods:

(1) Interconnection with another cable system operated in its service area. A cable service provider operating in the same service area as a provider under a State-issued franchise must interconnect its cable system on reasonable and competitively neutral terms with the other provider's cable system within 120 days after it receives a written request for interconnection and may not refuse to interconnect on these terms. The terms include compensation for costs incurred in interconnecting. Interconnection may be accomplished by direct cable, microwave link, satellite, or another method of connection.

(2) Transmission of the signal from each PEG channel programmer's origination site, if the origination site is in the provider's service area.

(b) Signal. - All PEG channel programming provided to a cable service provider for transmission must meet the federal National Television System Committee standards or the Advanced Television Systems Committee Standards. If a PEG channel programmer complies with these standards and the cable service provider cannot transmit the programming without altering the transmission signal, then the cable service provider must do one of the following:

(1) Alter the transmission signal to make it compatible with the technology or protocol the cable service provider uses to deliver its cable service.

(2) Provide to the county or city the equipment needed to alter the transmission signal to make it compatible with the technology or protocol the cable service provider uses to deliver its cable service. (2006-151, s. 1.)

§ 66-359: Repealed by Session Laws 2010-158, s. 11(a), effective July 1, 2010.

§ 66-360. Service to public building.

At the written request of a county or city, a cable service provider operating under a State-issued franchise must provide cable service without charge to a public building located within 125 feet of the provider's cable system. The required service is the basic, or lowest-priced, service the provider offers to customers. The terms and conditions that apply to service provided to a residential retail customer apply to the service provided to the public building. Only one service outlet is required for a building. The cable service provider is not required to provide inside wiring and is not required to provide service that conflicts with restrictions that apply in a program licensing agreement or another contract. A public building is a building used as a public school, a charter school, a county or city library, or a function of the county or city. (2006-151, s. 1.)

Article 43.

Service Agreements.

§ 66-370. Motor vehicle service agreement companies.

(a)   This section applies to all motor vehicle service agreement companies soliciting business in this State, but it does not apply to performance guarantees, warranties, or motor vehicle service agreements made by

(1)   A manufacturer,

(2)   A distributor, or

(3)   A subsidiary or affiliate of a manufacturer or a distributor, where fifty-one percent (51%) or more of the subsidiary or affiliate is owned directly or indirectly by

a.   The manufacturer,

b. The distributor, or

c. The common owner of fifty-one percent (51%) or more of the manufacturer or distributor

in connection with the sale of motor vehicles. This section does not apply to any motor vehicle dealer licensed to do business in this State (i) whose primary business is the retail sale and service of motor vehicles; (ii) who makes and administers its own service agreements with or without association with a third-party administrator or who makes its own service agreements in association with a manufacturer, distributor, or their subsidiaries or affiliates; and (iii) whose service agreements cover only vehicles sold by the dealer to its retail customer; provided that the dealer complies with G.S. 66-372 and G.S. 66-373. A motor vehicle dealer who sells a motor vehicle service agreement to a consumer, as defined in 15 U.S.C. § 2301(3), is not deemed to have made a written warranty to the consumer with respect to the motor vehicle sold or to have entered into a service contract with the consumer that applies to the motor vehicle, as provided in 15 U.S.C. § 2308(a), if: (i) the motor vehicle dealer acts as a mere agent of a third party in selling the motor vehicle service agreement; and (ii) the motor vehicle dealer would, after the sale of the motor vehicle service agreement, have no further obligation under the motor vehicle service agreement to the consumer to service or repair the vehicle sold to the consumer at or within 90 days before the dealer sold the motor vehicle service agreement to the consumer.

(b) The following definitions apply in this section and in G.S. 66-371, 66-372, and 66-373:

(1) Authorized insurer. - An insurance company authorized to write liability insurance under Articles 7, 16, 21, or 22 of Chapter 58 of the General Statutes.

(2) Distributor. - Defined in G.S. 20-286(3).

(3) Licensed insurer. - An insurance company licensed to write liability insurance under Article 7 or 16 of Chapter 58 of the General Statutes.

(4) Motor vehicle. - Defined in G.S. 20-4.01(23), but also including mopeds as defined in G.S. 20-4.01(27)d1.

(5) Motor vehicle service agreement. - Any contract or agreement indemnifying the motor vehicle service agreement holder against loss caused by failure, arising out of the ownership, operation, or use of a motor vehicle, of a mechanical or other component part of the motor vehicle that is listed in the agreement. The term does not mean a contract or agreement guaranteeing the performance of parts or lubricants manufactured by the guarantor and sold for use in connection with a motor vehicle where no additional consideration is paid or given to the guarantor for the contract or agreement beyond the price of the parts or lubricants.

(6) Motor vehicle service agreement company. - Any person that issues motor vehicle service agreements and that is not a licensed insurer.

(c) through (g) Repealed by Session Laws 1993 (Reg. Sess., 1994), c. 730, s. 3. (1991 (Reg. Sess., 1992), c. 1014, s. 1; 1993, c. 504, ss. 47, 48, 52; c. 539, s. 442; 1994, Ex. Sess., c. 24, s. 14(c); 1993 (Reg. Sess., 1994), c. 730, ss. 3, 4; 1995, c. 193, s. 3; 2007-95, ss. 2, 9.)

§ 66-371. Home appliance service agreement companies.

(a) This section applies to all home appliance service agreement companies soliciting business in this State, but it does not apply to performance guarantees or warranties made by manufacturers in connection with the sale of new home appliances. This section does not apply to any home appliance dealer licensed to do business in this State (i) whose primary business is the retail sale and service of home appliances; (ii) who makes and administers its own service agreements without association with any other entity; and (iii) whose service agreements cover primarily appliances sold by the dealer to its retail customers, provided that the dealer complies with G.S. 66-372 and G.S. 66-373. This section does not apply to any warranty made by a builder or seller of real property relating to home appliances that are sold along with real property. This section does not apply to any issuer of credit cards or charge cards that markets home appliance service agreements as an ancillary part of its business; provided, however, that such issuer maintains insurance in accordance with G.S. 66-373.

(b) The following definitions apply in this section:

(1) "Home appliance" means a clothes washing machine or dryer; kitchen appliance; vacuum cleaner; sewing machine; home audio or video electronic equipment; home electronic data processing equipment; home exercise and fitness equipment; home health care equipment; power tools; heater or air conditioner, other than a permanently installed unit using internal ductwork; or other personal consumer goods.

(2) "Home appliance service agreement" means any contract or agreement indemnifying the home appliance service agreement holder against loss caused by failure, arising out of the ownership, operation, or use of a home appliance, of a mechanical or other component part of the home appliance that is listed in the agreement.

(3) "Home appliance service agreement company" means any person that issues home appliance service agreements and that is not a licensed insurer.

(c) through (g) Repealed by Session Laws 1993 (Reg. Sess., 1994), c. 730, s. 3. (1991 (Reg. Sess., 1992), c. 1014, s. 1; 1993, c. 504, ss. 49, 52; c. 539, s. 443; 1994, Ex. Sess., c. 24, s. 14(c); 1993 (Reg. Sess., 1994), c. 730, ss. 3, 4, 6; 2003-290, s. 1(b); 2007-95, ss. 3, 10.)

§ 66-372. Miscellaneous requirements for motor vehicle and home appliance service agreement companies.

(a) The provisions of this section and G.S. 66-373 apply to companies specified in G.S. 66-370 and G.S. 66-371.

(b) The following definitions apply in this section and in G.S. 66-373:

(1) Service agreement. - Includes motor vehicle service agreements and home appliance service agreements.

(2) Service agreement company. - Includes motor vehicle service agreement companies and home appliance service agreement companies.

(c) Before the sale of any service agreement, the service agreement company shall give written notice to the customer clearly disclosing that the purchase of the agreement is not required either to purchase or to obtain financing for a motor vehicle or home appliance, as the case may be.

(d) No service agreement may be used in this State by any service agreement company if the agreement:

(1) In any respect violates, or does not comply with, the laws of this State;

(2) Contains, or incorporates by reference when incorporation is otherwise permissible, any inconsistent, ambiguous, or misleading clauses or any exceptions and conditions that deceptively affect the risk purported to be assumed in the general coverage of the agreement;

(3) Has any title, heading, or other indication of its provisions that is misleading; or

(4) Is printed or otherwise reproduced in a manner that renders any material provision of the agreement substantially illegible.

(e) All service agreements used in this State by a service agreement company shall:

(1) Not contain provisions that allow the company to cancel the agreement in its discretion other than for nonpayment of premiums or for a direct violation of the agreement by the consumer where the service agreement states that violation of the agreement would subject the agreement to cancellation;

(2) With respect to a motor vehicle service agreement as defined in G.S. 66-370(b)(1), provide for a right of assignability by the consumer to a subsequent purchaser before expiration of coverage if the subsequent purchaser meets the same criteria for motor vehicle service agreement acceptability as the original purchaser; and

(3) Contain a cancellation provision allowing the consumer to cancel at any time after purchase and receive a pro rata refund less any claims paid on the agreement and a reasonable administrative fee, not to exceed ten percent (10%) of the amount of the pro rata refund.

(f) Each service agreement company, as a minimum requirement for permanent office records, shall maintain:

(1)   A complete set of accounting records, including a general ledger, cash receipts and disbursements journals, accounts receivable registers, and accounts payable registers.

(2)   Memorandum journals showing the service agreement forms issued to the company salespersons and recording the delivery of the forms to dealers.

(3)   Memorandum journals showing the service agreement forms received by dealers and indicating the disposition of the forms by the dealers.

(4)   A detailed service agreement register, in numerical order by agreement number, of agreements in force. The register shall include the following: agreement number, date of issue, issuing dealer, name of agreement holder, description of item covered, service agreement period (and, if applicable, mileage), gross premium, total commission paid, and net premium.

(5)   A detailed claims register, in numerical order by service agreement number. The register shall include the following information: agreement number, date of issue, date claim paid, and, if applicable, disposition other than payment and reason for the disposition.

(g)   Repealed by Session Laws 1993 (Reg. Sess., 1994), c. 730, s. 3.

(h)   No insurer or service agreement company shall act as a fronting company for any unauthorized insurer or service agreement company that is not in compliance with this section. As used in this subsection, "fronting company" means a licensed insurer or service agreement company that, by reinsurance or otherwise, generally transfers to one or more unauthorized insurers or service agreement companies that are not in compliance with this section a substantial portion of the risk of loss under agreements it writes in this State.

(i)   All funds belonging to insurers, companies, or others received by a salesperson of a service agreement are trust funds received by the salesperson in a fiduciary capacity; and the salesperson, in the applicable regular course of business, shall account for and pay the funds to the person entitled to the funds. Any salesperson who, not being entitled to the funds, diverts or appropriates the funds or any portion of the funds, other than funds representing the salesperson's commission if authorized by the salesperson agreement, to his or her own use, upon conviction is guilty of embezzlement under G.S. 14-90.

(j) Any person who knowingly offers for sale or sells a service agreement for a company that has failed to comply with the provisions of this section is guilty of a Class 1 misdemeanor. All service agreement companies and individuals selling service agreements are subject to G.S. 75-1 through G.S. 75-19.

(k) Repealed by Session Laws 1993 (Reg. Sess., 1994), c. 730, s. 2.

(l) No service agreement company shall use in its name, contracts, literature, advertising in any medium, or any other printed matter the words "insurance", "casualty", "surety", "mutual", or any other words descriptive of the insurance business or deceptively similar to the name or description of any insurer doing business in this State, except to indicate that the obligations of the contract are insured by an insurance company.

(m) Repealed by Session Laws 2007-95, s. 11. (1991 (Reg. Sess., 1992), c. 1014, s. 1; 1993, c. 504, ss. 50, 51, 52; c. 539, s. 444; 1994, Ex. Sess., c. 24, s. 14(c); 1993 (Reg. Sess., 1994), c. 730, ss. 2, 3, 5; 1995, c. 193, ss. 4, 5; 2003-290, s. 2; 2007-95, ss. 4, 11.)

§ 66-373. Insurance policy requirements.

(a) Each company or person subject to this section shall maintain contractual liability insurance or service agreement reimbursement insurance with an authorized insurer for one hundred percent (100%) of claims exposure, including reported and incurred but not reported claims and claims expenses, on business written in this State unless the company or person complies with all of the following:

(1) Maintains an audited net worth of one hundred million dollars ($100,000,000).

(2) Has offered service agreement contracts or warranties, as applicable to the respective company, its parent company, or person, for at least the preceding 10 years.

(3) Either is required to file and has filed an SEC Form 10K or Form 20-F with the Securities and Exchange Commission (SEC) within the last calendar year or, if the company does not file with the SEC, can produce, upon request, a copy of the company's audited financial statements, which show a net worth of the company or person of at least one hundred million dollars ($100,000,000). A

company or person may utilize its parent company's Form 10-K, Form 20-F, or audited financial statements to satisfy this requirement if the parent company agrees to guarantee the obligations of the company or person relating to service agreement contracts or warranties, as applicable to the respective company or person, sold by the company or person in this State.

In lieu of complying with subdivisions (1), (2), and (3) of this subsection, the company or person may maintain a funded reserve account for the purpose of meeting its obligations under contracts issued and outstanding in this State. The reserves shall not be less than forty percent (40%) of gross consideration received, less claims paid, on the sale of the service contract for all in-force contracts.

(b) All forms relating to insurance policies written by authorized insurers under this section shall be filed with and approved by the Commissioner of Insurance before they may be used for any purpose in this State, irrespective of whether the insurers are licensed insurers.

(c) Each policy shall contain the following provisions:

(1) If the company or person does not fulfill its obligations under service agreements or warranties issued in this State for any reason, including federal bankruptcy or state receivership proceedings, the insurer will pay losses and unearned premium refunds directly to any person making the claim under the service agreement.

(2) The insurer shall assume full responsibility for the administration of claims if the company or person is unable to do so.

(3) The policy is subject to the cancellation, nonrenewal, and renewal provisions of G.S. 58-41-15, 58-41-20, 58-41-25, and 58-41-40.

(4) The policy shall insure all service agreements and warranties that were issued while the policy was in effect, regardless of whether the premium was remitted to the insurer.

(5) If the insurer is fulfilling any service agreement covered by the policy and if the service agreement holder cancels the service agreement, the insurer shall make a full refund of the unearned premium to the consumer pursuant to G.S. 66-372(e)(3). This subdivision applies only to service agreement companies.

(d) The Commissioner of Insurance may adopt rules, in addition to the requirements of this section, governing the terms and conditions of policy forms for the insurance required by this section.

(e) Persons and companies subject to G.S. 58-1-15, 58-1-20, 66-370, 66-371, and 66-374 are subject to and shall comply with this section. (1993 (Reg. Sess., 1994), c. 730, s. 1; 2003-290, s. 1(c); 2007-95, ss. 5, 12; 2011-222, s. 1.)

§ 66-374. Mechanical breakdown service agreements.

(a) Except as provided in subsection (c) of this section, all mechanical breakdown service agreement companies soliciting business in this State shall comply with G.S. 66-372 and G.S. 66-373.

(b) As used in this section, "mechanical breakdown service agreement companies" include any person that issues mechanical breakdown service agreements and is not a licensed insurer, and "mechanical breakdown service agreements" are applicable to mechanized equipment, including automobiles, riding mowers, scooters, generators, farm implements, logging equipment, road graders, bulldozers, and power equipment not licensed for road use, whether mobile or not.

(c) This section does not apply to performance guarantees, warranties, mechanical breakdown service agreements, or motor vehicle service agreements made by:

(1) A manufacturer.

(2) A distributor.

(3) A subsidiary of a manufacturer or distributor. (2003-290, s. 4; 2007-95, ss. 6, 13.)

§ 66-375: Reserved for future codification purposes.

§ 66-376: Reserved for future codification purposes.

§ 66-377: Reserved for future codification purposes.

§ 66-378: Reserved for future codification purposes.

§ 66-379: Reserved for future codification purposes.

Article 44.

Free Insurance.

§ 66-380. Definitions.

As used in this Article:

(1)   "Consumer goods" means goods that are used primarily for personal, family, or household purposes. For the purposes of this Article, consumer goods do not include automobiles or residences.

(2)   "Free insurance" means any of the following:

a.   Insurance for which no identifiable or additional charge is made to the purchaser or lessee of consumer goods or services directly or indirectly connected with the purchase of consumer goods.

b.   Insurance for which an identifiable or additional charge is made in an amount less than the cost of such insurance as to the seller, lessor, or other person other than the insurer providing the insurance. (2008-124, s. 9.1.)

§ 66-381. Free insurance.

No person shall advertise, offer, or provide free insurance for damage, loss, or theft as an inducement to the purchase, sale, or rental of consumer goods or services directly or indirectly connected with the purchase of consumer goods. (2008-124, s. 9.1.)

§ 66-382. Unfair trade practice.

A violation of G.S. 66-381 constitutes an unfair trade practice under G.S. 75-1.1. (2008-124, s. 9.1.)

Article 45.

Pawnbrokers, Metal Dealers, and Scrap Dealers.

Part 1. Pawnbrokers and Cash Converters.

§ 66-385. Short title.

This Part shall be known and may be cited as the Pawnbrokers and Cash Converters Modernization Act. (1989, c. 638, s. 2; 2011-325, s. 2; 2012-46, ss. 2, 4.)

§ 66-386. Purpose.

The making of pawn loans and the acquisition and disposition of tangible personal property by and through pawnshops and cash converters vitally affects the general economy of this State and the public interest and welfare of its citizens. In recognition of these facts, it is the policy of this State and the purpose of the Pawnbrokers and Cash Converters Modernization Act to do all of the following:

(1) Ensure a sound system of making loans and acquiring and disposing of tangible personal property by and through pawnshops, and to prevent unlawful

property transactions, particularly in stolen property, through licensing and regulating pawnbrokers.

(2) Ensure a sound system of acquiring and disposing of tangible personal property by and through cash converters and to prevent unlawful property transactions, particularly in stolen property, by requiring record keeping by cash converters.

(3) Provide for pawnbroker licensing fees and investigation fees of licensees.

(4) Ensure financial responsibility to the State and the general public.

(5) Ensure compliance with federal and State laws.

(6) Assist local governments in the exercise of their police authority. (1989, c. 638, s. 2; 2011-325, s. 3; 2012-46, ss. 2, 5.)

§ 66-387. Definitions.

The following definitions apply in this Part:

(1) Cash. - Lawful currency of the United States.

(2) Currency converter. - A person engaged in the business of purchasing goods from the public for cash at a permanently located retail store who holds himself or herself out to the public by signs, advertising, or other methods as engaging in that business. The term does not include any of the following:

a. Pawnbrokers.

b. Persons whose goods purchases are made directly from manufacturers or wholesalers for their inventories.

c. Precious metals dealers, to the extent that their transactions are regulated under Part 2 of this Article.

d. Purchases by persons primarily in the business of obtaining from the public, either by purchase or exchange, used clothing, children's furniture, and children's products, provided the amount paid for the individual item purchased is less than fifty dollars ($50.00).

 e. Purchases by persons primarily in the business of obtaining from the public, either by purchase or exchange, sporting goods and sporting equipment, provided the amount paid for the individual item purchased is less than fifty dollars ($50.00).

(3) Pawn or pawn transaction. - A written bailment of personal property as security for a debt, redeemable on certain terms within 180 days, unless renewed, and with an implied power of sale on default.

(4) Pawnbroker. - A person engaged in the business of lending money on the security of pledged goods and who may also purchase merchandise for resale from dealers and traders.

(5) Pawnshop. - The location at which, or premises in which, a pawnbroker regularly conducts business.

(6) Person. - Any individual, corporation, joint venture, association, or any other legal entity, however organized.

(7) Pledged goods. - Tangible personal property which is deposited with, or otherwise actually delivered into, the possession of a pawnbroker in the course of his business in connection with a pawn transaction.

(8) Purchase. - An item purchased from an individual for the purpose of resale whereby the seller no longer has a vested interest in the item. (1989, c. 638, s. 2; 2011-325, s. 4; 2012-46, ss. 2, 6; 2013-410, s. 26.)

§ 66-388. Pawnbroker authority.

A pawnbroker licensee is authorized to: (i) make loans on pledges of tangible personal property, (ii) deal in bullion stocks, (iii) purchase merchandise for resale from dealers, traders, and wholesale suppliers and (iv) use its capital and funds in any lawful manner within the general scope and purpose of its creation. Notwithstanding the provisions of this section, no pawnbroker has the authority enumerated in this section unless he has fully complied with the laws regulating the particular transactions involved. (1989, c. 638, s. 2; 2012-46, s. 2.)

§ 66-389. License required.

It is unlawful for any person, firm, or corporation to establish or conduct a business of pawnbroker unless such person, firm, or corporation has procured a license to conduct business in compliance with the requirements of this Part. (1989, c. 638, s. 2; 2012-46, ss. 2, 7.)

§ 66-390. Requirements for licensure.

(a)   To be eligible for a pawnbroker's license, an applicant must:

(1)   Be of good moral character; and

(2)   Not have been convicted of a felony within the last 10 years.

(b)   Every person, firm or corporation desiring to engage in the business of pawnbroker shall petition the appropriate city or county agency in the area in which the pawnshop is to be operated for a license to conduct such business. Such petitions shall provide:

(1)   The name and address of the person, and, in case of a firm or corporation, the names and addresses of the persons composing such firm or of the officers, directors, and stockholders of such corporation, excluding shareholders of publicly traded companies;

(2)   The name of the business and the street and mailing address where the business is to be operated;

(3)   A statement indicating the amount of net assets or capital proposed to be used by the petitioner in operation of the business; this statement shall be accompanied by an unaudited statement from an accountant or certified public accountant verifying the information contained in the accompanying statement;

(4)   An affidavit by the petitioner that he has not been convicted of a felony; and

(5) A certificate from the chief of police, or sheriff of the county, or the State Bureau of Investigation that the petitioner has not been convicted of a felony.

(c) Licenses shall be granted under this Part by the city if the pawnshop is to be operated within the corporate limits of a city as defined by G.S. 160A-1, and by a county if it is to be operated outside the corporate limits of any city as defined by G.S. 160A-1.

(d) Any license granted under this Part may be revoked by the county or city issuing it, after a hearing, for substantial abuses of this Part by the licensee. (1989, c. 638, s. 2; 2012-46, ss. 2, 8.)

§ 66-391. Record-keeping requirements for pawnbrokers.

(a) Every pawnbroker shall keep consecutively numbered records of each and every pawn transaction, which shall correspond in all essential particulars to a detachable pawn ticket or copy thereof attached to the record.

(b) The pawnbroker shall, at the time of making the pawn or purchase transaction, enter upon the pawn ticket a record of the following information which shall be typed or written in ink and in the English language:

(1) A clear and accurate description of the property, including model and serial number if indicated on the property;

(2) The name, residence address, phone number, and date of birth of pledgor;

(3) Date of the pawn transaction;

(4) Type of identification and the identification number accepted from pledgor;

(5) Description of the pledgor including approximate height, weight, sex, and race;

(6) Amount of money advanced;

(7) The date due and the amount due;

(8) All monthly pawn charges, including interest, annual percentage rate on interest, and total recovery fee; and

(9) Agreed upon "stated value" between pledgor and pawnbroker in case of loss or destruction of pledged item; unless otherwise noted, "stated value" is the same as the loan value.

(c) The following shall be printed on all pawn tickets:

(1) The statement that "ANY PERSONAL PROPERTY PLEDGED TO A PAWNBROKER WITHIN THIS STATE IS SUBJECT TO SALE OR DISPOSAL WHEN THERE HAS BEEN NO PAYMENT MADE ON THE ACCOUNT FOR A PERIOD OF 60 DAYS PAST MATURITY DATE OF THE ORIGINAL CONTRACT. NO FURTHER NOTICE IS NECESSARY.";

(2) The statement that "THE PLEDGOR OF THIS ITEM ATTESTS THAT IT IS NOT STOLEN, HAS NO LIENS OR ENCUMBRANCES, AND IS THE PLEDGOR'S TO SELL OR PAWN.";

(3) The statement that "THE ITEM PAWNED IS REDEEMABLE ONLY BY THE BEARER OF THIS TICKET OR BY IDENTIFICATION OF THE PERSON MAKING THE PAWN."; and

(4) A blank line for the pledgor's signature and the pawnbroker's signature or initials.

(d) The pledgor shall sign the pawn ticket and shall receive an exact copy of the pawn ticket which shall be signed or initialed by the pawnbroker or any employee of the pawnbroker. These records shall be available for inspection and pickup each regular workday by the sheriff of the county, or the sheriff's designee or the chief of police, or the chief's designee of the municipality in which the pawnshop is located. These records may be electronically reported to the sheriff of the county or the chief of police of the municipality in which the pawnshop is located by transmission over the Internet or by facsimile transmission in a manner authorized by the applicable sheriff or chief of police. These records shall be a correct copy of the entries made of the pawn or purchase transaction and shall be carefully preserved without alteration, and shall be available during regular business hours.

(e) Except as otherwise provided in this Part, any person presenting a pawn ticket to a pawnbroker is presumed to be entitled to redeem the pledged goods described on the ticket. (1989, c. 638, s. 2; 2007-415, s. 2; 2011-325, s. 5; 2012-46, ss. 2, 9.)

§ 66-392. Record-keeping requirements for currency converters.

(a) Every currency converter shall keep consecutively numbered records of each cash purchase. The currency converter shall, at the time of making the purchase, enter upon each record all of the following information, which shall be typed or written in ink and in the English language:

(1) A clear and accurate description of the property purchased by the currency converter from the seller, including model and serial number if indicated on the property.

(2) The name, residence address, phone number, and date of birth of the seller.

(3) The date of the purchase.

(4) The type of identification and the identification number accepted from the seller.

(5) A description of the seller, including approximate height, weight, sex, and race.

(6) The purchase price.

(7) The statement that "THE SELLER OF THIS ITEM ATTESTS THAT IT IS NOT STOLEN, HAS NO LIENS OR ENCUMBRANCES, AND IS THE SELLER'S TO SELL."

(b) The seller shall sign the record and shall receive an exact copy of the record, which shall be signed or initialed by the currency converter or any employee of the currency converter. These records shall be available for inspection and pickup each regular workday by the sheriff of the county or the sheriff's designee or the chief of police or the chief's designee of the municipality in which the currency converter is located. These records may be electronically reported to the sheriff of the county or the chief of police of the municipality in which the currency converter is located by transmission over the Internet or by facsimile transmission in a manner authorized by the applicable sheriff or chief of police. These records shall be a correct copy of the entries made of the purchase transaction, shall be carefully preserved without alteration, and shall be available during regular business hours.

(c)   This section does not apply to purchases directly from a manufacturer or wholesaler for a currency converter's inventory. (2011-325, s. 6; 2012-46, s. 2; 2013-410, s. 26.)

§ 66-393. Pawnbroker fees; interest rates.

No pawnbroker shall demand or receive an effective rate of interest greater than two percent (2%) per month, and no other charge of any description or for any purpose shall be made by the pawnbroker, except that the pawnbroker may charge, contract for, and recover an additional monthly fee for the following services, including but not limited to:

(1)   Title investigation;

(2)   Handling, appraisal, and storage;

(3)   Insuring a security;

(4)   Application fee;

(5)   Making daily reports to local law enforcement officers; and

(6)   For other expenses, including losses of every nature, and all other services.

In no event may the total of the above listed monthly fees on a pawn transaction exceed twenty percent (20%) of the principal up to a maximum of the following:

First month	$100.00
Second month	75.00

Third month   75.00

Fourth month and thereafter   50.00

In addition, pawnbrokers may charge fees for returned checks as allowed by G.S. 25-3-506. (1989, c. 638, s. 2; 1995 (Reg. Sess., 1996), c. 742, s. 37; 2012-46, s. 2.)

§ 66-394. Pawnbroker transactions.

In every pawn transaction:

(1)   The original pawn contract shall have a maturity date of not less than 30 days, provided that nothing herein shall prevent the pledgor from redeeming the property before the maturity date;

(2)   Any personal property pledged to a pawnbroker in this State is subject to sale or disposal when there has been no payment made on the account for a period of 60 days past maturity date of the original contract; provided that the contract between the pledgor and the pawnbroker is renewable if renewal is agreed upon by both the parties;

(3)   Every pawn ticket or receipt for such pawn shall have printed thereon the provisions of subdivision (1) of this section which shall constitute: (i) notice of such sale or disposal, (ii) notice of intention to sell or dispose of the property without further notice, and (iii) consent to such sale or disposal. The pledgor thereby forfeits all right, title and interest of, in, and to such pawned property to the pawnbroker who thereby acquires absolute title to the same, whereupon the debt is satisfied and the pawnbroker may sell or dispose of the unredeemed pledges as his own property. Any sale or disposal of property under this section terminates all liability of the pawnbroker and vests in the purchaser the right, title, and interest of the borrower and the pawnbroker;

(4)   If the borrower loses his pawn ticket he shall not thereby forfeit his right to redeem, but may, before the lapse of the redemption period, make an affidavit with indemnification for such loss. The affidavit shall describe the property pawned and shall take the place of the lost pawn ticket unless the pawned property has already been redeemed with the original pawn ticket; and

(5) A pledgor is not obligated to redeem pledged goods or make any payment on a pawn transaction. (1989, c. 638, s. 2; 2012-46, s. 2.)

§ 66-395. Prohibitions.

(a) A pawnbroker shall not:

(1) Accept a pledge from a person under the age of 18 years.

(2) Make any agreement requiring the personal liability of a pledgor in connection with a pawn transaction.

(3) Accept any waiver, in writing or otherwise, of any right or protection accorded a pledgor under this Part.

(4) Fail to exercise reasonable care to protect pledged goods from loss or damage.

(5) Fail to return pledged goods to a pledgor upon payment of the full amount due the pawnbroker on the pawn transaction. In the event such pledged goods are lost or damaged while in the possession of the pawnbroker, it shall be the responsibility of the pawnbroker to replace the lost or damaged goods with merchandise of like kind and equivalent value. In the event the pledgor and pawnbroker cannot agree as to replacement, the pawnbroker shall reimburse the pledgor in the amount of the value agreed upon pursuant to G.S. 66-391(b).

(6) Take any article in pawn, pledge, or as security from any person, which is known to such pawnbroker to be stolen, unless there is a written agreement with local or State law enforcement.

(7) Sell, exchange, barter, or remove from the pawnshop any goods pledged, pawned, or purchased before the earlier of seven days after the date the pawn ticket record is electronically reported in accordance with G.S. 66-391(d) or 30 days after the transaction, except in case of redemption by pledgor or items purchased for resale from wholesalers.

(8) Operate more than one pawnshop under one license, and such shop must be at a permanent place of business.

(9) Take as pledged goods any manufactured mobile home, recreational vehicle, or motor vehicle other than a motorcycle.

(b) A currency converter shall not purchase from any person property which is known to the currency converter to be stolen, unless there is a written agreement with local or State law enforcement. (1989, c. 638, s. 2; 2007-415, s. 1; 2011-325, s. 7; 2012-46, ss. 2, 10; 2013-410, s. 26.)

§ 66-396. Penalties.

(a) Every person, firm, or corporation, their guests or employees, who shall knowingly violate any of the provisions of this Part, shall, on conviction thereof, be deemed guilty of a Class 2 misdemeanor. If the violation is by an owner or major stockholder or managing partner of the pawnshop and the violation is knowingly committed by the owner, major stockholder, or managing partner of the pawnshop, then the license of the pawnshop may be suspended at the discretion of the court.

(b) The provision of subsection (a) of this section shall not apply to violations of G.S. 66-395(a)(6) or G.S. 66-395(b) which shall be prosecuted under the North Carolina criminal statutes.

(c) Any contract of pawn the making or collecting of which violates any provision of this Part, except as a result of accidental or bona fide error of computation, shall be void, and the licensee shall have no right to collect, receive or retain any interest or fee whatsoever with respect to such pawn. (1989, c. 638, s. 2; 1993, c. 539, s. 655; 1994, Ex. Sess., c. 24, s. 14(c); 2011-325, s. 8; 2012-46, ss. 2, 11.)

§ 66-397. Municipal or county authority.

All of the counties and cities as defined by G.S. 160A-1 may by ordinance adopt the provisions of this Part and may adopt such further rules and regulations as the governing bodies of the counties and cities deem appropriate; provided, however, no county or city may regulate:

(1) Interest, fees, or recovery charges;

(2) Hours of operation, unless such regulation applies to businesses generally;

(3) The nature of the business or type of pawn transaction; or

(4) License fees in excess of rates set by the State. (1989, c. 638, s. 2; 1993, c. 539, s. 655; 1994, Ex. Sess., c. 24, s. 14(c); 2011-325, s. 8; 2012-46, ss. 2, 12.)

§ 66-398. License renewal.

Notwithstanding any provision of this Part to the contrary, any person, firm, or corporation licensed as a pawnbroker on or before October 1, 1989, shall continue in force until the natural expiration thereof and all other provisions of this Part shall apply to such license. Such pawnbroker shall be eligible for renewal of his license upon its expiration or subsequent renewals, provided such license complies with the requirements for renewal that were in effect immediately prior to October 1, 1989. (1989, c. 638, s. 2; 2012-46, ss. 2, 13.)

§ 66-399. Bond.

Every person, firm, or corporation licensed under this Part shall, at the time of receiving the license, file with the city or county issuing the license a bond payable to such city or county in the sum of five thousand dollars ($5,000), to be executed by the licensee, and by two responsible sureties or a surety company licensed to do such business in this State, to be approved by the city or county, which shall be for the faithful performance of the requirements and obligations pertaining to the business so licensed. The city or county may sue for forfeiture of the bond upon a breach thereof. Any person who obtains a judgment against a pawnbroker and upon which judgment execution is returned unsatisfied may maintain an action in his own name upon the bond, to satisfy the judgment. (1989, c. 638, s. 2; 2012-46, ss. 2, 14.)

§ 66-400: Reserved for future codification purposes.

§ 66-401: Reserved for future codification purposes.

§ 66-402: Reserved for future codification purposes.

§ 66-403: Reserved for future codification purposes.

§ 66-404: Reserved for future codification purposes.

Part 2. Precious Metal Business.

§ 66-405. Legislative finding.

The General Assembly finds and declares that precious metal businesses in North Carolina vitally affect the general economy of the State and the public interest and public welfare, and in the exercise of its police power, it is necessary to regulate such businesses, in order to prevent thefts, disposal of stolen property, and other abuses upon its citizens. (1981, c. 956, s. 1; 2012-46, s. 15.)

§ 66-406. Definitions.

The following definitions apply in this Part:

(1) Dealer. - A person who purchases precious metals from the public, other than by an exempted transaction, in the form of jewelry, flatware, silver services, or other forms and holds himself or herself out to the public by signs, advertising, or other methods as engaging in such purchases, including any independent contractor purchasing precious metals under any arrangement in

any department store. An exempted transaction is one that is (i) not considered in determining whether a person is a dealer under this Part and (ii) not subject to the requirements of this Part, even if it is entered into by a person otherwise defined and regulated as a dealer. Exempted transactions are:

a. Purchases directly from manufacturers or wholesalers of precious metals by permanently located retail merchants for their inventories.

b. Pawns, pledges, or purchases of items made of precious metals, if the transaction is entered into by a licensed pawnbroker and the transaction is regulated under the provisions of Part 1 of this Article.

c. The acquisition of precious metals by a permanently located retail merchant through barter or exchange for other items sold in the ordinary course of the merchant's business, provided that the seller does not receive, as part of the transaction, any sum of money or any gift card or stored-value card, unless the card is redeemable only at that merchant's business.

(2) Local law enforcement agency. - The term means the following, as applicable:

a. The county police force, if the dealer's business is located within a county with a county police force and outside the corporate limits of a municipality.

b. The municipal police force, if the dealer's business is located within the corporate limits of a municipality having a police force.

c. The county sheriff's office of the county in which the dealer's business is located, if neither sub-subdivision a. nor b. of this subdivision applies.

(3) Precious metal. - Gold, silver, platinum, or palladium, as defined below, but excluding coins, medals, medallions, tokens, numismatic items, art ingots, or art bars.

a. Gold. - Any item or article containing 10 karats of gold or more which may be in combination or alloy with any other metal.

b. Silver. - Any item or article containing 925 parts per thousand of silver which may be in combination or alloy with any nonprecious metal or which is marked "sterling".

c. Platinum. - Any item or article containing 900 parts per thousand or more of platinum which may be in combination or alloy with any other metal.

d. Palladium. - Any item or article containing 950 parts per thousand or more of palladium which may be in combination or alloy with any other metal. (1981, c. 956, s. 1; c. 1001, s. 3; 1989 (Reg. Sess., 1990), c. 1024, s. 10(b); 2009-482, s. 1; 2012-46, ss. 15, 17.)

§ 66-407. Permits.

(a) Dealer Permit. - Except as provided in subsection (c) of this section, it is unlawful for any person to engage as a dealer in the business of purchasing precious metals either as a separate business or in connection with other business operations without first obtaining a permit for the business from the local law enforcement agency. The Department of Public Safety shall approve the forms for both the application and the permit. The application shall be given under oath and shall be notarized. A 30-day waiting period from the date of filing of the application is required prior to initial issuance of a permit. A separate permit shall be issued for each location, place, or premises within the jurisdiction of the local law enforcement agency which is used for conducting a precious metals business, and each permit shall designate the location, place or premises to which it applies. No business shall be conducted in a place other than that designated in the permit, or in a mobile home, trailer, camper, or other vehicle, or structure not permanently affixed to the ground or in any room customarily used for lodging in any hotel, motel, tourist court, or tourist home. The permit shall be posted in a prominent place on the designated premises. Permits shall be valid for a period of 12 months from the date issued and may be renewed without a waiting period upon filing of an application and payment of the annual fee. The annual fee for a permit within each jurisdiction is one hundred eighty dollars ($180.00) to provide for the administrative costs of the local law enforcement agency, including the purchase of required forms and the cost of conducting the criminal history record check of the applicant. The fee is not refundable even if the permits are denied or later suspended or revoked. A permit issued under this section is in addition to and not in lieu of other business licenses and is not transferable. No person other than the dealer named on the permit and that dealer's employees may engage in the business of purchasing precious metals under the authority of the permit.

Any dealer applying to the local law enforcement agency for a permit shall furnish the local law enforcement agency with the following information:

(1) The applicant's full name, and any other names used by the applicant during the preceding five years. In the case of a partnership, association, or corporation, the applicant shall list any partnership, association, or corporate names used during the preceding five years.

(2) Current address, and all addresses used by the applicant during the preceding five years.

(3) Physical description.

(4) Age.

(5) Driver's license number, if any, and state of issuance.

(6) Recent photograph.

(7) Record of felony convictions.

(8) Record of other convictions during the preceding five years.

(9) A full set of fingerprints of the applicant.

If the applicant for a dealer's permit is a partnership or association, all persons owning a ten percent (10%) or more interest in the partnership or association shall comply with the provisions of this subsection. These permits shall be issued in the name of the partnership or association.

If the applicant for a dealer's permit is a corporation, each officer, director and stockholder owning ten percent (10%) or more of the corporation's stock, of any class, shall comply with the provisions of this subsection. These permits shall be issued in the name of the corporation.

No permit shall be issued to an applicant who has been convicted of a felony involving a crime of moral turpitude, or larceny, or receiving stolen goods or of similar charges in any federal court or a court of this or any other state, unless the applicant has had his or her rights of citizenship restored pursuant to Chapter 13 of the General Statutes for five years or longer immediately preceding the date of application. In the case of a partnership, association, or corporation, no permit shall be issued to any applicant with an officer, partner, or director who has been convicted of a felony involving a crime of moral turpitude, or larceny, or receiving stolen goods or of similar charges in any federal court or a court of this or any other state, unless that person has had his or her rights of citizenship restored pursuant to Chapter 13 of the General Statutes for five years or longer immediately preceding the date of application.

The Department of Justice may provide a criminal history record check to the local law enforcement agency for a person who has applied for a permit through the agency. The agency shall provide to the Department of Justice, along with the request, the fingerprints of the applicant, any additional information required by the Department of Justice, and a form signed by the applicant consenting to the check of the criminal record and to the use of the fingerprints and other identifying information required by the State or national repositories. The applicant's fingerprints shall be forwarded to the State Bureau of Investigation for a search of the State's criminal history record file, and the State Bureau of Investigation shall forward a set of the fingerprints to the Federal Bureau of Investigation for a national criminal history record check. The agency shall keep all information pursuant to this subsection privileged, in accordance with applicable State law and federal guidelines, and the information shall be confidential and shall not be a public record under Chapter 132 of the General Statutes.

The Department of Justice may charge each applicant a fee for conducting the checks of criminal history records authorized by this subsection.

(b) Employee Requirements. - Every employee engaged in the precious metals purchasing business shall, within two business days of being so engaged, register his or her name and address with the local law enforcement agency and have his or her photograph taken by the agency. The employee also shall consent to a criminal history record check, which shall be performed by the local law enforcement agency. A person who refuses to consent to a criminal history record check shall not be employed by a dealer required to be licensed under this section. A person who has been convicted of a felony involving a crime of moral turpitude, larceny, receiving stolen goods, or of similar charges shall not be employed by a dealer required to be licensed under this section, unless the person has had his or her rights of citizenship restored pursuant to Chapter 13 of the General Statutes for five years or longer immediately preceding the date of registration. The agency shall issue to the employee a certificate of compliance with this section upon the applicant's payment of the sum of ten dollars ($10.00) to the agency. The certificate shall be renewed annually for a three-dollar ($3.00) fee and shall be posted in the work area of the registered employee. An employee is not subject to the requirements of this subsection if the employee is engaged in the precious metals purchasing business only incidentally to his or her main job responsibilities, and each precious metals transaction with which the employee is involved is overseen by a licensed dealer or registered employee. All records of transactions must be signed by the licensed dealer or registered employee at the time of the transaction, as required under G.S. 66-410(a).

The Department of Justice may provide a criminal history record check to the local law enforcement agency for an employee engaged in the precious metals business. The agency shall provide to the Department of Justice, along with the request, the fingerprints of the employee, any additional information required by the Department of Justice, and a form signed by the employee consenting to the check of the criminal record and to the use of the fingerprints and other identifying information required by the State or national repositories. The employee's fingerprints shall be forwarded to the State Bureau of Investigation for a search of the State's criminal history record file, and the State Bureau of Investigation shall forward a set of the fingerprints to the Federal Bureau of Investigation for a national criminal history record check. The agency shall keep all information pursuant to this subsection privileged, in accordance with applicable State law and federal guidelines, and the information shall be confidential and shall not be a public record under Chapter 132 of the General Statutes.

The Department of Justice may charge each employee a fee for conducting the checks of criminal history records authorized by this subsection.

(c) Special Occasion Permit. - A special occasion permit authorizes the permittee to purchase precious metals as a dealer participating in any trade shows, antique shows, and crafts shows conducted within the State. A special occasion permit shall be issued by any local law enforcement agency; provided, however, that a permittee under subsection (a) of this section shall apply for a special occasion permit with the local law enforcement agency that issued the dealer's permit. The Department of Public Safety shall approve the forms for both the application and the permit. The application shall be given under oath and notarized. A 30-day waiting period from the date of filing of the application is required prior to initial issuance of a permit.

Any dealer applying to a local law enforcement agency for a special occasion permit shall furnish the local law enforcement agency with the information required in an application for a dealer's permit as set forth in subsection (a) of this section. In addition, the applicant shall provide a physical address where any item included in a dealer purchase will be held for the period required under G.S. 66-411. The physical address shall be the location where the purchase was made, unless another physical address within the law enforcement jurisdiction where the purchase was made is approved by the law enforcement agency that issues the permit. The items shall be available at all reasonable times for inspection on the premises by law enforcement agencies.

If the applicant for a special occasion permit is a partnership or association, all persons owning a ten percent (10%) or more interest in the partnership or association shall comply with the provisions of this subsection. Any such permits shall be issued in the name of the partnership or association.

If the applicant for a special occasion permit is a corporation, each officer, director and stockholder owning ten percent (10%) or more of the corporation's stock, of any class, shall comply with the provisions of this subsection. Any such permits shall be issued in the name of the corporation.

No permit shall be issued to an applicant who has been convicted of a felony involving a crime of moral turpitude, or larceny, or receiving stolen goods or of similar charges in any federal court or a court of this or any other state, unless the applicant has had his or her rights of citizenship restored pursuant to Chapter 13 of the General Statutes for five years or longer immediately preceding the date of application. In the case of a partnership, association, or corporation, no permit shall be issued to any applicant with an officer, partner, or director who has been convicted of a felony involving a crime of moral turpitude, or larceny, or receiving stolen goods or of similar charges in any federal court or a court of this or any other state, unless that person has had his or her rights of citizenship restored pursuant to Chapter 13 of the General Statutes for five years or longer immediately preceding the date of application.

The Department of Justice may provide a criminal history record check to the local law enforcement agency for a person who has applied for a permit through the agency. The agency shall provide to the Department of Justice, along with the request, the fingerprints of the applicant, any additional information required by the Department of Justice, and a form signed by the applicant consenting to the check of the criminal record and to the use of the fingerprints and other identifying information required by the State or national repositories. The applicant's fingerprints shall be forwarded to the State Bureau of Investigation for a search of the State's criminal history record file, and the State Bureau of

Investigation shall forward a set of the fingerprints to the Federal Bureau of Investigation for a national criminal history record check. The agency shall keep all information pursuant to this subsection privileged, in accordance with applicable State law and federal guidelines, and the information shall be confidential and shall not be a public record under Chapter 132 of the General Statutes.

The Department of Justice may charge each applicant a fee for conducting the checks of criminal history records authorized by this subsection.

The filing fee for a special occasion permit application is one hundred eighty dollars ($180.00) to provide for the administrative cost of the local law enforcement agency including purchase of required forms and the cost of conducting the criminal history record check of the applicant. The fee is not refundable even if the permit is denied or is later suspended or revoked. A special occasion permit is in addition to and not in lieu of other business licenses and is not transferable. No person other than the dealer named on the permit and that dealer's employees may engage in the business of purchasing precious metals under the authority of the permit.

A special occasion permit is valid for 12 months from the date issued, unless earlier surrendered, suspended, or revoked. Application for renewal of a permit for an additional 12 months shall be on a form approved by the Department of Public Safety and shall be accompanied by a nonrefundable renewal fee of one hundred eighty dollars ($180.00).

Each special occasion permit shall be posted in a prominent place on the premises of any show at which the permittee purchases precious metals. (1981, c. 956, s. 1; 2002-147, s. 2; 2009-482, s. 2; 2011-145, s. 19.1(g); 2012-46, ss. 15, 18.)

§ 66-408. Perjury; punishment.

Any person who shall willfully commit perjury in any application for a permit or exemption filed pursuant to this Part shall be guilty of a Class 2 misdemeanor. (1981, c. 956, s. 1; 1993, c. 539, s. 525; 1994, Ex. Sess., c. 24, s. 14(c); 2012-46, ss. 15, 19.)

§ 66-409. Bond or trust account required.

Before any permit shall be issued to a dealer pursuant to G.S. 66-407, the dealer shall execute a satisfactory cash or surety bond or establish a trust account with a licensed and insured bank or savings institution located in the State of North Carolina in the sum of ten thousand dollars ($10,000). The bond or trust account shall be in favor of the State of North Carolina. A surety bond is to be executed by the dealer and by two responsible sureties or a surety company licensed to do business in the State of North Carolina and shall be on a form approved by the Department of Public Safety. Any bond shall be kept in full force and effect and shall be delivered to the law-enforcement agency which first issued a current permit to the dealer. A bond or trust account shall be for the faithful performance of the requirements and obligations of the dealer's business in conformity with this Part. Any law-enforcement agency shall have full power and authority to revoke the permit and sue for forfeiture of the bond or trust account upon a breach thereof. Any person who shall have suffered any loss or damage by any act of the permittee that constitutes a violation of this Part shall have the right to institute an action to recover against such permittee and the surety or trust account. Upon termination of the bond or trust account the permit shall become void. (1981, c. 956, s. 1; c. 1001, s. 4; 2011-145, s. 19.1(g); 2012-46, ss. 15, 20.)

§ 66-410. Records to be kept.

(a)   Every dealer to whom a permit has been issued pursuant to G.S. 66-407 shall maintain consecutively numbered records of each precious metals transaction. Each consecutively numbered record shall be made at the time of the transaction and shall contain a clear and accurate description of the transaction. A valid description shall include each of the following applicable and available items of information: the manufacturer's name, the model, the model number, the serial number, and any engraved numbers or initials found on the items; the date of the transaction; the name, sex, race, residence, telephone number and driver's license number of the person selling the items purchased; and the signature of both the dealer or registered employee and the seller. In the event the seller cannot furnish valid, unexpired photographic identification in the form of a drivers license, State-issued identification card, passport, or military identification card, the dealer shall require two forms of positive identification.

(b)   The consecutively numbered records required by this section shall be kept either (i) in a paginated, bound book or set of books with pages numbered in sequence or (ii) in an electronic database that prevents record deletion, tracks all modifications to records, and provides for electronic signatures.

(c)   The records shall be open at all reasonable times to inspection on the premises by law enforcement agencies, and an individual record shall be retained for at least two years after a transaction. If a dealer maintains a record book rather than an electronic database, the book shall be retained until at least two years following the last recorded transaction.

(d)   A copy of each consecutively numbered record entry shall be filed within 48 hours of the transaction in the office of the local law enforcement agency. Records shall be filed in the manner authorized by the local law enforcement agency, which may include reporting electronically by transmission over a computer network, by facsimile machine, or by hand delivering hard copies to the local law enforcement agency. In any case where a technological failure prevents a dealer from reporting electronically or by facsimile, the dealer shall have the option of hand delivering a hard copy of the record to the local law enforcement agency. Regardless of the manner in which the local law enforcement agency allows reporting, a dealer shall provide a hard copy of records upon the request of a law enforcement agency.

(e)   The files of local law enforcement agencies that contain copies of records shall not be subject to inspection and examination as authorized by G.S. 132-6. Any public official or employee who shall knowingly and willfully permit any person to have access to or custody or possession of any portion of such files, unless the person is one specifically authorized by the local law enforcement agency to have access for purposes of law enforcement investigation or civil or criminal proceedings, shall be guilty of a Class 3 misdemeanor and upon conviction shall only be fined up to five hundred dollars ($500.00) in the discretion of the court. (1981, c. 956, s. 1; 1993, c. 539, s. 526; 1994, Ex. Sess., c. 24, s. 14(c); 2009-482, s. 4; 2012-46, ss. 15, 21.)

§ 66-411. Items not to be modified.

No item included in a dealer purchase shall be sold, traded or otherwise disposed of, melted, cut or otherwise changed in form nor shall any item be removed from the licensed premises, or other location specified on the application for a special occasion permit, for a period of seven days from the date the transaction was reported in accordance with G.S. 66-410. (1981, c. 956, s. 1; 2009-482, s. 5; 2012-46, ss. 15, 22.)

§ 66-412. Purchasing from juvenile.

No dealer or employee or agent thereof shall purchase from any juvenile under 18 years of age any article made, in whole or in part, of precious metal. (1981, c. 956, s. 1; 2012-46, s. 15.)

§ 66-413. Penalties.

Any dealer who violates the provisions of this Part shall be deemed guilty of a Class 2 misdemeanor. In addition any dealer so convicted shall be ineligible for a dealer's permit for a period of three years from the date of conviction. Each and every violation shall constitute a separate and distinct offense. (1981, c. 956, s. 1; 1993, c. 539, s. 527; 1994, Ex. Sess., c. 24, s. 14(c); 2012-46, ss. 15, 23.)

§ 66-414. Portable smelters prohibited.

It shall be unlawful for any person to possess or operate a smelter in any mobile home, trailer, camper, or other vehicle or structure not permanently affixed to the ground, for the purpose of refining precious metals. Violation of the provisions of this section shall constitute a Class 2 misdemeanor. (1981, c. 956, s. 1; 1993, c. 539, s. 528; 1994, Ex. Sess., c. 24, s. 14(c); 2012-46, s. 15.)

§ 66-415: Reserved for future codification purposes.

§ 66-416: Reserved for future codification purposes.

§ 66-417: Reserved for future codification purposes.

§ 66-418: Reserved for future codification purposes.

§ 66-419: Reserved for future codification purposes.

Part 3. Regulation of Sales and Purchases of Metals.

§ 66-420. Definitions.

The following definitions apply in this Part:

(1) Cash card system. - A system of payment that provides payment in cash or in a form other than cash and that when providing payment in the form of cash (i) captures a photograph of the seller at the time payment is received and (ii) uses an automated cash dispenser, including, but not limited to, an automated teller machine.

(1a) Copper. - Nonferrous metals, including, but not limited to, copper wire, copper clad steel wire, copper pipe, copper bars, copper sheeting, copper tubing and pipe fittings, and insulated copper wire. The term shall not include brass alloys, bronze alloys, lead, nickel, zinc, or items not containing a significant quantity of copper.

(2) Fixed site. - A site occupied by a secondary metals recycler as the owner of the site or as a lessee of the site under a lease or other rental agreement providing for occupation of the site by a nonferrous metals purchaser for a total duration of not less than 364 days.

(3) Law enforcement officer. - Any duly constituted law enforcement officer of the State or of any municipality or county.

(4) Nonferrous metals. - Metals not containing significant quantities of iron or steel, including, but not limited to, copper, aluminum other than aluminum cans, a product that is a mixture of aluminum and copper, catalytic converters, lead-acid batteries, and stainless steel beer kegs or containers. The term shall not include precious metals as defined and regulated in Part 2 of this Article.

(5) Nonferrous metals purchaser. - A secondary metals recycler who purchases, gathers, or obtains nonferrous metals.

(6) Permit. - A permit issued pursuant to G.S. 66-426(a).

(7) Regulated metals property. - All ferrous and nonferrous metals.

(8) Secondary metals recycler. - Any person, firm, or corporation in the State:

a. That is engaged in the business of gathering or obtaining ferrous or nonferrous metals that have served their original economic purpose or is in the business of performing the manufacturing process by which ferrous metals or nonferrous metals are converted into raw material products consisting of prepared grades and having an existing or potential economic value; or

b. That has facilities for performing the manufacturing process by which ferrous metals or nonferrous metals are converted into raw material products consisting of prepared grades and having an existing or potential economic value, by methods including, but not limited to, the processing, sorting, cutting, classifying, cleaning, baling, wrapping, shredding, shearing, or changing the physical form or chemical content of the metals, but not including the exclusive use of hand tools. (2012-46, s. 28; 2013-169, s. 1.)

§ 66-420.1. Applicability.

This Chapter shall not apply to a salvage yard regulated pursuant to Chapter 20 of the General Statutes, unless the salvage yard is engaged in the business of gathering or obtaining ferrous or nonferrous metals that have served their original economic purpose and is in the business of performing the manufacturing process by which ferrous metals or nonferrous metals are converted into raw material products consisting of prepared grades and having an existing or potential economic value. (2013-410, s. 30.5.)

§ 66-421. Required records and receipts for regulated metals transactions.

(a)   Receipt Required. - A secondary metals recycler shall issue a receipt for all purchase transactions in which the secondary metals recycler purchases regulated metals property. This receipt shall be issued to and signed by the person delivering the property, and the secondary metals recycler shall be able to provide documentation regarding the employee who completed the transaction.

(b)   Records Required. - A secondary metals recycler shall maintain a record of all purchase transactions in which the secondary metals recycler purchases regulated metals property. The record of each transaction shall contain the following information:

(1)   The name and address of the secondary metals recycler.

(2)   The name, initials, or other identification of the individual entering the information.

(3)   The date of the transaction.

(4)   The weight of the regulated metals property purchased.

(5)   The description made in accordance with the custom of the trade of the type of regulated metals property purchased and the physical address where the regulated metals were obtained by the seller and the date when purchased, and a statement signed by the seller or the seller's agent certifying that the seller or the seller's agent has the lawful right to sell and dispose of the property.

(6)   The amount of consideration given for the regulated metals property.

(7)   The name and address of the vendor of the regulated metals property and the license plate number, make, model, and color of the vehicle used to deliver the regulated metals.

(8)   A photocopy or electronic scan of the unexpired drivers license or state or federally issued photo identification card of the person delivering the regulated metals property to the secondary metals recycler. If the secondary

metals recycler has a copy of the valid photo identification of the person delivering the regulated metals property on file, the secondary metals recycler must examine the photo identification and verify that it has not expired, but may reference the photo identification that is on file without making a separate photocopy or electronic scan for each subsequent transaction. If the person delivering the regulated metals property does not have an unexpired drivers license or an unexpired state or federally issued photo identification card, the secondary metals recycler shall not complete the transaction.

(9) A copy of the receipt required under subsection (a) of this section when all the information required under subsection (a) of this section is clear and legible or, in the event the copy of the receipt is not clear or not legible, the original receipt.

(10) A video or digital photograph of the seller together with the regulated metals property being delivered by the seller. The video or photograph required by this section shall be of a quality that is sufficient to allow a person of ordinary faculties to identify the person recorded or photographed.

(11) In transactions involving catalytic converters that are not attached to a vehicle, and central air conditioner evaporator coils or condensers, the person delivering the materials shall place next to that person's signature on the receipt required under subsection (a) of this section, a clear impression of that person's index finger that is in ink and free of any smearing. A secondary metals recycler may elect to obtain the fingerprint electronically. If the secondary metals recycler has a copy of the fingerprint of the person delivering the nonferrous metal on file, the secondary metals recycler must examine the photo identification, but may reference the fingerprint that is on file without making a separate fingerprint for each subsequent transaction. (2012-46, s. 28.)

§ 66-422. Inspection of regulated metals property and records.

(a) Retention of Records. - A secondary metals recycler shall keep and maintain the information required under G.S. 66-421(b) for not less than two years from the date of the purchase of the regulated metals property. Records shall be securely maintained at all times and shall be destroyed in a manner that protects the identity of the owner of the property, the seller of the property, and the purchaser of the property.

(b) Inspection of Regulated Metals Property and Records. - During the usual and customary business hours of a secondary metals recycler, a law enforcement officer shall have the right to inspect all of the following:

(1) Any and all purchased regulated metals property in the possession of the secondary metals recycler.

(2) Any and all records required to be maintained under G.S. 66-421(b).

(c) Making Receipts Available for Inspection by Law Enforcement. - A secondary metals recycler shall make receipts for the purchase of regulated metals property available for pickup each regular workday if requested by the sheriff or chief of police of the county or the chief of police of the municipality in which the secondary metals recycler is located. The sheriff or the chief of police may request these receipts to be electronically transferred directly to the law enforcement agency. Records retained by a law enforcement agency shall be securely retained as required by law and destroyed in a manner that protects the identity of the owner of the property, the seller of the property, and the purchaser of the property.

(d) Records Are Not Public. - Records submitted to any public law enforcement agency pursuant to this section are records of criminal investigations or records of criminal intelligence information as defined in G.S. 132-1.4 and are not public records as defined by G.S. 132-1. (2012-46, s. 28.)

§ 66-423. Hold notices for nonferrous metals; retention of nonferrous metals.

(a) Hold Notices. - When a law enforcement officer has reasonable suspicion to believe that any item of nonferrous metal in the possession of a nonferrous metals purchaser has been stolen, the law enforcement officer may issue a hold notice to the nonferrous metals purchaser. The hold notice must be in writing, be delivered to the nonferrous metals purchaser, specifically identify those items of nonferrous metal that are believed to have been stolen and that are subject to the notice, and inform the nonferrous metals purchaser of the information contained in this section. Upon receipt of the notice, the nonferrous metals purchaser must not process or remove the items of nonferrous metal identified in the notice, or any portion thereof, from the secondary metal recycler's fixed site for 15 calendar days after receipt of the notice unless released prior to the 15-day period by the law enforcement officer. A hold notice may be renewed for an additional 30 days by the law enforcement officer. A renewal must satisfy the same requirements as an initial hold notice in order to be valid.

(b) Retention of Nonferrous Metals. - Any secondary metals recycler owner convicted of a felonious violation of this Article, G.S. 14-71, 14-71.1, or 14-72 shall hold and retain nonferrous metals for seven days from the date of purchase before selling, dismantling, crushing, defacing, or in any manner altering or disposing of the regulated metals property. (2012-46, s. 28.)

§ 66-424. Prohibited activities and transactions.

(a) A secondary metals recycler shall not do any of the following:

(1) Operate any business that cashes checks at a fixed site at which the secondary metals recycler purchases regulated metals property.

(2) Purchase nonferrous metals for the purpose of recycling the nonferrous metals, unless the nonferrous metals purchaser possesses a valid permit.

(3) Purchase any central air conditioner evaporator coils or condensers, or catalytic converters that are not attached to a vehicle, except that a secondary metals recycler may purchase these items from a company, contractor, or individual that is in the business of installing, replacing, maintaining, or removing these items.

(4) Purchase any regulated metals property that the secondary metals recycler knows or reasonably should know to be stolen.

(b) It shall be unlawful to transport or possess on highways of this State an amount of copper weighing in the aggregate more than 25 pounds, unless at least one of the following is true:

(1) The vehicle is used in the ordinary course of business for the purpose of transporting nonferrous metals. This term includes vehicles used by gas, electric, communications, water, plumbing, electrical, and climate conditioning service providers, and their employees, agents, and contractors, in the course of providing these services.

(2) The person transporting or possessing the copper possesses, and presents when requested, a valid bill of sale for the copper.

(3) A law enforcement officer determines that the copper is not stolen and is in the rightful possession of the person.

(c) A secondary metals recycler shall not purchase any of the following:

(1) Any regulated metal marked with the initials or other identification of a telephone, cable, electric, water, or other public utility, or any brewer.

(2) Any utility access cover.

(3) Any street light pole or fixture.

(4) Any road or bridge guard rail.

(5) Any highway or street sign.

(6) Any water meter cover.

(7) Any metal beer keg, including any made of stainless steel that is clearly marked as being the property of the beer manufacturer.

(8) Any traffic directional or control sign.

(9) Any traffic light signal.

(10) Any regulated metal marked with the name of a government entity.

(11) Any spikes, plates, or other railroad track components or signs, and any property owned by a railroad and marked and otherwise identified as such.

(12) Any historical marker or any grave marker or burial vase. (2012-46, s. 28.)

§ 66-425. Permissible payment methods for nonferrous metals purchasers.

Limitation on Cash Purchases. No nonferrous metals purchaser shall enter into a cash transaction for the purchase of copper, and no nonferrous metals purchaser shall purchase any nonferrous metal property for any cash consideration greater than one hundred dollars ($100.00) per transaction. Any payment in excess of one hundred dollars ($100.00) per transaction shall be made by check, money order or cash card system. A nonferrous metals purchaser shall not make more than one cash purchase per day from any individual, business, corporation or partnership. (2012-46, s. 28.)

§ 66-426. Issuance of nonferrous metals purchase permits by Sheriff; form; fees; recordkeeping.

(a) Issuance of Permits. - The sheriff of each county shall issue a nonferrous metals purchase permit to an applicant if the applicant (i) has a fixed site in the sheriff's county; (ii) declares on a form provided by the sheriff that the applicant is informed of and will comply with the provisions of this Part; (iii) does not have a permit that has been revoked pursuant to G.S. 66-429(b) at the time of the application; and (iv) has not been convicted of more than three violations of this Part. A permit shall be valid for 12 months and shall be valid only for fixed sites in the county of issuance. A permit shall be obtained for each fixed site at which nonferrous metals are purchased.

(b) Form. - The Attorney General shall prescribe a standard application form and a standard permit form to be used by sheriffs. The permit form shall contain, at a minimum, the date of issuance and the name and address of the permit holder.

(c) Fees; Record-Keeping Requirements. - The sheriff shall not charge a fee for a permit, and shall retain a copy of any permit issued. (2012-46, s. 28; 2012-194, s. 46(a).)

§ 66-427. Exemptions.

This Part does not apply to:

(1) Purchases of regulated metals property from a manufacturing, industrial, government, or other commercial vendor that generates or sells regulated metals property in the ordinary course of its business.

(2) Purchases of regulated metals property that involve only beverage containers, except that G.S. 66-423 shall apply in that case. (2012-46, s. 28.)

§ 66-428. Preemption.

A county or municipality shall not enact any local law, ordinance, or regulation regulating secondary metals recyclers or regulated metals property that conflicts with this Part, and this Part preempts all existing laws, ordinances, or regulations that conflict with it. (2012-46, s. 28.)

§ 66-429. Violations.

(a) Punishment Generally. - Unless the conduct is covered by some other provision of law providing greater punishment, any person knowingly and willfully violating any of the provisions of this Part shall be guilty of a Class 1 misdemeanor for a first offense. A second or subsequent violation of this Part is a Class I felony.

(b) Revocation of Permits. - If the owner or the employees of a fixed site are convicted of an aggregate of three or more violations of this Part within a 10 year period, the permit associated with that fixed site shall be immediately revoked by the sheriff for a period of six months. Any attempt to circumvent this subsection by procuring a permit through a family member shall result in extension of the revocation period for an additional 18 months. (2012-46, s. 28.)

§ 66-430. Restitution.

The court may order a defendant to make restitution to the secondary metals recycler or property owner, as appropriate, for any damage or loss caused by the defendant and arising out of a violation of G.S. 14-71, G.S. 14-71.1, G.S.

14-72, G.S.14-159.4, G.S. 66-424(a)(3), or G.S. 66-424(a)(4) committed by the defendant. (2012-46, s. 28.)

§ 66-431. Forfeiture of vehicles used to transport unlawfully obtained regulated metals property.

(a) Vehicles which are used or intended for use to convey or transport, or in any manner to facilitate the conveyance or transportation of unlawfully obtained regulated metals property, as defined by this Part, are subject to forfeiture, except that:

(1) No conveyance shall be forfeited under the provisions of this section by reason of any act or omission, committed or omitted while such conveyance was unlawfully in the possession of a person other than the owner in violation of the criminal laws of the United States, or of any state;

(2) No conveyance shall be forfeited unless the violation involved is a felony;

(3) A forfeiture of a vehicle encumbered by a bona fide security interest is subject to the interest of the secured party who had no knowledge of or consented to the act or omission;

(4) No conveyance shall be forfeited under the provisions of this section unless the owner knew or had reason to believe the vehicle was being used in the commission of any violation that may subject the conveyance to forfeiture under this section.

(b) Any vehicle subject to forfeiture under this section may be seized by any law enforcement officer upon process issued by any district or superior court having jurisdiction over the vehicle except that seizure without such process may be made when:

(1) The seizure is incident to an arrest or a search under a search warrant;

(2) The vehicle subject to seizure has been the subject of a prior judgment in favor of the State in a criminal injunction or forfeiture proceeding under this section.

(c) Vehicles taken or detained under this section shall not be repleviable, but shall be deemed to be in custody of the law enforcement agency seizing it, which may:

(1) Place the vehicle under seal; or

(2) Remove the vehicle to a place designated by it; or

(3) Request that the North Carolina Department of Justice take custody of the vehicle and remove it to an appropriate location for disposition in accordance with law.

Any vehicle seized by a State, local, or county law enforcement officer shall be held in safekeeping as provided in this subsection until an order of disposition is properly entered by the judge.

(d) Whenever a vehicle is forfeited under this section, the law enforcement agency having custody of it may:

(1) Retain the vehicle for official use; or

(2) Sell any forfeited vehicle, provided that the proceeds be disposed of for payment of all proper expenses of the proceedings for forfeiture and sale, including expense of seizure, maintenance of custody, advertising, and court costs; or

(3) Transfer any vehicles which are forfeited under the provisions of this section to the North Carolina Department of Justice when, in the discretion of the presiding judge and upon application of the North Carolina Department of Justice, said vehicle may be of official use to the North Carolina Department of Justice;

(4) Upon determination by the director of any law enforcement agency that a vehicle transferred pursuant to the provisions of this section is of no further use to said agency for use in official investigations, such vehicle may be sold as surplus property in the same manner as other vehicles owned by the law enforcement agency, and the proceeds from such sale after deducting the cost of sale shall be paid to the treasurer or proper officer authorized to receive fines and forfeitures to be used for the school fund of the county in the county in which said vehicle was seized; provided, that any vehicle transferred to any law enforcement agency under the provisions of this section which has been

modified to increase speed shall be used in the performance of official duties only and not for resale, transfer, or disposition other than as junk. (2007-301, s. 3; 2012-46, ss. 27, 29.)

§ 66-432: Reserved for future codification purposes.

§ 66-433: Reserved for future codification purposes.

§ 66-434: Reserved for future codification purposes.

§ 66-435: Reserved for future codification purposes.

§ 66-436: Reserved for future codification purposes.

§ 66-437: Reserved for future codification purposes.

§ 66-438: Reserved for future codification purposes.

§ 66-439: Reserved for future codification purposes.

Article 46.

Guaranteed Asset Protection Waivers.

§ 66-440. Definitions.

The following definitions apply in this Article:

(1)   Administrator. - A person that performs administrative or operational functions with respect to guaranteed asset protection waivers.

(2)   Borrower. - A debtor, retail buyer, or lessee under a vehicle finance agreement.

(3)   Creditor. - Any of the following:

a.   A lender in a loan or credit transaction.

b.   A lessor in a lease transaction.

c.   A vehicle dealer, including a motor vehicle dealer as that term is defined in G.S. 20-286(11), that provides credit to or arranges financing for a purchaser of a vehicle.

d.   A seller in a commercial retail installment transaction.

e.   An assignee of any of the foregoing to whom the credit obligation is payable.

(4)   Free-look period. - The period of time from the effective date of a guaranteed asset protection waiver until the date the borrower may cancel the contract without penalty, fees, or costs to the borrower.

(5)   Guaranteed asset protection waiver. - A contractual agreement in which a creditor agrees for a separate charge to cancel or waive all or part of amounts due on a borrower's vehicle finance agreement in the event of a total physical damage loss or unrecovered theft of the vehicle, which agreement shall be part of, or a separate addendum to, the vehicle finance agreement.

(6)   Insurer. - An insurance company licensed, registered, or otherwise authorized to do business under Chapter 58 of the General Statutes.

(7) Vehicle. - A motor vehicle, as that term is defined in G.S. 20-286(10), as well as self-propelled or towed vehicles designed for personal or commercial use, including, but not limited to, automobiles, trucks, motorcycles, recreational vehicles, all-terrain vehicles, snowmobiles, campers, boats, personal watercraft, and trailers for motorcycles, boats, campers, and personal watercraft.

(8) Vehicle finance agreement. - A loan, lease, or retail installment sales contract for the purchase or lease of a vehicle. (2013-193, s. 1.)

§ 66-441. Scope of Article.

(a) Complete Exemptions. - This Article shall not apply to any of the following:

(1) An insurance policy offered by an insurer under Chapter 58 of the General Statutes, except as provided in G.S. 66-443.

(2) A debt cancellation or debt suspension contract being offered pursuant to 12 C.F.R. Part 37, 12 C.F.R. Part 721, or any other federal law.

(b) Partial Exemption for Commercial Transactions. - G.S. 66-444, 66-446(c), and 66-447 are not applicable to a guaranteed asset protection waiver offered in connection with a lease or retail installment sale associated with a commercial transaction. (2013-193, s. 1.)

§ 66-442. Guaranteed asset protection waivers not subject to insurance laws.

Guaranteed asset protection waivers are not insurance and are exempt from the provisions of Chapter 58 of the General Statutes, as are persons administering, marketing, selling, or offering to sell guaranteed asset protection waivers to borrowers. (2013-193, s. 1.)

§ 66-443. Insurance of guaranteed asset protection waivers.

(a) Insurance for Creditors. - Creditors may insure guaranteed asset protection waiver obligations under a contractual liability policy or other similar policy issued by an insurer but shall not be required to do so.

(b) Required Terms. - Contractual liability or other insurance policies insuring guaranteed asset protection waivers shall include terms that do all of the following:

(1) Obligate the insurer to reimburse or pay to the creditor any sums the creditor is legally obligated to waive under guaranteed asset protection waivers issued by the creditor and purchased or held by the borrower.

(2) Provide that the policy covers any subsequent assignee upon the assignment, sale, or transfer of the vehicle finance agreement.

(3) Provide that the policy remains in effect unless cancelled or terminated in compliance with applicable insurance laws of this State.

(4) Provide that the cancellation or termination of policy shall not reduce the insurer's responsibility for guaranteed asset protection waivers issued by the creditor prior to the date of cancellation or termination and for which premiums have been received by the insurer.

(c) Administrators May Procure Insurance. - An insurance policy obtained pursuant to this section may be directly obtained by a creditor or may be procured by an administrator to cover the creditor's obligations. (2013-193, s. 1.)

§ 66-444. Mandatory terms.

A guaranteed asset protection waiver shall include all of the following written terms in clear, easily understandable language:

(1) The name and address of the initial creditor and the borrower at the time of sale and the identity of any administrator if different from the creditor.

(2) The purchase price and the terms of the guaranteed asset protection waiver, including without limitation, the requirements for protection, conditions, or exclusions associated with the guaranteed asset protection waiver.

(3) The length of the free-look period, which shall be at least 30 days, and the procedure by which a borrower may exercise the borrower's rights during that period.

(4) The terms required by G.S. 66-445.

(5) The methodology for calculating any refund of the unearned purchase price of the guaranteed asset protection waiver due in the event of cancellation of the guaranteed asset protection waiver or early termination of the vehicle finance agreement.

(6) The procedure the borrower must follow, if any, to obtain guaranteed asset protection waiver benefits under the terms and conditions of the waiver, including a telephone number and address where the borrower may apply for waiver benefits.

(7) A statement that neither the extension of credit, the terms of the credit, nor the terms of the related vehicle sale or lease may be conditioned upon the purchase of the guaranteed asset protection waiver. (2013-193, s. 1.)

§ 66-445. Cancellation.

(a) Cancellation During Free-Look Period. - A guaranteed asset protection waiver shall include a term stating that if a borrower cancels the waiver within the free-look period, the borrower will be entitled to a full refund so long as no benefits have been provided under the guaranteed asset protection waiver.

(b) Cancellation After the Free-Look Period. - A guaranteed asset protection waiver may be either cancellable or noncancellable after the free-look period. A guaranteed asset protection waiver shall include the following terms regarding cancellation after the free-look period:

(1) A statement of whether or not the guaranteed asset protection waiver is cancellable or noncancellable after the expiration of the free-look period.

(2) If the waiver is cancellable, all of the following terms:

a. A statement that in the event of a borrower's cancellation of the guaranteed asset protection waiver or early termination of the vehicle finance agreement, the borrower may be entitled to a refund of any unearned portion of the purchase price of the waiver unless the waiver provides otherwise.

b. The procedures by which a borrower may cancel the waiver. This term shall include a requirement that in the event the underlying vehicle finance agreement is terminated, cancellation shall be made by providing a written request to the creditor, administrator, or other party within 90 days of the event terminating the vehicle finance agreement.

(c) Cancellation in the Event of Default. - Any cancellation refund under subsections (a) and (b) of this section may be applied by the creditor as a reduction of the amount owed under the vehicle finance agreement unless the borrower can show that the vehicle finance agreement has been paid in full. A guaranteed asset protection waiver shall include a term stating that notwithstanding subsections (a) and (b) of this section, if cancellation of the waiver occurs as a result of a default under the vehicle finance agreement or the repossession of the vehicle associated with the vehicle finance agreement or any other termination of the vehicle finance agreement, any refund due may be paid directly to the creditor or administrator and applied as set forth in this subsection. (2013-193, s. 1.)

§ 66-446. Miscellaneous provisions.

(a) Article Controls. - The offering and sale of guaranteed asset protection waivers in this State shall be subject to the provisions of this Article.

(b) Manner of Payment. - Guaranteed asset protection waivers may, at the option of the creditor, be sold for a single payment or may be offered with a monthly or periodic payment option.

(c) Compliance With Truth in Lending Act. - Notwithstanding any other provision of law, any cost to the borrower for a guaranteed asset protection waiver subject to the Truth in Lending Act (15 U.S.C. § 1601, et seq.) and its implementing regulations, as they may be amended from time to time, shall be separately stated and is not to be considered a finance charge or interest.

(d) Preservation Upon Transfer. - A guaranteed asset protection waiver shall remain a part of the vehicle finance agreement upon its assignment, sale, or transfer by a creditor.

(e) Cannot Be Required. - Neither the extension of credit, the term of credit, nor the term of a related vehicle sale or lease may be conditioned upon the purchase of a guaranteed asset protection waiver.

(f) Forwarding of Proceeds. - A creditor that offers a guaranteed asset protection waiver shall report the sale of and forward funds received on all such waivers to the designated party, if any, as prescribed in any applicable administrative services agreement, contractual liability policy, other insurance policy, or other specified program documents.

(g) Fiduciary Duty. - Funds received or held by a creditor or administrator and belonging to an insurer, creditor, or administrator, pursuant to the terms of a written agreement, shall be held by the creditor or administrator in a fiduciary capacity. (2013-193, s. 1.)

§ 66-447. Enforcement.

The Attorney General may take action which is necessary or appropriate to enforce the provisions of this Article and to protect guaranteed asset protection waiver holders in this State. After proper notice and opportunity for hearing, the Attorney General may:

(1) Order a creditor, administrator, or any other person not in compliance with this Article to cease and desist from further guaranteed asset protection waiver-related operations which are in violation of this Article.

(2) Impose a penalty of not more than five hundred dollars ($500.00) per violation and no more than ten thousand dollars ($10,000) in the aggregate for all violations of a similar nature. For purposes of this Article, violations are of a similar nature if the violation consists of the same or similar course of conduct, action, or practice, irrespective of the number of times the conduct or practice that is determined to be a violation of the Article occurred. (2013-193, s. 1.)

§ 66-448. Severability.

If any provision of this Article or the application of the provision to any person or circumstances is held invalid, the remainder of the Article and the application of the provision to persons or circumstances other than those as to which it is held invalid shall not be affected. (2013-193, s. 1.)

Chapter 67.

Dogs.

Article 1.

Owner's Liability.

§ 67-1. Liability for injury to livestock or fowls.

If any dog, not being at the time on the premises of the owner or person having charge thereof, shall kill or injure any livestock or fowls, the owner or person having such dog in charge shall be liable for damages sustained by the injury, killing, or maiming of any livestock, and costs of suit. (1911, c. 3, s. 1; C.S., s. 1669.)

§ 67-2. Permitting bitch at large.

If any person owning or having any bitch shall knowingly permit her to run at large during the erotic stage of copulation he shall be guilty of a Class 3 misdemeanor. (1862-3, c. 41, s. 2; Code, s. 2501; Rev., s. 3303; C.S., s. 1670; 1993, c. 539, s. 529; 1994, Ex. Sess., c. 24, s. 14(c).)

§ 67-3. Sheep-killing dogs to be killed.

If any person owning or having any dog that kills sheep or other domestic animals, or that kills a human being, upon satisfactory evidence of the same being made before any judge of the district court in the county, and the owner duly notified thereof, shall refuse to kill it, and shall permit such dog to go at liberty, he shall be guilty of a Class 3 misdemeanor, and the dog may be killed by anyone if found going at large. (1862-3, c. 41, s. 1; 1874-5, c. 108, s. 2; Code, s. 2500; Rev., s. 3304; C.S., s. 1671; 1973, c. 108, s. 24; 1977, c. 597; 1993, c. 539, s. 530; 1994, Ex. Sess., c. 24, s. 14(c).)

§ 67-4. Failing to kill mad dog.

If the owner of any dog shall know, or have good reason to believe, that his dog, or any dog belonging to any person under his control, has been bitten by a mad dog, and shall neglect or refuse immediately to kill the same, he shall forfeit and pay the sum of fifty dollars ($50.00) to him who will sue therefor; and the offender shall be liable to pay all damages which may be sustained by anyone, in his property or person, by the bite of any such dog, and shall be guilty of a Class 3 misdemeanor. (R.C., c. 67; Code, s. 2499; Rev., s. 3305; C.S., s. 1672; 1993, c. 539, s. 531; 1994, Ex. Sess., c. 24, s. 14(c).)

Article 1A.

Dangerous Dogs.

§ 67-4.1. Definitions and procedures.

(a)   As used in this Article, unless the context clearly requires otherwise and except as modified in subsection (b) of this section, the term:

(1)   "Dangerous dog" means

a.   A dog that:

1.   Without provocation has killed or inflicted severe injury on a person; or

2.   Is determined by the person or Board designated by the county or municipal authority responsible for animal control to be potentially dangerous because the dog has engaged in one or more of the behaviors listed in subdivision (2) of this subsection.

b. Any dog owned or harbored primarily or in part for the purpose of dog fighting, or any dog trained for dog fighting.

(2) "Potentially dangerous dog" means a dog that the person or Board designated by the county or municipal authority responsible for animal control determines to have:

a. Inflicted a bite on a person that resulted in broken bones or disfiguring lacerations or required cosmetic surgery or hospitalization; or

b. Killed or inflicted severe injury upon a domestic animal when not on the owner's real property; or

c. Approached a person when not on the owner's property in a vicious or terrorizing manner in an apparent attitude of attack.

(3) "Owner" means any person or legal entity that has a possessory property right in a dog.

(4) "Owner's real property" means any real property owned or leased by the owner of the dog, but does not include any public right-of-way or a common area of a condominium, apartment complex, or townhouse development.

(5) "Severe injury" means any physical injury that results in broken bones or disfiguring lacerations or required cosmetic surgery or hospitalization.

(b) The provisions of this Article do not apply to:

(1) A dog being used by a law enforcement officer to carry out the law enforcement officer's official duties;

(2) A dog being used in a lawful hunt;

(3) A dog where the injury or damage inflicted by the dog was sustained by a domestic animal while the dog was working as a hunting dog, herding dog, or predator control dog on the property of, or under the control of, its owner or keeper, and the damage or injury was to a species or type of domestic animal appropriate to the work of the dog; or

(4) A dog where the injury inflicted by the dog was sustained by a person who, at the time of the injury, was committing a willful trespass or other tort, was

tormenting, abusing, or assaulting the dog, had tormented, abused, or assaulted the dog, or was committing or attempting to commit a crime.

(c)   The county or municipal authority responsible for animal control shall designate a person or a Board to be responsible for determining when a dog is a "potentially dangerous dog" and shall designate a separate Board to hear any appeal. The person or Board making the determination that a dog is a "potentially dangerous dog" must notify the owner in writing, giving the reasons for the determination, before the dog may be considered potentially dangerous under this Article. The owner may appeal the determination by filing written objections with the appellate Board within three days. The appellate Board shall schedule a hearing within 10 days of the filing of the objections. Any appeal from the final decision of such appellate Board shall be taken to the superior court by filing notice of appeal and a petition for review within 10 days of the final decision of the appellate Board. Appeals from rulings of the appellate Board shall be heard in the superior court division. The appeal shall be heard de novo before a superior court judge sitting in the county in which the appellate Board whose ruling is being appealed is located. (1989 (Reg. Sess., 1990), c. 1023, s. 1.)

§ 67-4.2. Precautions against attacks by dangerous dogs.

(a)   It is unlawful for an owner to:

(1)   Leave a dangerous dog unattended on the owner's real property unless the dog is confined indoors, in a securely enclosed and locked pen, or in another structure designed to restrain the dog;

(2)   Permit a dangerous dog to go beyond the owner's real property unless the dog is leashed and muzzled or is otherwise securely restrained and muzzled.

(b)   If the owner of a dangerous dog transfers ownership or possession of the dog to another person (as defined in G.S. 12-3(6)), the owner shall provide written notice to:

(1)   The authority that made the determination under this Article, stating the name and address of the new owner or possessor of the dog; and

(2)   The person taking ownership or possession of the dog, specifying the dog's dangerous behavior and the authority's determination.

(c)   Violation of this section is a Class 3 misdemeanor. (1989 (Reg. Sess., 1990), c. 1023; 1993, c. 539, s. 532; 1994, Ex. Sess., c. 24, s. 14(c).)

§ 67-4.3. Penalty for attacks by dangerous dogs.

The owner of a dangerous dog that attacks a person and causes physical injuries requiring medical treatment in excess of one hundred dollars ($100.00) shall be guilty of a Class 1 misdemeanor. (1989 (Reg. Sess., 1990), c. 1023; 1993, c. 539, s. 533; 1994, Ex. Sess., c. 24, s. 14(c).)

§ 67-4.4. Strict liability.

The owner of a dangerous dog shall be strictly liable in civil damages for any injuries or property damage the dog inflicts upon a person, his property, or another animal. (1989 (Reg. Sess., 1990), c. 1023, s. 1.)

§ 67-4.5. Local ordinances.

Nothing in this Article shall be construed to prevent a city or county from adopting or enforcing its own program for control of dangerous dogs. (1989 (Reg. Sess., 1990), c. 1023, s. 1.)

Article 2.

License Taxes on Dogs.

§§ 67-5 through 67-11: Repealed by Session Laws 1973, c. 822, s. 6.

§ 67-12. Permitting dogs to run at large at night; penalty; liability for damage.

No person shall allow his dog over six months old to run at large in the nighttime unaccompanied by the owner or by some member of the owner's family, or some other person by the owner's permission. Any person intentionally, knowingly, and willfully violating this section shall be guilty of a Class 3 misdemeanor, and shall also be liable in damages to any person injured or suffering loss to his property or chattels. (1919, c. 116, s. 5; C.S., s. 1680; 1993, c. 539, s. 534; 1994, Ex. Sess., c. 24, s. 14(c).)

§ 67-13. Repealed by Session Laws 1973, c. 822, s. 6.

§ 67-14. Mad dogs, dogs killing sheep, etc., may be killed.

Any person may kill any mad dog, and also any dog if he is killing sheep, cattle, hogs, goats, or poultry. (1919, c. 116, s. 8; C.S., s. 1682.)

§ 67-14.1. Dogs injuring deer or bear on wildlife management area may be killed; impounding unmuzzled dogs running at large.

(a)   Any dog which trails, runs, injures or kills any deer or bear on any wildlife refuge, sanctuary or management area, now or hereafter so designated and managed by the Wildlife Resources Commission, during the closed season for hunting with dogs on such refuge or management area, is hereby declared to be a public nuisance, and any wildlife protector or other duly authorized agent or employee of the Wildlife Resources Commission may destroy, by humane method, any dog discovered trailing, running, injuring or killing any deer or bear in any such area during the closed season therein for hunting such game with dogs, without incurring liability by reason of his act in conformity with this section.

(b)   Any unmuzzled dog running at large upon any wildlife refuge, sanctuary, or management area, when unaccompanied by any person having such dog in charge, shall be seized and impounded by any wildlife protector, or other duly authorized agent or employee of the Wildlife Resources Commission.

(c) The person impounding such dog shall cause a notice to be published at least once a week for two successive weeks in some newspaper published in the county wherein the dog was taken, or if none is published therein, in some newspaper having general circulation in the county. Such notice shall set forth a description of the dog, the place where it is impounded, and that the dog will be destroyed if not claimed and payment made for the advertisement, a catch fee of one dollar ($1.00) and the boarding, computed at the rate of fifty cents (50¢) per day, while impounded, by a certain date which date shall be not less than 15 days after the publication of the first notice. A similar notice shall be posted at the courthouse door.

(d) The owner of the dog, or his agent, may recover such dog upon payment of the cost of the publication of the notices hereinbefore described together with a catch fee of one dollar ($1.00) and the expense, computed at the rate of fifty cents (50¢) per day, incurred while impounding and boarding the dog.

(e) If any impounded dog is not recovered by the owner within 15 days after the publication of the first notice of the impounding, the dog may be destroyed in a humane manner by any wildlife protector or other duly authorized agent or employee of the North Carolina Wildlife Resources Commission, and no liability shall attach to any person acting in accordance with this section. (1951, c. 1021, s. 1.)

§ 67-15. Repealed by Session Laws 1983, c. 35, s. 2.

§ 67-16. Failure to discharge duties imposed under this Article.

Any person failing to discharge any duty imposed upon him under this Article shall be guilty of a Class 3 misdemeanor. (1919, c. 116, s. 10; C.S., s. 1684; 1993, c. 539, s. 535; 1994, Ex. Sess., c. 24, s. 14(c).)

§ 67-17. Deleted.

§ 67-18. Application of Article.

This Article, G.S. 67-5 to 67-18, inclusive, is hereby made applicable to every county in the State of North Carolina, notwithstanding any provisions in local, special or private acts exempting any county or any township or municipality from the provisions of the same enacted at any General Assembly commencing at the General Assembly of 1919 and going through the General Assembly of 1929. (1929, c. 318.)

Article 3.

Special License Tax on Dogs.

§§ 67-19 through 67-28. Repealed by Session Laws 1973, c. 822, s. 6.

Article 4.

Guide Dogs.

§ 67-29. Repealed by Session Laws 1973, c. 493, s. 2.

Article 5.

Protection of Livestock and Poultry from Ranging Dogs.

§ 67-30. Appointment of animal control officers authorized; salary, etc.

A county may appoint one or more animal control officers and may fix their salaries, allowances, and expenses. (1951, c. 931, s. 1; 1955, c. 1333, s. 1; 1957, cc. 81, 840; 1973, c. 822, s. 6.)

§ 67-31. Powers and duties of dog warden.

The powers and duties of the county dog warden shall be as follows:

(1)   He shall have the power of arrest and be responsible for the enforcement within his county of all public and public-local laws pertaining to the ownership and control of dogs, and shall cooperate with all other law-enforcement officers operating within the county in fulfilling this responsibility.

(2)   In those counties having a rabies control officer, the county dog warden shall act as assistant to the rabies control officer, working under the supervision of the county health department, to collect the dog tax. In those counties having no rabies control officer, the county dog warden shall serve as rabies control officer. (1951, c. 931, s. 2.)

§ 67-32: Repealed by Session Laws 1983, c. 891, s. 9.

§§ 67-33 through 67-35. Repealed by Session Laws 1973, c. 822, s. 6.

§ 67-36. Article supplements existing laws.

The provisions of this Article are to be construed as supplementing and not repealing existing State laws pertaining to the ownership, taxation, and control of dogs. (1951, c. 931, s. 7.)

Chapter 68.

Fences and Stock Law.

Article 1.

Lawful Fences.

§§ 68-1 through 68-2. Repealed by Session Laws 1969, c. 691.

§§ 68-3 through 68-4. Repealed by Session Laws 1971, c. 741, s. 2.

§ 68-5. Repealed by Session Laws 1969, c. 619.

Article 2.

Division Fences.

§§ 68-6 through 68-14: Repealed by Session Laws 1971, c. 741, s. 2.

Article 3.

Livestock Law.

§ 68-15. Term "livestock" defined.

The word "livestock" in this Chapter shall include, but shall not be limited to, equine animals, bovine animals, sheep, goats, llamas, and swine. (Code, s. 2822; Rev., s. 1681; C.S., s. 1841; 1971, c. 741, s. 1; 1997-84, s. 2.)

§ 68-16. Allowing livestock to run at large forbidden.

If any person shall allow his livestock to run at large, he shall be guilty of a Class 3 misdemeanor. (Code, s. 2811; 1889, c. 504; Rev., s. 3319; C.S., s. 1849; 1971, c. 741, s. 1; 1993, c. 539, s. 536; 1994, Ex. Sess., c. 24, s. 14(c).)

§ 68-17. Impounding livestock at large; right to recover costs and damages.

Any person may take up any livestock running at large or straying and impound the same; and such impounder may recover from the owner the reasonable costs of impounding and maintaining the livestock as well as damages to the impounder caused by such livestock, and may retain the livestock, with the right to use with proper care until such recovery is had. Reasonable costs of impounding shall include any fees paid pursuant to G.S. 68-18.1 in order to locate the owner. (Code, s. 2186; Rev., s. 1679; C.S., s. 1850; 1951, c. 569; 1971, c. 741, s. 1; 1991, c. 472, s. 3.)

§ 68-18. Notice and demand when owner known.

If the owner of impounded livestock is or becomes known to the impounder, actual notice of the whereabouts of the impounded livestock must be immediately given to the owner and the impounder must then make demand upon the owner of the livestock for the costs of impoundment and the damages to the impounder, if any, caused by such livestock. (Code, s. 2817; Rev., s. 1680; C.S., s. 1851; 1971, c. 741, s. 1.)

§ 68-18.1. Notice when owner not known.

If the owner of the impounded livestock is not known or cannot be found, the impounder shall inform the sheriff of the county in which the livestock was found of the impoundment, giving a full description of the livestock impounded, including all marks or brands on the livestock, and shall state when and where the animal was taken up. (1874-5, c. 258, s. 2; Code, s. 3768; Rev., s. 2833; C.S., s. 3951; 1991, c. 472, s. 2; 2012-18, s. 1.10.)

§ 68-19. Determination of damages by selected landowners or by referee.

If the owner and impounder cannot agree as to the cost of impounding and maintaining such livestock, as well as damages to the impounder caused by such livestock running at large, then such costs and damages shall be determined by three disinterested landowners, one to be selected by the owner of the livestock, one to be selected by the impounder and a third to be selected by the first two. If within 10 days a majority of the landowners so selected cannot agree, or if the owner of the livestock or the impounder fails to make his selection, or if the two selected fail to select a third, then the clerk of superior court of the county where the livestock is impounded shall select a referee. The determination of such costs and damages by the landowners or by the referee shall be final. (Code, s. 2186; Rev., s. 1679; C.S., s. 1850; 1951, c. 569; 1971, c. 741, s. 1.)

§ 68-20. Notice of sale and sale where owner fails to redeem or is unknown; application of proceeds.

If the owner fails to redeem his livestock within three days after the notice and demand as provided in G.S. 68-18 is received or within three days after the determination of the costs and damages as provided in G.S. 68-19, then, upon written notice fully describing the livestock, stating the place, date, and hour of sale posted at the courthouse door and three or more public places in the township where the owner resides, and after 10 days from such posting, the impounder shall sell the livestock at public auction. If the owner of the livestock remains unknown to the impounder, then, 30 days after publication of the notice required by G.S. 68-18.1, the impounder shall post at the courthouse door and three public places in the township where the livestock is impounded a written notice fully describing the livestock, and stating the place, date, and hour of sale. After 20 days from such posting, the impounder shall sell the livestock at public auction. The proceeds of any such public sale shall be applied to pay the reasonable costs of impounding and maintaining the livestock and the damages to the impounder caused by the livestock. Reasonable costs of impounding shall include any fees paid pursuant to G.S. 68-18.1 in an attempt to locate the owner of the livestock. The balance, if any, shall be paid to the owner of the livestock, if known, or, if the owner is not known, then to the school fund of the county where the livestock was impounded. (Code, s. 2817; Rev., s. 1680; C.S., s. 1851; 1971, c. 741, s. 1; 1991, c. 472, s. 4.)

§ 68-21. Illegally releasing or receiving impounded livestock misdemeanor.

If any person willfully releases any lawfully impounded livestock without the permission of the impounder or receives such livestock knowing that it was unlawfully released, he shall be guilty of a Class 3 misdemeanor. (Code, s. 2819; 1889, c. 504; Rev., s. 3310; C.S., s. 1853; 1971, c. 741, s. 1; 1993, c. 539, s. 537; 1994, Ex. Sess., c. 24, s. 14(c).)

§ 68-22. Impounded livestock to be fed and watered.

If any person shall impound or cause to be impounded any livestock and shall fail to supply to the livestock during the confinement a reasonably adequate quantity of good and wholesome feed and water, he shall be guilty of a Class 3 misdemeanor. (1881, c. 368, s. 3; Code, s. 2484; 1891, c. 65; Rev., s. 3311; C.S., s. 1854; 1971, c. 741, s. 1; 1993, c. 539, s. 538; 1994, Ex. Sess., c. 24, s. 14(c).)

§ 68-23. Right to feed impounded livestock; owner liable.

When any livestock is impounded under the provisions of this Chapter and remains without reasonably adequate feed and water for more than 24 hours, any person may lawfully enter the area of impoundment to supply the livestock with feed and water. Such person shall not be liable in trespass for such entry and may recover of the owner or, if the owner is unknown, of the impounder of the livestock, the reasonable costs of the feed and water. (1881, c. 368, s. 4; Code, s. 2485; Rev., s. 1682; C.S., s. 1855; 1971, c. 741, s. 1.)

§ 68-24. Penalties for violation of this Article.

A violation of G.S. 68-16, 68-21 or 68-22 is a Class 3 misdemeanor. (1971, c. 741, s. 1; 1993, c. 539, s. 539; 1994, Ex. Sess., c. 24, s. 14(c).)

§ 68-25. Domestic fowls running at large after notice.

(a) If any person shall permit any turkeys, geese, chickens, ducks or other domestic fowls to run at large on the lands of any other person while such lands are under cultivation in any kind of grain or feedstuff or while being used for gardens or ornamental purposes, after having received actual or constructive notice of such running at large, the person is guilty of a Class 3 misdemeanor.

(b) If any person permits any domestic fowls to run at large on the lands of a commercial poultry operation of any other person after having received actual or constructive notice of such running at large, the person is guilty of a Class 3 misdemeanor. For purposes of this subsection, a commercial poultry operation means any premises or operation where domestic poultry are fed, caged, housed, or otherwise kept for meat or egg production until sold or marketed.

(b1)   Repealed by Session Laws 2011-412, s. 3.1, effective October 15, 2011.

(c)   If it shall appear to any magistrate that after three days' notice any person persists in allowing his fowls to run at large in violation of this section and fails or refuses to keep them upon his own premises, then the said magistrate may, in his discretion, order any sheriff or other officer to kill the fowls when they are running at large as herein provided. (C.S., s. 1864; 1971, c. 741, s. 1; 1993, c. 539, s. 540; 1994, Ex. Sess., c. 24, s. 14(c); 2011-313, s. 1; 2011-412, s. 3.1.)

§§ 68-26 through 68-41: Repealed by Session Laws 1971, c. 741, s. 2.

Article 4.

Stock along the Outer Banks.

§ 68-42. Stock running at large prohibited; certain ponies excepted.

From and after July 1, 1958, it shall be unlawful for any person, firm or corporation to allow his or its horses, cattle, goats, sheep, or hogs to run free or at large along the outer banks of this State. This Article shall not apply to horses known as marsh ponies or banks ponies on Ocracoke Island, Hyde County. This Article shall not apply to horses known as marsh ponies or banks ponies on Shackleford Banks between Beaufort Inlet and Barden's Inlet in Carteret County. Saving and excepting those animals known as "banker ponies" on the island of Ocracoke owned by the Boy Scouts and not exceeding 35 in number. (1957, c. 1057, s. 1; 1997-456, s. 9.)

§ 68-43. Authority of Secretary of Environment and Natural Resources to remove or confine ponies on Ocracoke Island and Shackleford Banks.

Notwithstanding any other provisions of this Article, the Secretary of Environment and Natural Resources shall have authority to remove or cause to be removed from Ocracoke Island and Shackleford Banks all ponies known as banks ponies or marsh ponies if and when he determines that such action is essential to prevent damage to the island. In the event such a determination is made, the Secretary, in lieu of removing all ponies, may require that they be restricted to a certain area or corralled so as to prevent damage to the island. In the event such action is taken, the Secretary is authorized to take such steps and act through his duly designated employees or such other persons as, in his opinion, he deems necessary and he may accept any assistance provided by or through the National Park Service. (1957, c. 1057, s. 11/2; 1973, c. 1262, s. 86; 1977, c. 771, s. 4; 1989, c. 727, s. 218(10); 1997-443, s. 11A.119(a); 1997-456, s. 10.)

§ 68-44. Penalty for violation of G.S. 68-42.

Any person, firm or corporation violating the provisions of G.S. 68-42 shall be guilty of a Class 3 misdemeanor. (1957, c. 1057, s. 2; 1993, c. 539, s. 541; 1994, Ex. Sess., c. 24, s. 14(c).)

§ 68-45. Impounding stock.

The provisions of G.S. 68-24 to 68-30, relative to the impounding of stock running at large shall apply with equal force and effect along the outer banks of this State. (1957, c. 1057, s. 3.)

§ 68-46. "Outer banks of this State" defined.

For the purposes of this Article, the terms "outer banks of this State" shall be construed to mean all of that part of North Carolina which is separated from the mainland by a body of water, such as an inlet or sound, and which is in part bounded by the Atlantic Ocean. (1957, c. 1057, s. 4.)

Chapter 69.

Fire Protection.

Article 1.

Investigation of Fires and Inspection of Premises.

§§ 69-1 through 69-7.1: Recodified as Article 79 of Chapter 58.

Article 2.

Fire Escapes.

§§ 69-8 through 69-13: Repealed by Session Laws 1987, c. 864, s. 51.

Article 3.

State Volunteer Fire Department.

§§ 69-14 through 69-25: Recodified as Article 80 of Chapter 58.

Article 3A.

Rural Fire Protection Districts.

§ 69-25.1. Election to be held upon petition of voters.

Upon the petition of thirty-five percent (35%) of the resident freeholders living in an area lying outside the corporate limits of any city or town, which area is described in the petition and designated as "_____

(Here insert name)

Fire District," the board of county commissioners of the county shall call a special election in said district for the purpose of submitting to the qualified voters therein the question of levying and collecting a special tax on all taxable property in said district, of not exceeding fifteen cents (15¢) on the one hundred dollars ($100.00) valuation of property, for the purpose of providing fire protection in said district. The county tax office shall be responsible for checking the freeholder status of those individuals signing the petition and confirming the location of the property owned by those individuals. Unless specifically excluded by other law, the provisions of Chapter 163 of the General Statutes concerning petitions for referenda and special elections shall apply. If the voters reject the special tax under the first paragraph of this section, then no new election may be held under the first paragraph of this section within two years on the question of levying and collecting a special tax under the first paragraph of this section in that district, or in any proposed district which includes a majority of the land within the district in which the tax was rejected.

Upon the petition of thirty-five percent (35%) of the resident freeholders living in an area which has previously been established as a fire protection district and in which there has been authorized by a vote of the people a special tax not exceeding ten cents (10¢) on the one hundred dollars ($100.00) valuation of property within the area, the board of county commissioners shall call a special election in said area for the purpose of submitting to the qualified voters therein the question of increasing the allowable special tax for fire protection within said district from ten cents (10¢) on the one hundred dollars ($100.00) valuation to fifteen cents (15¢) on the one hundred dollars ($100.00) valuation on all taxable property within such district. Special elections on the question of increasing the allowable tax rate for fire protection shall not be held within the same district at intervals less than two years. (1951, c. 820, s. 1; 1953, c. 453, s. 1; 1959, c. 805, ss. 1, 2; 1983, c. 388, ss. 1, 1.1; 2002-159, s. 55(g); 2013-381, s. 10.6.)

§ 69-25.2. Duties of county board of commissioners regarding conduct of elections; cost of holding.

The board of county commissioners, after consulting with the county board of elections, shall set a date for the special election in accordance with G.S. 163-287 by resolution adopted. The county board of elections shall hold and conduct the election in the district. The county board of elections shall advertise and conduct said election, in accordance with the provisions of this Article and with the procedures prescribed in Chapter 163 governing the conduct of special and general elections. The cost of holding the election to establish a district shall be paid by the county, provided that if the district is established, then the county shall be reimbursed the cost of the election from the taxes levied within the district, but the cost of an election to increase the allowable tax under G.S. 69-25.1 or to abolish a fire district under G.S. 69-25.10 shall be paid from the funds of the district. (1951, c. 820, s. 2; 1975, c. 706; 1981, c. 786, s. 2; 2013-381, s. 10.7.)

§ 69-25.3. Ballots.

At said election those voters who are in favor of levying a tax in said district for fire protection therein shall vote a ballot on which shall be written or printed, "In favor of tax for fire protection in _____

(Here insert name)

Fire Protection District." Those who are against levying said tax shall vote a ballot on which shall be written or printed the words, "Against tax for fire protection in_____ Fire Protection District."

(Here insert name)

Whenever an election is called pursuant to this Article on the question of increasing the tax limit for fire protection in any area, those voters in favor of such increase therein shall vote a ballot on which shall be printed, "In favor of tax increase for fire protection in __ Fire Protection District." Those who are against increasing the tax limit for fire protection therein shall vote a ballot on which shall be printed, "Against tax increase for fire protection in Fire Protection District."

The failure of the election on the question of an increase in the tax for fire protection shall not be deemed to be the abolishment of the special tax for fire protection already in effect in said district. (1951, c. 820, s. 3; 1959, c. 805, s. 3.)

§ 69-25.4. Tax to be levied and used for furnishing fire protection.

(a) If a majority of the qualified voters voting at said election vote in favor of levying and collecting a tax in said district, then the board of county commissioners is authorized and directed to levy and collect a tax in said district in such amount as it may deem necessary, not exceeding ten cents (10¢) on the one hundred dollars ($100.00) valuation of property in said district from year to year, and shall keep the same as a separate and special fund, to be used only for furnishing fire protection within said district, as provided in G.S. 69-25.5.

Provided, that if a majority of the qualified voters voting at such elections vote in favor of levying and collecting a tax in such district, or vote in favor of increasing the tax limit in said district, then the board of county commissioners is authorized and directed to levy and collect a tax in such districts in such amount as it may deem necessary, not exceeding fifteen cents (15¢) on the one hundred dollars ($100.00) valuation of property in said district from year to year.

(b) For purposes of this Article, the term "fire protection" and the levy of a tax for that purpose may include the levy, appropriation, and expenditure of funds for furnishing emergency medical, rescue and ambulance services to protect persons within the district from injury or death; and the levy, appropriation, and expenditure of the tax to provide such services are proper, authorized and lawful. In providing these services the fire district shall be subject to G.S. 153A-250.

(c) For purposes of this Article, a fire protection district is a municipal corporation organized for a special purpose. Except in cases when a fire protection district commission is appointed to govern the district, the board of county commissioners, or joint boards of county commissioners when the area lies in more than one county, shall serve as the governing body. (1951, c. 820, s. 4; 1959, c. 805, s. 4; 1981, c. 217; 2001-414, s. 33.)

§ 69-25.5. Methods of providing fire protection.

Upon the levy of such tax, the board of county commissioners shall, to the extent of the taxes collected hereunder, provide fire protection for the district -

(1) By contracting with any incorporated city or town, with any incorporated nonprofit volunteer or community fire department, or with the Department of Environment and Natural Resources to furnish fire protection, or

(2) By furnishing fire protection itself if the county maintains an organized fire department, or

(3) By establishing a fire department within the district, or

(4) By utilizing any two or more of the above listed methods of furnishing fire protection. (1951, c. 820, s. 5; 1973, c. 1262, s. 86; 1977, c. 771, s. 4; 1989, c. 727, s. 218(11); 1997-443, s. 11A.119(a).)

§ 69-25.6. Municipal corporations empowered to make contracts.

Municipal corporations are hereby empowered to make contracts to carry out the purposes of this Article. (1951, c. 820, s. 6.)

§ 69-25.7. Administration of special fund; fire protection district commission.

The special fund provided by the tax herein authorized shall be administered to provide fire protection as provided in G.S. 69-25.5 by the board of county commissioners or the joint boards of county commissioners, if the area lies in more than one county, or by a fire protection district commission of three qualified voters of the area, to be known as

_____

___

(Here insert name)

Fire Protection District Commission, said board to be appointed by the board of county commissioners or the joint boards of county commissioners, if the area lies in more than one county, for a term of two years, said commission to serve at the discretion of and under the supervision of the board of county commissioners or boards of county commissioners if the area lies in more than one county. (1951, c. 820, s. 7; 1953, c. 453, s. 2.)

§ 69-25.8. Authority, rights, privileges and immunities of counties, etc., performing services under Article.

Any county, municipal corporation or fire protection district performing any of the services authorized by this Article shall be subject to the same authority and immunities as a county would enjoy in the operation of a county fire department within the county, or a municipal corporation would enjoy in the operation of a fire department within its corporate limits.

No liability shall be incurred by any municipal corporation on account of the absence from the city or town of any or all of its fire-fighting equipment or of members of its fire department by reason of performing services authorized by this Article.

Members of any county, municipal or fire protection district fire department shall have all of the immunities, privileges and rights, including coverage by workers' compensation insurance, when performing any of the functions authorized by this Article, as members of a county fire department would have in performing their duties in and for a county, or as members of a municipal fire department would have in performing their duties for and within the corporate limits of the municipal corporation. (1951, c. 820, s. 8; 1979, c. 714, s. 2.)

§ 69-25.9. Procedure when area lies in more than one county.

In the event that an area petitioning for a tax election under this Article lies in more than one county said petition shall be submitted to the board of county commissioners of all the counties in which said area lies and election shall be called which shall be conducted jointly by the county board of elections and the cost of same shall be shared equally by all counties.

Upon passage, the tax herein provided shall be levied and collected by each county on all of the taxable property in its portion of the fire protection district; the tax collected shall be paid into a special fund and used for the purpose of providing fire protection for the district. (1953, c. 453, s. 3; 1985, c. 563, s. 5.)

§ 69-25.10. Means of abolishing tax district.

Upon a petition of fifteen percent (15%) of the resident freeholders of any special fire protection district or area, at intervals of not less than two years, the board of county commissioners or the joint boards of county commissioners, if the area lies in more than one county, shall call an election to abolish the special tax for fire protection for the area, the election to be called and conducted as provided in G.S. 69-25.2; if a majority of the registered voters vote to abolish said tax, the commissioners shall cease levy and collecting same and any unused funds of the district shall be turned over to and used by the county commissioners of the county collecting same as a part of its general fund, and any property or properties of the district or the proceeds thereof shall be distributed, used or disposed of equitably by the board of county commissioners or the boards of county commissioners. (1953, c. 453, s. 4.)

§ 69-25.11. Changes in area of district.

After a fire protection district has been established under the provisions of this Article and fire protection commissioners have been appointed, changes in the area may be made as follows:

(1) The area of any fire protection district may be increased by including within the boundaries of the district any adjoining territory upon the application of the owner, or a two-thirds majority of the owners, of the territory to be included, the unanimous recommendation in writing of the fire protection commissioners of said district, the approval of a majority of the members of the board of directors of the corporation furnishing fire protection to the district, and the approval of the board or boards of county commissioners in the county or counties in which said fire protection district is located. However, before said fire protection district change is approved by the county commissioners, notice shall be given once a week for two successive calendar weeks in a newspaper having general circulation in said district, and notice shall be posted at the courthouse door in each county affected, and at three public places in the area to be included, said notices inviting interested citizens to appear at a designated meeting of said county commissioners, said notice to be published the first time and posted not less than fifteen days prior to the date fixed for hearing before the county commissioners.

(2) The area of any fire protection district may be decreased by removing therefrom any territory, upon the application of the owner or owners of the territory to be removed, the unanimous recommendation in writing of the fire protection commissioners of said district, the approval of a majority of the members of the board of directors of the corporation furnishing fire protection to

the district, and the approval of the board or boards of county commissioners of the county or counties in which the district is located.

(3) In the case of adjoining fire districts having in effect the same rate of tax for fire protection, the board of county commissioners, upon petition of the fire protection commissioners and the boards of directors of the corporations furnishing fire protection in the districts affected, shall have the authority to relocate the boundary lines between such fire districts in accordance with the petition or in such other manner as to the board may seem proper. Upon receipt of such petition, the board of county commissioners shall set a date and time for a public hearing on the petition, and notice of such hearing shall be published in some newspaper having general circulation within the districts to be affected once a week for two weeks preceding the time of the hearing. Such hearings may be adjourned from time to time and no further notice is required of such adjourned hearings. In the event any boundaries of fire districts are altered or relocated under this section, the same shall take effect at the beginning of the next succeeding fiscal year after such action is taken.

(4) In the case of adjoining fire districts having in effect a different rate of tax for fire protection, the board of county commissioners, upon petition of two thirds of the owners of the territory involved and after receiving a favorable recommendation of the fire protection commissioners and the boards of directors of the corporations furnishing fire protection in the districts affected, may transfer such territory from one district to another and therefore relocate the boundary lines between such fire districts in accordance with the petition or in such other manner as the board may deem proper. Upon receipt of such petition, the board of county commissioners shall set a date and time for a public hearing on the petition, and notice of such hearing shall be published in some newspaper having general circulation within the districts to be affected once a week for two weeks preceding the time of the hearing. Such hearings may be adjourned from time to time and no further notice is required of such adjourned hearings. In the event any boundaries of fire districts are relocated under this section, the same shall take effect at the beginning of the next succeeding fiscal year after such action is taken.

(5) The area of any fire protection district may be increased by including within the boundaries of the district any adjoining territory lying within the corporate limits of the city if the territory is not already included within a fire protection district, provided both the city governing body and the county commissioners of the county or counties in which the fire protection district is

located all agree by resolution to such inclusion. (1955, c. 1270; 1959, c. 805, s. 5; 1965, cc. 625, 1101; 1987, c. 711, s. 2.)

§ 69-25.12. Privileges and taxes where territory added to district.

In case any territory is added to any fire protection district, from and after such addition, the taxpayers and other residents of said added territory shall have the same rights and privileges and the taxpayers shall pay taxes at the same rates as if said territory had originally been included in the said fire protection district. (1955, c. 1270.)

§ 69-25.13. Privileges and taxes where territory removed from district.

In case any territory is removed from any fire protection district from and after said removal, the taxpayers and other residents of said removed territory shall cease to be entitled to the rights and privileges vested in them by their inclusion in said fire protection district, and the taxpayers shall no longer be required to pay taxes upon their property within said district. (1955, c. 1270.)

§ 69-25.14. Contract with city or town to which all or part of district annexed concerning property of district and furnishing of fire protection.

Whenever all or any part of the area included within the territorial limits of a fire protection district is annexed to or becomes a part of a city or town, the governing body of such district may contract with the governing body of such city or town to give, grant or convey to such city or town, with or without consideration, in such manner and on such terms and conditions as the governing body of such district shall deem to be in the best interests of the inhabitants of the district, all or any part of its property, including, but without limitation, any fire-fighting equipment or facilities, and may provide in such contract for the furnishing of fire protection by the city or town or by the district. (1957, c. 526.)

§ 69-25.15. When district or portion thereof annexed by municipality furnishing fire protection.

(a) When the whole or any portion of a fire protection district has been annexed by a municipality furnishing fire protection to its citizens, then such fire protection district or the portion thereof so annexed shall immediately thereupon cease to be a fire protection district or a portion of a fire protection district; and such district or portion thereof so annexed shall no longer be subject to G.S. 69-25.4 authorizing the board of county commissioners to levy and collect a tax in such district for the purpose of furnishing fire protection therein.

(b) Nothing herein shall be deemed to prevent the board of county commissioners from levying and collecting taxes for fire protection in the remaining portion of a fire protection district not annexed by a municipality, as aforesaid.

(c) When all or part of a fire protection district is annexed, and the effective date of the annexation is a date other than a date in the month of June, the amount of the fire protection district tax levied on property in the district for the fiscal year in which municipal taxes are prorated under G.S. 160A-58.10 shall be multiplied by the following fraction: the denominator shall be 12 and the numerator shall be the number of full calendar months remaining in the fiscal year following the day on which the annexation becomes effective. For each owner, the product of the multiplication is the prorated fire protection payment. The finance officer of the city shall obtain from the assessor or tax collector of the county where the annexed territory was located a list of the owners of property on which fire protection district taxes were levied in the territory being annexed, and the city shall, no later than 90 days after the effective date of the annexation, pay the amount of the prorated fire protection district payment to the owners of that property. Such payments shall come from any funds not otherwise restricted by law.

(d) Whenever a city is required to make fire protection district tax payments by subsection (c) of this section, and the city has paid or has contracted to pay to a rural fire department funds under G.S. 160A-37.1 or G.S. 160A-58.57, the county shall pay to the city from funds of the rural fire protection district an amount equal to the amount paid by the city (or to be paid by the city) to a rural fire department under G.S. 160A-37.1 or G.S. 160A-58.57 on account of annexation of territory in the rural fire protection district for the number of months in that fiscal year used in calculating the numerator under subsection (c) of this section; provided that the required payments by the county to the city shall not exceed the total of fire protection district payments made to taxpayers in the district on account of that annexation. (1957, c. 1219; 1985, c. 707, ss. 1, 2; 1987, c. 45, s. 1.)

§ 69-25.16. Exclusion from rural fire protection districts.

There shall be excluded from any rural fire protection district, and the provisions of this Article shall not apply to, an electric generating plant, together with associated land and facilities, which provides electricity to the public; provided that this section shall not apply to any rural fire protection district in existence on May 1, 1971. (1971, c. 297.)

§ 69-25.17. Validation of fire protection funds appropriated in providing rescue and ambulance services.

All prior appropriations and expenditures by any county board of commissioners of funds derived from taxes levied in rural fire protection districts, but used to provide rescue and ambulance services within said districts, are hereby approved, confirmed, validated, and declared to be proper, authorized, and legal. (1977, c. 131, s. 1.)

Article 4.

Hotels; Safety Provisions.

§§ 69-26 through 69-38: Recodified as Article 81 of Chapter 58.

Article 5.

Authority and Liability of Firemen.

§ 69-39 through 69-39.1: Recodified as Article 82 of Chapter 58.

Article 6.

Mutual Aid between Fire Departments.

§ 69-40: Recodified as Article 83 of Chapter 58.

Vision Books Order Form

Fax Orders:	1-980-299-5965
Phone Orders:	1-704-898-0770
E-mail Orders:	www.visionbooks.org
Mail Orders:	Vision Books, LLC P.O. Box 42406 Charlotte, NC 28215

Shipp To:
Name_____
Address_____
City_____State_____Zip_____
Phone_____Fax_____
Email_____@_____

Bill To: We can bill a third party on your behalf.
Name_____
Address_____
City_____State_____Zip_____
Phone____(_____)_____Fax_____
Email_____@_____

Pamphlet Number ($15.00 Each)	Qty	Total Cost
_____	_____	_____
_____	_____	_____
_____	_____	_____
_____	_____	_____
_____	_____	_____
_____	_____	_____
_____	_____	_____
Full Volume Set 1-92	92 Pamphlets	1,380.00

Free Shipping Shipping & Handling on Full Volume Orders
Add $1.00 Shipping & Handling per pamphlet $_____

Total Cost $_____

Thank you for your order. Management!

DID YOU ENJOY THIS BOOK?

Vision Books, LLC would like to hear from you! If you or someone you know has been fasely imprisoned, we would like to hear your story. If the 'North Carolina Criminal Law and Procedure' has had an effect in your life or if you have suggestions, we would like to hear from you. Send your letters to:

Vision Books, LLC
Attn: Staff Writers
P.O. Box 42406
Charlotte, NC 28215
Email: staff@visionbooks.org

Order Additional Copies:

Fax Orders:	1-980-299-5965
Phone Orders:	1-704-898-0770
E-mail Orders:	www.visionbooks.org
Mail Orders:	Vision Books, LLC P.O. Box 42406 Charlotte, NC 28215

www.ingramcontent.com/pod-product-compliance
Lightning Source LLC
Chambersburg PA
CBHW051629170526
45167CB00001B/117